THE
LAST
CHOICE

THE LAST CHOICE

Preemptive Suicide
in Advanced Age, Second Edition

C. G. Prado

Westport, Connecticut
London

The Library of Congress has cataloged the hardcover edition as follows:

Prado, C. G.
    The last choice : preemptive suicide in advanced age / C. G. Prado.
—2nd ed.
        p. cm. — (Contributions in philosophy, ISSN 0084–926X ; no.
63)
    Includes bibliographical references and index.
    ISBN 0–313–30584–6 (alk. paper)
    1. Aged—Suicidal behavior. 2. Suicide—Moral and ethical
aspects. 3. Euthanasia—Moral and ethical aspects. I. Title.
II. Series.
HV6545.2.P7 1998
362′.28′084′6—dc21   98–11103

British Library Cataloguing in Publication Data is available.

A hardcover edition of *The Last Choice* is available from
Greenwood Press, an imprint of Greenwood Publishing Group, Inc.
(Contributions in Philosophy, Number 63; ISBN 0–313–30584–6).

Library of Congress Catalog Card Number: 98–11103
ISBN: 0–275–96150–8

First published in 1998

Praeger Publishers, 88 Post Road West, Westport, CT 06881
An imprint of Greenwood Publishing Group, Inc.

Printed in the United States of America

♾™

The paper used in this book complies with the
Permanent Paper Standard issued by the National
Information Standards Organization (Z39.48–1984).

10 9 8 7 6 5 4 3 2 1

For
Rose Candeloro Williams

One said of suicide, "As long as one has brains one should not blow them out." And another answered, "But when one has ceased to have them, too often one cannot."

F. H. Bradley, *Aphorisms*, #48

CONTENTS

PREFACE

When *The Last Choice* was first published in 1990, I felt the book was timely; now I feel it was somewhat ahead of its time. I agreed then with Margaret Battin's dust-jacket comment that suicide would "replace abortion as *the* social issue" of the 1990s, and seven years into the decade, she's certainly been proven right. But the focus of public debate hasn't been suicide per se; it's been physician-assisted suicide as an alternative to slow and agonizing death. While we've seen considerable "right to die" and "death with dignity" activism,[1] professional, public, and media interest in physician-assisted suicide hasn't yet extended to the broader issue of elective death in general, nor in particular to what I introduced in the first edition as preemptive suicide in advanced age.

The idea of preemptive suicide, of self-destruction as an unforced anticipatory option as opposed to suicide forced by actual circumstances, remains disturbing to many. Consider that even such ardent supporters of the right to die as Derek Humphry and Jack Kevorkian haven't pressed the cause of preemptive suicide. Humphry, who at the time was head of the Hemlock Society, made it clear in his review of *The Last Choice* that his concern is limited to affording people the opportunity to end lives that are already irredeemably jeopardized.[2] Humphry's much-read and much-debated *Final Exit* is a manual devoted to curtailment of the process of dying, not to anticipatory self-destruction.³ And regardless of varying views on his practice, Kevorkian's many cases and numerous trials have had to do either with helping people shorten the course of their fatal pathological afflictions, or with helping them to escape unbearable chronic conditions, not with preempting occurrence of those afflictions or conditions.

My view still is that there are good reasons to end one's life in anticipation of punishing and demeaning developments, just as there are good reasons to end one's life when one actually is in desperate and hopeless circumstances. What prompted this revised edition is that I think the current interest in assisted suicide strongly suggests it may be time to consider preemptive suicide as an option in advanced age. I also think that there are now some additional good reasons for preemptive suicide in advanced age. Since publication of the first edition of *The Last Choice*, I've worked on physician-assisted suicide,⁴ and have learned that some reasons for preemptive suicide have less to do with individuals than with how our social world is changing. The single most important thing I've learned is that some of the reasons why suicide has replaced abortion as the major social issue are hidden beneath a welter of distracting developments, at least a few of which only *look* like they are motivated by compassion for those whose lives are ending.

If you ask why suicide has become a major social issue, you'll be told about our aging population, about pressures on the health-care system, about the prohibition-challenging activities of people like Timothy Quill, and certainly about Holland's and Australia's experiments with condoned and legalized assisted suicide.⁵ You'll also be told about greater cultural maturity and increasing realism about the value of dependent and punishing survival, and about growing medical awareness that life-sustaining treatment can be counterproductive. And you'll repeatedly be told about the need to oppose some physicians' efforts to keep people alive against their wishes and interests, and the need to empower patients against those efforts.

These various factors are presented as the causes of the new interest in suicide. But some of these so-called causes may not be that at all; they may be effects of something quite different. Our values and beliefs are shaped to a worrying extent by influences of which we are unaware or that we obscure by rationalizing them in numerous ways. We exist in a social environment that is as much a life medium as air or water. And like air and water, the social medium has currents and eddies that affect us but which are transparent to us. There are now eddies and currents that are changing our views on life and death,[6] and they aren't any better understood at present than other social forces were in their own time.

The main way our social medium influences us is by presenting us with many "truths" in the form of "common knowledge" or what's taken for granted in a culture or society. As members of a society with a certain culture, we perceive a world that contains not only mundane truths about physical things and events, but equally mundane truths about our own "nature," about what is or isn't of value, what is or isn't reasonable, what is or isn't moral, and, above all, what is or isn't normal. In short, as social beings we exist in what Michel Foucault calls "a regime of truth."[7] Until recently, the "normal" view, the truth of our cultural perspective, was that suicide is irrational and cowardly. That is changing. There's a sea change taking place in our regime of truth, in our social medium, and at base it has to do with the value of "dependent life."[8] *That's* what explains the 1990s' concern with assisted suicide and voluntary euthanasia. The detailed whys and wherefores of the change are best left to sociologists and social psychologists. The important thing is that assisted suicide has become a major social issue less because of the supposed causes mentioned than because we're coming to terms with a fundamental reconception of human life. The real causes of change, what is driving the reconception, are population pressures—in terms of both aging and sheer numbers—and related generational tensions. What we're witnessing in all the discussion of assisted suicide and voluntary euthanasia is a wholesale adjustment of our "regime of truth" and a reshaping of the "normal" view of self-destruction.

What most concerns me is that the population pressures and generational tensions, which I believe underlie some of the causes of greater interest in assisted suicide, are changing our social medium in ways that constitute new, additional reasons for preemptive suicide in advanced age. We may be seeing the beginning of attitudes that won't allow time for slow death. Most have heard of cases where patients are kept alive in great pain and to no good end, such as a woman dying an agonizingly slow death of cervical cancer, her "diseased tissues . . . literally rotting so that desolate family members could barely stand the stench."[9] There is great awareness now, especially with regard to cancer and AIDS, of the cruelty of demeaning, pain-filled, lingering death. But on the other side are cases like that of a woman dying of disseminated breast cancer whose hastened death was justified on the grounds that her imminent death "could have taken another week," and the attending physician "just needed that bed."[10] However, these contrasting cases are not what's of most fundamental importance; that is our new tolerance of the taking of life. I'm not for a moment suggesting that the taking of life isn't sometimes justified, warranted, and wise. What's novel is the reasons. We're seeing an essential change that turns on its being accepted as normal that some lives shouldn't be lived, aren't worth living, at least not to their ends. This idea seems to have come on us almost unnoticed in the furor about justification of particular instances of suicide and assisted suicide. I think that a new reason for preemptive suicide is that we're beginning to accept as a "truth" the fact that life has a *volitional* terminus.

C. G. Prado
Kingston, 1997

NOTES

1. See the updated and expanded bibliography.
2. Humphry 1992c
3. Humphry 1992a.
4. Prado and Taylor 1998.
5. See Kolata 1997c for the opposed positions taken on the Netherlands case.
6. Note that throughout I speak of North American and Western European culture. I don't intend my generalizations to extend to cultures in which attitudes toward life and death may be significantly different.
7. See Prado 1995.
8. Here I borrow from Sandel 1997. Dependent life is life lived at the convenience of others. The very old, the severely disabled, and many terminal patients are totally dependent on others for their survival.
9. Kolata 1997c.
10. Ibid.

THE
LAST
CHOICE

1

COHERENCE, CHOICE, AND DEATH

Free to die and free in death,
able to say a holy No
when the time for Yes has passed . . .
Nietzsche, *Zarathustra*

My aim in this book is basically to recapture for our time the pre-Judeo-Christian view of suicide as sometimes the wisest course of action, and as not necessarily an irrational or dishonorable act. In particular I want to show that suicide in advanced age can be a rational alternative to demeaning and punishing decline. My basic strategy is criterial: I offer and discuss criteria for determining when suicide is rational, in the sense of being a warranted course of action according to established reasoning and evaluatory standards.

The project may seem at once timely and unnecessary: timely because of our aging population and the historically recent rise in elderly suicides, and unnecessary because of "growing acceptance of the concept of 'rational suicide.' "[1] But this book is necessary because suicide is currently judged rational only when contextually or circumstantially coerced,[2] that is, when suicide is release from actual, unendurable suffering. Recent tolerance in societal attitudes has been toward "surcease" suicide,[3] or suicide as release from hopeless and irremediable agony. Social attitudes toward other forms of suicide remain obstructive. It needs to be established that suicide can be rational as a preemptive choice and act.

What follows is devoted to showing how an aging individual may rationally choose to commit what I call "preemptive suicide," which differs from surcease suicide or self-destruction forced by immediate torment and desperation. The point of preemptive suicide isn't escaping actual, intolerable circumstances, but avoiding foreseen demeaning decline and needless suffering. I intend what follows as a contribution to broad societal reconsideration of suicide as an *elective* choice, rather than only as the most drastic response to irremediable wretchedness.

THE CENTRAL QUESTIONS

The question most basic to my project is whether suicide can be rational: whether suicide can be a fully warranted course of action, the deliberation and enactment of which meet established standards of sound reasoning and equally sound valuation of options and relevant factors. The answer to this question is most straightforward in cases of surcease suicide, or when reason and values recommend and warrant suicide because there's really no other option. Paradigms of these cases are those where individuals are in agony that can't be alleviated and can be escaped only through death. Yet, as will emerge in the course of this book, suicide can be rational in cases where there isn't any contextual coercion of this sort.

In contrast with rational suicide are self-destruction that is *a*rational because of pathological circumstances, and self-destruction that is *irra*tional because of impaired reasoning or unwarranted valuations of circumstances and prospects. However, "rational" has several different contextually determined senses, and to claim that suicide can be rational is to say several different things about the taking of one's own life. What concerns me, and is at the heart of my project, is whether suicide can make good sense; whether it can be coherent to choose to die for anticipatory reasons, or whether there's some conceptual inconsistency in a living being's electing to cease to live except as escape from insupportable torment. Reference to coherence and consistency shouldn't be taken as the posing of a purely logical question. The issue isn't a logical or abstractly formal one about whether it's contradictory to exist yet choose not to exist. Existing and choosing not to exist are a fact and an intention, which can't conflict in the same way that two propositions conflict when one contradicts the other. The coherency issue is one of whether we're capable of fully understanding our own death as the consequence of suicidal action, and whether possible understanding can carry over to enactment, in the sense of whether we're able to carry out a well-understood intention to die without self-deception or a significant measure of impetuosity or heedless abandon. The coherency issue arises in a special way for preemptive suicide, because understanding of consequences and enactment of the well-understood intention to die aren't facilitated by the pressure of present, actual torment. In surcease suicide, understanding of the consequences of suicidal action is mediated by the fact that what's desperately sought is escape, so enactment of suicidal decisions is in turn mediated by the need to gain release. Many think that the only way we can willfully embrace our own death *is* as escape, and that without the spur of agony or horrendous fear, we can take our own lives only while not in our "right minds."

Understanding the consequences of suicide can't be a matter of mere literal understanding. We can't require that potential suicidists do the impossible and actually imagine being dead as the result of the action they're contemplating, but the enormity and irrevocable nature of suicide requires more than literal understanding of death as the end of life to serve as the key deliberative element in rational consideration of suicide and the intended result of its commission. What's required is a depth of understanding that's hard to articulate precisely, but that seems intuitively clear and has been described as "vivid awareness of . . . consequences" in deliberation.[4] What's most problematic about the consideration and commission of suicide, and poses the issue of coherency, is whether there can be "vivid awareness" of the consequences of killing ourselves. We aren't sure what it is to have adequately vivid awareness of our own deaths as ends to action. Freudians think that at the unconscious level no one truly can accept the reality of personal death, so no one can fully understand the consequences of committing suicide. If the Freudians are right, then it's difficult to see the force of saying that choosing to die could be coherent and a decision to die could be rational. It could be that even when abstract criteria for coherence and sound deliberation are satisfied, taking one's own life still falls short of being rational because, in the event, some overriding self-deceptive factor obscures what one is actually doing. If there is psychological preclusion of adequate understanding of death, then choosing to die can't be coherent, because in every instance the choice would actually be for something other than death. Killing oneself couldn't be an act in accordance with rational deliberation because, whatever the deliberative antecedents, in acting we would be intentionally doing something else.

The likeliest way suicidal decision and action are distorted or "redirected" toward more acceptable outcomes is by the belief that one will survive death. This belief is given content by the idea that death is only the end of one's "earthly" life, and that after death one continues to exist in some other mode. Religious and secular belief in an afterlife is extremely common, and I'm not suggesting that believing in an afterlife is itself irrational. However, to be rational, suicidal deliberation, decision, and action must minimally involve serious consideration and acknowledgment of the possibility that there's no afterlife and that death is personal annihilation. If one commits suicide without taking into account that doing so may be annihilating oneself, the act won't be rational because it will lack vivid awareness of consequences. But while this is conceptually clear, what's less clear is whether we *can* achieve vivid awareness of death as likely or even just possibly self-annihilation. That's the core of the coherency issue: whether in destroying ourselves we really grasp what we're doing. As we'll see below, the haunting idea is that *in the event* our most rational deliberations and decisions fail to carry through to the act of self-killing itself. Our nature could be such that we can achieve rational self-destruction only when hard-pressed by immediate circumstances. If so, preemptive suicide wouldn't be fully rational, even if warranted.

Another difficult point has to do with what one can intend or hope to gain in committing suicide. It's perfectly intelligible to sacrifice one's life for another person, for a cause, as atonement, or for personal honor, but the question here is what potential suicidists themselves stand to gain from dying. As we'll see later, nonsacrificial suicide must be in one's own interests to be rational, and it seems, again, that the only way it can be of benefit to the suicidist is when dying provides escape from something. The end of one's own existence is a very strange objective, and we appear to understand it only as either sacrifice or escape. That's why justifiable, nonsacrificial self-destruction is usually described in comparative terms, that is, in terms of being better than a more dreadful alternative. But if suicide is in one's interests only as sacrifice or escape, preemptive suicide looks highly problematic because it isn't sacrifice for others and is escape only in an attenuated sense. The point of preemptive suicide is avoidance; preemptive suicide is relinquishment of life before one is in a position to need to escape some punishing circumstance. It could be that, given the irretrievable nature of human life, justification of self-destruction doesn't extend to avoidance of anticipated developments as a warrant for suicide, because the certainty gained that one won't face those developments is outweighed by the value of the life forgone.

A preliminary sorting of issues, then, sets out some basic questions regarding whether suicide can be rational. Chief among these is whether it's coherent to choose to die; whether one can act on a coherent decision to die in a knowing and resolute manner; and what it is one can intend to achieve for oneself by dying. Suicide can't be rational if it makes no sense to choose to die, or if we can't willfully and mindfully cause our own deaths, or if we can gain nothing by dying.

A DIFFERENT EMPHASIS

My reason for undertaking the somber project of showing preemptive suicide to be sometimes rational derives from my work on aging.[5] I believe that elective death in advanced age should be recognized as a justifiable alternative to demeaning deterioration and stultifying dependency. My belief is supported by evidence that much of the historically recent increase in elderly suicides is due to growing unwillingness by the old to endure the very mixed benefits of increasingly dependent and debilitated survival.[6] However, mere recognition of suicide as a rational option would be insufficient. The reason is that advanced age itself raises questions about our reasoning and valuations of our circumstances and prospects, as I outline in Chapter 2. Therefore, the advice and judgment of others is critical for testing the soundness of preemptive suicidal deliberation and decisions. Even if suicide is coming to be accepted as sometimes rational, still-dominant negative attitudes inhibit, if they don't preclude, effective consultative help in the consideration of elective death. Moreover, given the advanced age of potential preemptive suicidists, and hence the likelihood that family members and health-care practitioners are closely involved in their activities, attitudes must be changed to prevent well-intentioned but essentially patronizing intervention in suicide. The crucial role of consultative support and nonintervention in preemptive suicide makes it essential not only to gain recognition of the rationality of suicide and preemptive suicide, but also to change prevalent attitudes enough for potential preemptive suicidists to get productive and non-obstructive counseling, and then to be allowed to carry out their soundly reasoned decisions. It's also necessary that there be medical willingness to provide painless ways to end life for others than patients enduring great suffering.[7] The option of preemptive suicide in advanced age must be made a practical reality. Preemptive suicide needs to be recognized as a rational option in advanced age, and its consideration and enactment need to be facilitated where warranted.[8]

My project differs from current treatments of suicide, assisted suicide, and voluntary euthanasia because it doesn't focus on surcease suicide or self-inflicted death as escape from pressing and desperate circumstances. Suicide forced by life's becoming literally unbearable, suicide as escape or release, has always been recognized, albeit grudgingly, as a sometimes justifiable option. It's surcease suicide that's now being more generally accepted and that right-to-die movements want legalized and, if necessary, assisted. What we've lost in Judeo-Christian culture isn't so much the option of choosing to die rather than endure greatly punishing or morally unacceptable situations. What we've lost is the option to "will at the right time to die,"[9] when that decision is made on the basis of what we expect to happen, rather than on the basis of what has already happened to us. Suicide committed in anticipation of something usually is regarded as irrational or cowardly. As Montaigne puts the common view, "It is the part of cowardliness . . . to shun the strokes of fortune."[10] We need to defeat this view and reclaim the right to decide that we've lived long enough, the right to decide that by living longer, we risk the value of what we've achieved in our lives merely for the sake of sheer survival. What needs to be rediscovered and acknowledged is that anticipatory judgments may suffice to justify suicide, that a time does come when it's best to trade whatever life is left for the privilege of ending our lives on our own terms.

We don't have to go back to the ancient Greeks and Romans to find acceptance of suicide as an elective preemptive option. David Hume shared Seneca's convictions and argued "that a man of sixty-five, by dying, cuts off only a few years of infirmities."[11] Toward the end of his life, Hume thought that even the enjoyment of the literary fame he'd sought for so long would add only short-lived pleasure to a life from which he felt distanced and that had become threatening with the onset of serious illness. Despite his sensible views on suicide, Hume didn't take his own life, but he was saved the need to do so by being very fortunate in the manner of his terminal illness and death. Once his illness was diagnosed, he tells us, he "reckon[ed] upon a speedy dissolution." His death was enviable in that he was still, at the very end, capable of bantering with the likes of James Boswell.[12] But the sad fact is that few of us can count on an easy death. Much more often death comes cruelly, its onset destroying us as persons well before death itself destroys us as organisms. It's the possibility of trading good time left for the certainty of avoiding a bad death that our present culture denies us. Hume anticipated Nietzsche's admonition that everyone should "practice the difficult art of leaving at the right time,"[13] but few in our era accept, much less act on, that admonition. Not only is anything less than surcease suicide thought irrational, suicide is often thought morally wrong, even when justified by immediately catastrophic alternatives. The Judeo-Christian view is that our lives simply aren't ours to take, so suicide is prohibited as a presumptuous and illegitimate disposition of God-created, and thus God-owned, life. Duties to one's community and family are invariably used to bolster the prohibition and to extend it to the secular realm, but whether backed up with appeals to divinity or community or both, the root of the prohibition and of the attitudes behind it is the belief that our lives are not our own.[14]

Aside from proposing suicide as an option in less-than-desperate circumstances, another way my project differs from more standard treatments of suicide is that it doesn't center on moral questions. The reason I defer moral questions about suicide and preemptive suicide is that regardless of commonly held opinions, the issue of whether suicide can be rational is prior to questions about its moral permissibility.[15] First, moral questions about elective death can't be resolved in the abstract; there are no universal, objective standards available to us that determine the moral rightness or wrongness of suicide independently of time, place, and circumstance. Moral questions about suicide require specification of the particular moral code prohibiting suicide. Second, and more fundamental, is that moral questions about suicide are secondary to the issue of whether suicide can be rational because of the conceptual fact that if suicide isn't rational, it can't be a responsible act, and if suicide isn't a responsible act, it can't be morally culpable or, for that matter, morally commendable.

Clearly, moral beliefs will figure prominently in potential suicidists' deliberations, and just as clearly some moral values, and certainly most religious ones, preclude the possibility of suicide for many. However, I'm not concerned to argue against specific moral codes or religious creeds. The questions I'm raising are, first, whether suicide can be rational, and second, whether preemptive suicide can be rational. Only if both questions are answered in a positive manner can suicide and preemptive suicide pose moral questions. My thesis that suicide and preemptive suicide can be rational is conceptually compatible with, though doctrinally opposed to, moral codes prohibiting suicide because of alleged wrongness. Any moral code that judges suicide to be wrong must allow that suicide can be rational, in order for suicide to be culpably contrary to the code in question. It's not my intention to challenge any moral codes. What I want to defeat is the view that suicide is never rational, or that it's never rational unless forced by the most extreme and pressing circumstances. These views aren't moral stands against suicide, though they're dubiously used to support moral prohibition of it. The views are basically classifications of suicide as either always an irresponsible act, because always a consequence of confusion or compulsion, or as a responsible act only when considered and committed under great duress. Defeating these views means showing how suicide and preemptive suicide can be rational; it's a further matter to establish that one or another moral code does or doesn't condone rational suicide. If suicide is never rational, if it's always a consequence of compulsion, coercion, or confusion, moral and religious questions about its permissibility, like moral and religious prohibitions against it, are pointless.

As our population ages, and as modern medicine keeps alive more people whose survival would otherwise be highly problematic, it becomes pressing to appreciate that it's within our power to rationally and responsibly judge, at some point, that we have lived long enough, and that further survival could be against our own best interests. At present, acknowledgment that life should sometimes be given up is limited to cases where life is burdened by great suffering. What's new is that suicide is coming to be more openly discussed and more widely accepted as warranted when life is being sustained at huge effort and cost, and in ways that make people utterly dependent and impose often overwhelming frustration and stress on them. This is why we're seeing a good deal of "right to die" and "death with dignity" activism. It's also why we're witnessing much more widespread use of advance directives or "living wills" and do-not-resuscitate orders to forestall excessive efforts to keep patients alive. People are beginning to think twice about life being worth preserving at all costs. There's significant evidence that as more people become aware of the nature of medicotechnological extension of life, and of the personal and economic costs involved, the quality of the life thus gained increases in importance.[16] The result has been greater resistance to maintenance of life for its own sake. But it isn't only the terminally ill and the hopelessly incapacitated who might better die sooner than medical technology may allow. We should all be able to choose to end our lives before deteriorating to a point where meaningless survival is all we have left. This means that our culture must come to recognize the legitimacy of some cases of preemptive suicide, that people must learn to respect someone's choice to die in anticipation of demeaning deterioration, and that potential suicidists must not be burdened with the weight of societal disapproval. Peer pressure can be as imprisoning to people wanting to die as any doctor's ill-advised and overly diligent efforts to keep them alive.

My argument for preemptive suicide's rationality is intended to show that people are capable of freely and sensibly choosing to die before their minds and bodies betray them. It's also intended to show that the option to end our lives before the onset of demeaning dependence and infirmity should be accepted by society and stripped of the present connotations of irrationality and cowardice—and possibly of moral prohibition. The argument's success would be the enhancement of lives lived to their ends *by choice*. The argument's aim is to foster adoption of Nietzsche's—unrealized—desire for a "free death" of his own choosing.[17] Nietzsche didn't want to be like the ropemakers who "drag out their threads and always walk backwards."[18] As Antonin Artaud puts it, in the commission of suicide we can "for the first time give things the shape of [our] will."[19]

CLARIFICATION OF TERMS

Assuming the foregoing sections have succeeded in sketching the nature of the discussion to follow, it's now necessary to clarify in a preliminary way the key terms used in this and subsequent chapters. As noted, the sense of "rational" in "rational suicide" has to do with suicide being a warranted course of action according to established reasoning and evaluatory standards. Its being so first requires the coherency of choosing to die. At the most basic level, suicide must be rational in the sense that choosing to die is intelligible. What can most readily make this fatal choice intelligible is great suffering or compelling sacrifice. Preemptive suicide is more difficult. The potential preemptive suicidist isn't someone choosing death over immediate, unbearable agony, but one choosing to die rather than risk living under anticipated abhorrent conditions. In either case the choice to die is rational only if it can be made with vivid awareness that dying most likely is ceasing to exist. That's what's hard to get hold of: how one might choose not to exist, especially when that option isn't presented as the only way out of immediate suffering. As mentioned above, the likeliest answer is that individuals can choose to die because they don't believe that death is personal annihilation. Choosing to die doesn't pose a coherency problem if the choice is perceived as opting for a better existence. But if someone commits suicide on this basis, if an individual's choice to die actually is to enter another state of continued existence, and the possibility of doing so is unquestioned, suicide wouldn't be fully rational. The reason is that the choice being made wouldn't really be to die, since that entails choosing a course of action that entails at least possible annihilation, but to continue to exist in a different way. There isn't conclusive evidence that there's any kind of afterlife, so choosing to die must include acknowledgment of the possibility that doing so is choosing annihilation. Otherwise, suicide is committed without adequate appreciation of possible consequences.

A second preliminary clarification regarding "rational" is that I'm not appealing to some eternal, ahistorical conception of rationality. First, "rational" here simply contrasts or opposes the sense in which suicide is commonly thought *irrational*. Second, "rational," as used, appeals only to our present common standards for judging the soundness of thought and action. We *do* make judgments about the rationality of action without producing philosophical warrants for the use of terms like "rational" and "reasonable." Rationality is minimally defined as satisfying "two conditions: consistency and fulfillment of . . . aims."[20] With respect to consistency, the relevant sense isn't the strictly logical one, but rather that "in the same circumstances the same course of action is always taken."[21] With respect to fulfillment of aims, the instrumental sense of "rational" is that behavior is rational in proportion to how effectively and efficiently it achieves a desired end. But the standards by which something is deemed consistent and instrumentally optimal may vary historically. Operant standards may be interpreted as ahistorical, or they may be interpreted as conventional, and arguments can be made in support of both interpretations. For my purposes, common or received standards of rationality suffice. My use of "rational" is the one used by Margaret Battin when she says that in "the absence of any compelling evidence to the contrary," we have to accept that someone may choose to die "on the basis of reasoning which is *by all usual standards* adequate."[22] I'm trying to make a case for judging preemptive suicide as rational by our usual standards; I'm neither arguing for nor appealing to a particular philosophical conception of rationality.

A similar point needs to be made about interests. Interests are to be assessed by our usual standards, just as is rationality. Some understand people's basic interests to be objective, drawing a hard distinction between "real" interests and "perceived" interests; others reject the distinction and in effect make perceived interests exhaustive. But a distinction can be drawn between what's in people's interests, and what they believe is in their interests, without introducing objective interests carrying metaphysical baggage. My position is that if potential suicidists and their peers judge suicide to be in the suicidists' interests after cool, reflective consideration, including significant efforts to gather and assess necessary data and enough time to ensure evaluative stability and avoidance of impulsive decisions, then that judgment is sufficient to warrant suicide as in those individuals' interests. Some argue that it still makes sense to say that suicide is objectively not in the suicidists' interests, regardless of personal and peer judgment. I think the only way this claim can make sense is in the philosophically uninteresting case of something's not being known that, if known, would significantly affect deliberation and alter the judgment. However, the hard fact is that none of our interesting decisions can be made on the basis of certainty that all the facts are in, and to require such certainty wouldn't only rule out suicide but would preclude all significant action.

A last preliminary clarification has to do with suicide itself. I use Tom L. Beauchamp's definition of suicide, which holds that "[a] person commits suicide if: (1) that person intentionally brings about his or her own death; (2) others do not coerce him or her to do the action; and (3) death is caused by conditions arranged by the person for the purpose of bringing about his or her own death."[23]

I can now offer a first approximation of how suicide and preemptive suicide may be rational. Assuming full understanding of precisely what is being considered and may be chosen, rational suicide must also meet the following requirements: the deliberation leading to suicide must be free of error or confusion; suicidal deliberation and choice must be cogent in the sense that, given the same circumstances and the same evaluation of relevant factors, others would draw the same conclusions; and self-destruction must best serve the individual's interests in the particular circumstances. I'll need to expand on each of these requirements, and it'll emerge that preemptive rational suicide requires qualification of the third requirement, but for the moment they suffice to indicate the basic conditions for rational suicide.

These requirements are all complex, and considerably more will be said about each, but there's another, and likely contentious, point to be made here about the rationality of suicide. The other side of the coin to claims about objective rationality and/or interests is relativism.[24] But as I'm using the term "rational," the rationality of suicide can't be relativized to individuals or even small groups. The *Dictionary of Modern Thought* assures us that someone's suicide "may be regarded as rational, if he [or she] prefers death to any other possible future."[25] However, the *Dictionary* goes on to say that "society may regard his [or her] death as an undesirable aim." In our time of tolerance for different perspectives, some are inclined to accept individuals' or special-interest groups' valuations and decisions too uncritically, and to disregard broader social standards and traditions. The rationale is that those standards and traditions are entrenched but have no greater authority than any others. I believe broad societal standards and traditions carry considerably more weight than that, and that they define the contexts

within which we have our social being.[26] While I reject ahistorical conceptions of rationality, I also reject allowing too broad a gap between what's
thought rational—or moral—by an individual or small group, and what's
thought rational—or moral—by society at large. The way that I'm using
"rational" appeals to a critical commonality of judgment in a culture or
society, and suicide can't be regarded as rational simply because it is deemed
so by an individual or a small group. I appreciate that we're dealing here
with ill-defined boundaries, but they're nonetheless quite real. Acceptance
of suicide as rational can't be mere tolerance of individuals' or groups'
perceptions and preferences. Rationality may not be ahistorical and absolute, but it's broader than the perspectives of individuals and small groups.
Consider that regardless of individual or group judgments, we wouldn't
accept suicide by a demented person or a child as rational.[27]

Nonetheless, the relativistic understanding of rationality does highlight
something important. The rationality of suicide can't be addressed purely
in terms of abstract and anonymous requirements. To be rational, suicide
must accord with individual suicidists' values. This is the sense of "rational"
that is rendered relativistic when it's mistakenly thought to be exhaustive—that is, when it's thought that all that matters are suicidists' value-
laden perspectives. But possible distortion or exaggeration doesn't decrease
the importance of suicide's accordance with suicidists' deeply held values.
A major problem with the relativist view of suicide's rationality as subjec-
tive, or at most relative to a group, is that consistency with values needn't
be consistency with interests. As will become clear, people's values may
conflict with their interests, and vice versa. For instance, a deeply held
religious doctrine prohibiting suicide may be against a person's interests
because it forces that individual to endure unnecessary suffering. Again, a
person's interest in survival may clash with that individual's values by
barring suicide for the sake of personal honor. What relativistic stress on
individuals' value-laden perspectives reminds us of is that in assessing the
rationality of suicide, we have to both give values their due weight and
distinguish between values and interests. To be rational, suicide must be in
accord with suicidists' values *and* best serve their interests.

AN ADDENDUM REGARDING THE POLITICAL
ASPECT

Given the burden put on resources by a rapidly aging population, it's an
undeniable fact that "*suicide is cheap.*"[28] The practice of preemptive suicide
in advanced age obviously would have important economic benefits for

government-supported health-care systems. The cost of caring for and maintaining the lives of very elderly people is increasing alarmingly, and barring miracles, it won't be very long before there's social pressure on the elderly to follow practices we now associate with groups living under the most marginal conditions. The principle at work in the old Inuit practice of the elderly wandering out on an ice floe, when they could no longer carry their weight in a hard-pressed community, may come to be seen as socially responsible action by our culture instead of as a barbaric practice.[29] I realize that my project of establishing the rationality of preemptive suicide will be attractive to pragmatic governments and tough-minded policy groups. However, my interest in the socioeconomic consequences of preemptive suicide is limited to how they may figure in potential suicidists' deliberations. My concern is with individual decisions, not public policy. Preemptive suicide in advanced age must be shown to be a rational option before we can consider whether public policies should support it or might wrongly endorse the practice to exploit it. Questions about the rationality of suicide are complex enough, and can be properly dealt with only if I put aside issues that, if addressed, would render my project practically impossible. I shall argue that preemptive suicide is sometimes in one's interests, through preventing anticipated (worse) harm, and hence that it may be rational to choose to die at an advanced age but prior to the onset of desperate circumstances. If those basic points can be established, then the moral, religious, social, legal, economic, and political questions can be taken in their turn.

In closing this chapter, I warn the reader that the difficulty of the points I need to make calls for frequent reiteration—as may already be evident. But reiteration isn't always simple repetition. What's required for clarity is that points be made in slightly different ways and from slightly different perspectives. I turn now to how advanced age is itself a reason for contemplating suicide. In Chapter 2 I discuss why someone close to "three score and ten" should consider that "the time for Yes has passed."

NOTES

1. Tolchin 1989.
2. Contextual or circumstantial coercion of course excludes coercion on the part of some*one*.
3. De Spelder and Strickland 1987:413.
4. Harman 1986.
5. Prado 1983, 1986, 1988; see also McKee 1988.

6. See, e.g., Angell 1997b, 1990; Outhit 1997; Hamel and DuBose 1996; Battin 1994; H. Brody 1992; Sanders 1992; Foley 1991; Tolchin 1989; McIntosh and Osgood 1986.

7. Percy Bridgman, a Nobel laureate in physics, shot himself in 1961. He wrote in his suicide note, "[i]t is not decent for society to make a man do this to himself." Kolata 1997c.

8. This raises the issue of *assisted* suicide, which I consider elsewhere. See Prado and Taylor 1998.

9. Nietzsche 1967:484.

10. Montaigne 1995.

11. Hume 1963:615.

12. Ibid.; Boswell 1947.

13. Nietzsche 1954:184.

14. See Sandel 1997.

15. There's serious confusion in much opposition to suicide due to incorporation of the incompatible ideas that suicide is wrong *and* that suicide is irrational.

16. See bibliography.

17. Nietzsche presents a case of how someone can want to die before being destroyed as a person, but be overtaken by events that make realizing that desire impossible.

18. Nietzsche 1954:184.

19. Artaud 1995.

20. Bullock, et al. 1988:721.

21. Ibid.

22. Battin 1982a:301; my emphasis.

23. Beauchamp 1980:77; quoted in Rachels 1986:81.

24. Relativism is the view that "cognitive, moral, or aesthetic claims involving . . . truth, meaningfulness, rightness [and] reasonableness . . . are relative to the contexts in which they appear." Krausz 1989:1.

25. Bullock et al. 1988:721.

26. My view is closest to that of Alisdair MacIntyre. For a brief account see Bond 1996:28–37.

27. E.g., a twelve-year-old and a thirteen-year-old killed themselves emulating rock star Kurt Cobain. Cohen 1997.

28. Battin 1987:169.

29. See Caplan 1996.

2

THE CRISIS OF AGING

Some become too old even for their truths.
Nietzsche, *Zarathustra*

The common view is that aging itself doesn't pose philosophical problems—though this is less a view than the absence of one. The most readily acknowledged problems posed by aging are practical; they have to do with social and economic matters, such as increased use of health-care resources. These are largely problems posed by the aged for society at large. Where the focus is on the aged's own problems, what are acknowledged are age-related difficulties like isolation, debility, and decreased competence. When there's recognition of more subtle problems, it tends to be limited to psychological ones, such as loneliness and depression. But aging itself does pose philosophical problems. One sort is epistemological; another has to do with self-identity or self-conception: who and what one is.

The most basic epistemological question is "How do you know?" That is, epistemology is all about justification, about telling knowledge from unconfirmed or unconfirmable belief. Age-related deterioration in reasoning, even if only suspected, leaves us not knowing if we know what we think we know. Age-related problems about self-identity or self-conception have to do with decreasing interpretive flexibility[1]—again, even if only suspected—and its effect on who we think we are. Self-identity problems arise when elderly individuals have to rethink who they are because of changes in themselves and how others deal with them. The core of these problems is that aging forces people to change as subjects. Age impugns our ability to cope, and in doing so it impugns our identity. Whereas real or suspected deterioration in reasoning impugns our knowledge, real or suspected deterioration in interpretive flexibility leaves us unsure that we *can* make good sense of what we encounter, and doubly unsure that we can check whether we *are* making good sense of what we encounter.

Epistemological problems posed by aging are critical to what's best described as the maintenance of intellectuality. For some, imperilment of intellectuality poses a more ominous and exigent threat than do the more familiar chronic maladies that characterize old age. Physical maladies may cause great discomfort, but the threat to intellectuality is a threat to the capacities and sensibilities that make us the persons we are. In what follows, I'll speak of "reflective aging individuals" to mean people who are sixty-five and older, who are perspicaciously self-aware, and whose intellectuality shapes and defines their existence as persons and social entities. The point isn't to make invidious comparisons with elderly people who possibly don't value their intellectuality. The point is about priorities. All aging individuals fear mental decline, but some fear mental decline primarily because it threatens their ability to continue their activities, while others fear mental decline because it threatens their very existence as persons. Consider a parallel: arthritis may be only an irritation to an aging individual who delights in listening to violin concertos, but it is a preclusive obstacle to an aging individual who delights in playing violin concertos. Reflective aging individuals equate significant erosion of reasoning and interpretive flexibility with proportionate loss of personal essence, and so with a kind of death.

Perhaps the most difficult aspect of epistemological problems posed by advanced age for reflective individuals is that erosion of mental proficiency is self-masking. Erosion of reasoning and interpretive flexibility not only disrupts conclusions reached and construals put on events and situations; it also hinders effective monitoring and assessment of reasoning and interpretation. The result is that deterioration of reasoning and interpretive capacity is at best sporadically evident to afflicted individuals. Matters are worsened by our apparently limitless capacity for rationalization and self-deception, because these do not just slow recognition of deterioration; they ensure that even when there is recognition of deterioration, self-serving maneuvers will be used to explain it away. The consequence is that reflective aging individuals face the bleak realization that their decline will be masked from them until they no longer exist as the persons they are, despite living on. This realization may prompt the thought that it may be preferable to end lives that will continue only in sadly and unacceptably reduced ways.

If the epistemological aspect of age-related deterioration is frightening, the self-identity aspect is even more frightening. The reason is that rather than affecting what individuals believe and do, the deterioration diminishes their very selves. Once deterioration occurs, affected individuals effectively cease to exist as the persons they are. Affected individuals can't even remember who they were before deterioration set in, because memories are distorted by being the memories of new, diminished selves. The diminishment of the self is a matter of people becoming new subjects. Their subjectivity is redefined; they come to see themselves and their world differently. But while deterioration of reasoning and interpretive flexibility is something that happens to us, something that has identifiable physical and psychological causes, diminishment of the self is only partly so. This diminishment is usually thought to be a function of neurological decline, but that's too simple a view. Malcolm Cowley—whose writings at eighty show he suffered very little age-related deterioration—comments that "we start by growing old in other people's eyes, then slowly we come to share their judgment."[2] Cowley's remark underscores that age-related change in subjectivity isn't caused only from within. Age-related redefinition of who someone is results in part from interaction with others, and in part from acceptance of cultural and societal models or paradigms.[3] Part of becoming old is accepting how we're treated by others; another part is accepting what our society tells us it is to be old.

Understanding deterioration in reasoning and interpretive capacity is fairly straightforward in comparison to understanding deteriorative change in self-conception. The former is basically a matter of mapping impairment of abilities, whereas the latter is a matter of grasping how a person becomes someone else while remaining the same individual.[4] Understanding this transformation begins with appreciation of how, in our society, we're presented with norms that prompt and enable adoption of a new subjectivity as an aged person: a "senior." These norms range from categorizing practices to scientific theories about our nature at various stages of our lives. We don't come to consider ourselves old only because we can't do things we did when younger as well or at all, but because others treat us differently and because we relate our chronological age to the many sociological and psychological descriptions of what people of certain ages are all about.

The mechanics of how subjects are molded and remolded have to do with others' behavior toward them and the "truths" of a culture or society: the ideas and beliefs that are taken as given, and are rarely questioned or reflected on. The key is what's considered and accepted as normal. But normalcy is neither willfully imposed nor knowingly accepted; normalcy is presented to us in what we're taught, in how we're treated, in how others behave, and in reactions to our remarks and actions. We don't accept "the normal" and conform to it; we adopt it, we internalize it, we become normal. And just as teenagers are notoriously molded by their peers' actions and expectations, so the elderly are remade in the image of society's conception of the old.

Epistemological problems attendant on advanced age, then, are comple- mented and completed by profound shifts in our conceptions of ourselves. Not only do reflective aging individuals face possible masked deterioration in their reasoning and interpretive capacities, they face that possibility as redefined subjects, as persons reduced in their own eyes by internalized "truths" about what's normal for their age. These "truths" range from characterization of the old as forgetful to a quite recent and ominous view of the aged as too socially costly.[5] Reflective aging individuals must deal with and adjust to changes for the worse in themselves and imposed on them. The question they have to ask themselves is whether the life left to them is worth the struggle.

CHANGES

Even the healthiest and most favored of us aren't as quick, resilient, or adaptive at seventy years of age as at twenty. Physical deterioration is obvious and, though now more controlled by better nutrition and improved medical treatment, it has yet to be reversed. Less obvious but just as real are mental changes for the worse. While aging isn't simply a matter of wholesale and persistent deterioration, we're complex organisms and do degenerate in various ways and at varying rates. While vocabulary, articu- lateness, and comprehension are only slightly diminished by age seventy- five, cognitive efficiency may be down by 40 percent due to slowness of uptake and response. Nonpathological, age-related neural deterioration begins in the frontal lobes, which means that even where there's no appreciable decline in purely cognitive capacity, there are broad psycho- logical changes for the worse, such as heightened emotionality and self- centeredness, which are usually seen as intensification of personality traits. Often these changes are wrongly conflated with impairment of reasoning, which is usually pathological when evident. But while these changes may not affect reasoning, they affect the priorities and values that reasoning serves by affecting moods and attitudes. So the difference between deteriorative changes in reasoning and psychological changes is of less practical importance than might be thought, because psychological changes may indirectly cripple even undiminished reasoning by directing it in unproductive ways. There are also numerous more specific deteriorative changes, such as shortened attention span, difficulty with concentration, and, most notorious, unreliable short-term memory. Some negative changes have no neurophysiological basis, and may be due to lack of challenge and practice, or to the distraction of chronic ailments, but their reality is undeniable.

"Natural" age-related deterioration is a long way from the onset of major afflictions such as acute confusion, Alzheimer's disease, arteriosclerotic dementia, and clinical depression.[6] But the point is that precisely because there *is* deterioration, advanced age itself, and not just its pathological afflictions, renders intellectuality problematic. To the extent that negative changes in reasoning and interpretive flexibility are suspected or anticipated by reflective aging individuals, and to the extent that those changes are assumed in how others treat the aged, those growing old are faced with constant reassessment of their intellectuality, and so of their identities. And the crucial point is that this reassessment isn't directed at discerning problems that might be set right; the reassessment has to do with understanding what aging persons are becoming. Aging individuals have to accommodate themselves to such realizations as that certain levels of thought not only have become unattainable, but may become unrecognizable for reasons that fall short of conditions we would characterize as clinical. People may be a long way from senility and still have lost their aptitude for abstract thought or, more important, a certain order of rigorous and penetrating self-reflection. Nor is it just an ability that's lost. Even highly intelligent people have to face the fact that the abstract thought they regularly achieve might be lost to them not only in the sense of their not being able to do it, but also in the sense of their not being able to appreciate it. The more they value their intellectuality, the harder it is to acknowledge that double loss, and the harder it would be for them to be sanguine about their futures as intellectual entities. Reflective aging individuals who begin to suspect deteriorative changes in themselves must envisage a time when they'll have lost not only the intellectuality they prize but also their understanding of why they valued it and how it defined who they were. Reorientation of the self in old age, then, goes beyond doubts about reasoning and interpretive capacities, to realization that even awareness of what's been lost may be lost. That realization must prompt the soberest thoughts about the value of continued existence.

Many will reject the idea that the considerations just outlined properly occasion serious thoughts of suicide. They'll argue that the intellectual aspect of our nature is being given exaggerated importance, and some will deny that there are adequate grounds to anticipate the sort of deterioration described. It's fashionable now to think that age doesn't inevitably bring serious holistic deterioration, to blame such views on cultural factors, and even to describe old age as now conceived as itself a social construct. Much of what I've said will be suspect to many, who'll see it as arising from a disproportionate valuation of a single dimension of human life. Those who think this way see no general epistemological problems peculiar to aging; they attribute the self-identity problems mentioned to the prejudicial social construction of "old age." I understand this point of view, because I held it for some time. I used to be a "constructivist" regarding old age, and my earlier work on aging was directed against stereotypic thinking about advanced age and the aged. In *Rethinking How We Age*[7] and elsewhere, I maintained that some age-related decline in interpretive flexibility is due to learned, practical factors, and argued against a stereotypic conception of aging as inherently deteriorative because of wholesale neurological decline. I even sketched a form of therapy for reversing the loss of interpretive flexibility.[8]

I still think some interpretive difficulties that attend old age are practical, but no longer believe that's enough to render aging any less destructive. I've learned too much about the magnitude of the problems. One of the most difficult things to do, at any age, is rigorously to examine our construals of whatever we encounter. Any decrease of interpretive flexibility must be one of the most worrying things to suspect in oneself: it amounts to suspecting that we can't tell what's going on; it amounts to suspecting that we've begun to create our own isolated little world by imposing preconceived ideas on people and events. Reflective aging individuals may well see recognition or even suspicion of decreasing interpretive flexibility as the beginning of the end of their existence as intellectual entities. They'll realize that even if their reasoning remains largely unimpaired, what they reason about may be too much of their own making to be sound. Failure to see these suspicions and realizations as cause for consideration of preemptive suicide is something I can attribute only to either preclusive moral or religious convictions, or a kind of aspect blindness.

INTERPRETIVE PARSIMONY

Loss or impairment of reasoning is intuitively clear. Loss or impairment of interpretive flexibility needs some clarification to show its relevance as a factor in consideration of preemptive suicide. In "Ageing and Narrative"[9] I introduced the notion of "interpretive parsimony" to explain how some age-related interpretive difficulties are the consequences of learned practices, and not the effects of neurophysiological deterioration. Basically, interpretive parsimony is extension to a counterproductive degree of the necessary activity of organizing experience. Its scope is as wide as that of experience, and it may condition everything from recognizing objects in one's environment, through understanding others' actions, to comprehension of abstract ideas. In the main, parsimonious conditioning is gerrymandering of anomalous experiences to fit expectations. At whatever level of application, it is the employment of and reliance on too few and too rigid anticipatory construals of ideas, events, and people's actions—including one's own.

It isn't my intent to rehearse what I've said elsewhere, but three points need to be made about interpretive parsimony. First, even though interpretive economy is familiar to us as stereotypic thinking and the constraints of habit on construal of what we encounter, my term designates a more unified pattern of mental behavior than particular stereotypes and habits. Even though we think of individuals and of groups, like the elderly, as close-minded in various ways, we tend to do so in terms of fairly specific interpretive biases and practices. For instance, we consider stereotypic thinking primarily in connection with racism and sexism, and we think of constraining habit in connection with adaptive difficulties of a narrow sort, such as learning new job procedures. Interpretive parsimony is broader; in particular, it includes construal of one's own situation and actions. Second, interpretive parsimony enables us to understand some attitudinal and behavioral changes in the elderly as the cumulative effect of learned economy of construal, as opposed to the consequence of neurological deterioration. It thereby forces us to realize that we unknowingly collaborate with neurophysiological deterioration in the undermining of our own adaptive capacities. We do so by adding learned restrictions to any imposed on us by deterioration. This means that while our most recently identified prejudice, ageism,[10] has no adequate basis in fact, nonetheless age itself may be a better reason for negative attitudes toward the elderly than we would like.[11] Third, interpretive parsimony increases precisely because of success. That is, given our fairly stable environment, we manage relatively well with narrower and fewer interpretive practices than we might ideally employ. Parsimonious construals of people and their actions often are adequate for our purposes, even though not generous enough for productive understanding of others and rewarding interaction with them.

The essence of interpretive parsimony is that rather than letting new and varied experience broaden our interpretive practices as we age, we force experience to fit our interpretive practices. And because of relative success, this economy tends to increase to a point where it becomes self-defeating and we no longer deal effectively with the people and events we encounter. At that point we start hearing and addressing characters largely of our own making, and live through events we reshape to fit our expectations. As Patrick McKee points out in commenting on interpretive parsimony, we seem to be "left in old age with a pronounced tendency . . . to see the world in narrower terms."[12]

Interpretive decline is self-masking in the same way impairment of reasoning is. Recognition of growing interpretive parsimony, if it occurs, is usually diffuse awareness that something is wrong. This may take the form of concerned bafflement about others' reactions to our remarks and actions. Parsimonious interpretation of what others say and do produces occasions in which interaction with others proves frustrating and unproductive. Unfortunately, these situations are often dealt with by most people through use of still narrower interpretation. If interaction with others goes wrong, interpretively parsimonious individuals encountering discordance in their relations with others will be confirmed in their stereotypic views and consequently will apply them more broadly rather than considering whether the trouble may lie in their own attitudes and behavior. The result is that occasions for recognition of interpretive parsimony are lost, and relations with others are made that much more difficult.

Reflective aging individuals are considerably more likely to recognize interpretive parsimony in themselves than individuals not given to introspection. Interpretive parsimony may be recognized by reflective individuals when the behavior of those with whom they interact begins to fall systematically short of their expectations or otherwise raises questions about why those others respond as they do. Interpretive parsimony may also be recognized by reflective individuals when their own behavior falls short of expectations or is puzzling. In the first sort of case, reflective people won't simply dismiss how they're treated by others as due entirely to those others' own perceptions and biases. Reflective individuals will consider that they may somehow be eliciting perplexing responses; if they're treated condescendingly, they'll ponder whether they've acted in some way that invites condescension. In the second sort of case, reflective people will look more closely at their own motives and intentions when they surprise themselves by, say, making an overly hasty judgment about someone or some situation. Interpretive parsimony is accessible to reflection in a way that decreased interpretive flexibility due to neurophysiological deterioration isn't—though the latter may be intermittently recognized. If reflective individuals realize they've grown interpretively parsimonious, and they understand that interpretive economy is learned, they may initially feel confidence in their ability to assess their parsimony and to reverse it. Against this, if reflective individuals realize they've suffered neurophysiological deterioration, they'll have no illusions about their ability to reverse that deterioration.

Unfortunately, at present there's little reason to think that interpretive parsimony is ultimately any more reversible than is neurological deterioration.[13] Regardless of the greater likelihood that reflective people may recognize interpretive parsimony in themselves, it's by no means as likely that they'll be able to deal with it effectively. The main thing is that there's no way of telling if the growing interpretive rigidity, which occasions the recognition of parsimony, is conditioning efforts to counter parsimonious interpretation. Self-assessment of interpretive activity is, of course, itself interpretive. Individuals considering their interpretations of ideas, events, actions, or situations can test their construals only by considering alternative interpretations. But the alternative interpretations may well be parsimonious themselves in both specific content and variety,[14] as may be the exercise of assessment. Coping with interpretive parsimony isn't just a matter of taking more care, because the point is that what's affected is our very thinking, and in turn who we are, not just particular beliefs or ideas we may have.

EPISTEMOLOGICAL CRISES

Alisdair MacIntyre introduced the notion of an epistemological crisis in considering how individuals may fail, in a serious and paralyzing way, to understand what is taking place around them. MacIntyre contends that people may be at a complete loss as to what to do because they realize there are systematically different and mutually exclusive interpretations of important situations they face. They may become aware "of the existence of alternative and rival schemata which yield mutually incompatible accounts of what is going on."[15] Using Hamlet's predicament on his return to Elsinore as an apt fictive example, MacIntyre remarks that what Hamlet finds on his return from Wittenberg poses a crisis because there are "too many schemata available for interpreting the events at Elsinore. . . . There is the revenge schema of the Norse sagas; there is the renaissance courtier's schema; there is a Machiavellian schema about competition for power."[16] Hamlet doesn't know whether to believe his mother, Rosencrantz and Guildenstern, or his father's ghost about what occurred during his absence, so he looks for corroborative evidence for one or another interpretation. What makes the situation a crisis is that until Hamlet "has adopted some schema he does not know what to treat as evidence," but on the other hand, "until he knows what to treat as evidence he cannot tell what schema to adopt."[17] The resolution of the epistemological crisis can't be a matter of choosing among competing schemes by having recourse to "the facts," because what counts as facts is a function of whatever interpretive scheme is adopted. The epistemological crisis isn't a matter of not knowing enough; it's a matter of not knowing what to make of what's available.

Epistemological crises may go deeper than the need to make sense of particular events. The crises may be about ourselves. Interpretive schemes we use not only shape and define who others are and what they're up to, they shape and define who we are and what we're up to. When there's reason to think we're changing in advanced age, the schemes available to us for interpreting how we may be changing are determined by the deterioration considered in the last section. Responses to that deterioration include the "senility scheme" of inevitable decline, the "constructivist" scheme that attributes the negative aspects of aging to a prejudicial social construct, the "complacency" scheme that simply denies deterioration, and the "defiance" scheme that casts aging individuals as able to cope with and overcome possible deterioration. MacIntyre's epistemological crises are posed by challenges to the interpretive schemes within which we're subjects. The subjects of epistemological crises are unable to act until they can act on the basis of one or another interpretive scheme, because without a scheme, there's no coherent self to act. Subjects' identities are determined by the complex narratives that organize their lives. If those narratives are sufficiently disrupted, the subjects' identities are rendered as uncertain as their understanding of the problematic events that initiated their doubts. Because they're unable to adopt an explanatory scheme to construe the events in question in one way or another, the subjects of epistemological crises find their interpretive practices suddenly problematic, and that in turn jeopardizes the identities those practices define.

Epistemological crises, then, are interpretive failures and consequent paralyses resulting from the unresolved need to choose among alternative interpretive schemes. If the crises are serious enough, subjects' inability to deal with the events that prompt the crises disrupt the mechanisms they use to interpret other events in a holistic way. If that happens, the interpreting subjects can't function; they can't be subjects. That's when epistemological crises become crises of identity and aging individuals come to be at a loss as to who they are. This is the predicament that Robert Kastenbaum, paralleling MacIntyre, describes as the "crisis of explanation" in old age. Kastenbaum uses empirical data that show elderly people usually don't know how to deal with old age, and argues that the self-identity of the elderly is threatened by interpretive difficulties. He tells us that many elderly persons "*literally do not know what has happened to them, cannot explain to themselves . . . who they are, and cannot determine in which direction to move and for what purpose.*"[18]

Identity crises in advanced age can be understood as having several stages, though they're not necessarily temporally sequential. First, aging individuals realize that they "can't go on,"[19] that their lives no longer have substantial futures. This is key to identity crises because the realization makes aging individuals immensely vulnerable. Second, they begin to find their memory, attitudes, and behavior unreliable. For instance, they may be surprised at their new sentimentality or obsessive concern with health. Third, they're dealt with differently by others—as less responsible and with vaguely problematic thought and action. The result is that, like scientists who can no longer accommodate the experimental anomalies of an unviable theory, aging individuals no longer can accommodate anomalies in both their own attitudes and behavior and how they're treated by others. At that point their interpretive schemes fail, and they can't sustain the identity those schemes define. The identities their interpretive practices presuppose and delineate become precarious when those practices become suspect and when those identities cease to be accepted by others. Aging individuals find themselves treated by others in a manner too much at odds with their own expectations for them to deal in turn with those others as the persons they take themselves to be. For a time their interpretive schemes can be adjusted, but like theories burdened with too many qualifications, they soon become unworkable. As Kastenbaum puts it, aging individuals come not to know who they are, because the persons they've taken themselves to be are not only undermined by their own occasionally puzzling behavior, they're no longer acknowledged by those with whom they deal.

The difference between MacIntyre's epistemological crises and Kastenbaum's crises of explanation is mainly one of the measure of reflective awareness. The crisis of explanation is an epistemological crisis when experienced by a reflective person who understands that the crisis of explanation is caused by interpretive failure, is generated by interpretive conflicts, and calls for adoption of a new identity-defining and life-organizing scheme. Whereas unreflective individuals may accept their puzzlement and frustration as part of whatever is happening to them, and adapt to their circumstances in a way I discuss in the next section, reflective individuals will appreciate that they're being treated according to one or another of our culture's stereotypes of the aged, and that they must rethink their situations. They must assess to what extent the stereotype applies, and how they may best acknowledge irremediable changes and improve the still-manageable aspects of their circumstances. But rather than reducing their difficulties, understanding may only make matters worse. Recognition of stereotypic thinking applied to themselves invites parsimonious interpretation of disruptive incidents as due to stereotypic thinking on the part of others. Because it threatens diminishment of self, the possibility that the stereotyping has real grounds may be shunned. This tends to isolate aging individuals, to entrench unproductive views and attitudes, and superficially and temporarily to ease their crises with facile defiance. The result can be escalation of their crises into even more crippling ones.

The very reflectiveness that enables recognition of interpretive failure affords an opportunity for self-deception. In trying to deal with what they'll see as unfair stereotyping of themselves by others, reflective aging individuals may concede a certain amount of reason for worry, but insist on construing some of the changes that elicit unwelcome behavior on the part of others as positive rather than deteriorative. They may see those changes as products of growth and new wisdom rather than of decline. For example, they may see an increase in self-centeredness not as a product of negative attitudinal and emotive changes, but as finally giving themselves their due; they may accept a narrowing of interests and perspectives as new focusing on what is truly important. These partial concessions and reconstruals are misguided efforts to work out new interpretive schemes, and though misguided, they may succeed for a time. However, they are extremely dangerous maneuvers. First, they inevitably introduce greater cognitive dissonance. Second, they virtually ensure that reflective aging individuals will become more interpretively parsimonious, and so more isolated, and finally face more devastating crises. Third, because they're essentially no more than postponements of the inevitable, the time these maneuvers buy could well leave individuals with no scope for the hard decisions they might eventually make about ending their lives.

SETTLING FOR SENILITY

People facing Kastenbaum's crisis of explanation in old age, whether or not they're particularly reflective, are under tremendous psychological pressure to understand their situations, to adopt interpretive schemes that resolve their crises. But they'll be loath to confront the fact that it is *they* who are changing. And because few are equal to the task of understanding, let alone dealing with, large-scale failure and revision of interpretive schemes, aging individuals will strongly tend to look for something external to themselves to explain what has happened to them. Kastenbaum remarks that many elderly people see old age as a misfortune, almost as if, with luck, it might have been avoided.[20] Aging individuals tend to see themselves as people to whom something has happened, rather than as people in the process of natural transformation. This means that the crisis of explanation is prone to be half-resolved by adoption of our culture's "senility script," the experience-organizing narrative that portrays advanced age as an affliction. This model of aging "has tended to 'blame the victim' by explaining the problems of the aged as consequences of . . . deterioration and decline."[21] What the model fails to acknowledge is "the way social forces contribute to the difficulties faced by the aged."[22] The crises the aged face are prompted in part by how others treat them. Resolving those crises by adoption of the age-as-affliction model is acceptance that how they're treated by others is entirely justified. In MacIntyre's terms, what happens is that an interpretive scheme is adopted that recasts the self as diminished and impaired by inescapable degeneration, and others as treating that self in ways determined by that degeneration. This is unknowingly complicitous adoption by aging individuals of a senility imposed on them by others; it's internalization of our youth-oriented culture's model of age as affliction.

People don't usually think of their thought and action as functions of the employment of interpretive schemes. When aging individuals realize that something has gone seriously wrong, when anomalies begin to pile up, they aren't prepared to recognize that their interpretive schemes have failed because those schemes defined and served different, younger persons with different capacities, interests, and roles. Lacking understanding of how we're in part defined by others, aging individuals will be inclined to accept redefinition as increasingly dependent and lessened persons. The basis for this acquiescence was established in their own youth, when they internalized the same monolithic stereotype of old age that is now applied to them. That stereotype represents old age as a time of inevitable and holistic decline, and so as necessarily a time of decreasing autonomy and responsibility. The stereotype largely precludes the possibility of aging individuals' making significant decisions about themselves and their prospects, and condemns them to dependency and sufferance. "[T]he official psychology . . . portrays the old in terms of deficiency and personal deterioration, . . . elderly people are not given a voice in defining their condition."[23] And the ready-made interpretive scheme diminishes aging individuals in their own eyes as it diminishes them in the eyes of others. Nonetheless, though abhorrent, the senility script our culture offers furnishes the aged with apparent understanding of what's happened to them, and so with an interpretive scheme they so desperately need. The scheme is then unthinkingly adopted and used to define themselves into a sad and powerless old age.

The elderly thus are deprived of a voice in saying who they are and what the ends of their lives might be like. And what's most significant in the present context is that adoption of the senility script robs the old of the chance to forgo the worst of those lives by committing preemptive suicide. The old are denied the opportunity to assess their situations and prospects by being made to take themselves as victims of affliction, rather than as persons changing in ways they can't prevent but might avoid. But by the time the aged might want to hasten their deaths, they're assumed, by others and by themselves, to be past having the capacity to make so important a decision.

At present our culture's contribution to coping with old age is pressure to accept the interpretive scheme just described, whose intellectual parent is Aristotle and that has aging individuals deteriorating equally and inexorably in every aspect of their being. An alternative scheme, whose intellectual parent is Cicero and that is gaining favor, is far more optimistic. In its contemporary "constructivist" incarnation it conceives of old age as a cultural product and—barring diagnosable clinical conditions—denies that advanced age brings systematic deteriorative mental changes. But in spite of the attractiveness of this second scheme, both schemes are unacceptable because they are simplistic. The first facilely generalizes about an extremely complex process and glosses over very real differences among individuals. Worst of all, it yokes autonomy and responsibility to chronological age, so the soundness of the aged's assessments and decisions is rendered problematic prior to any symptoms of senescence.[24] The second scheme insouciantly ignores changes that are real enough to prompt Kastenbaum's explanatory crises and MacIntyre's epistemological crises. On the constructivist model, all but the most debilitating negative symptoms will be discounted as the products of unfortunate socialization and cultural stereotypes. Moreover, the epistemological implications of both schemes are unacceptable. Adoption of the senility model means that reasoning and interpretive flexibility are taken as increasingly untrustworthy, even if no negative symptoms are evident. Deterioration is assumed to be inevitable and, if not evident, presumed to be hidden. Adoption of the constructivist model means that called-for assessment of reasoning and interpretive flexibility in advanced age is precluded by refusal to allow special need. What may well be impaired reasoning and narrowed interpretation are then taken as basically reliable, and anomalies are explained away.

Our culture's view of old age ensures that too many aging individuals understand neither that their age-generated cognitive crises are in part interpretive, nor that the stereotypic "solution" our culture offers for those crises is itself interpretive. Though such understanding wouldn't change factual situations, it would go some way toward enabling aging individuals to better cope with what they face. Most important, understanding of the interpretive nature of the crises would enable individuals to appreciate that the crises are an occasion for assessment and decision, not acquiescence, and that there's still time for productive assessment and decision. It's crucial to understand that the crises are often a kind of prelude, not the occasion for acceptance that something irremediable has already occurred. Aging individuals have to appreciate that they can and must decide how they'll deal with old age, as opposed to simply acknowledging and accepting that old age has overtaken them. Adoption of a cultural stereotype is in effect abandonment of any possibility of controlling old age, especially the possibility of simply forgoing some part of it. The stereotype also ensures that even if persons I'm calling "reflective" understand that their culture's stereotype is operant in how they're seen and treated, and perhaps in their own thinking, they face a problem Hamlet didn't face in his epistemological crisis. Aging individuals must contend with the fact that just when they most need productive interaction with others, they're seen by others through distorting filters that warp or even preclude the interaction that alone can provide external checks on their assessments of their situations and prospects. If the responses of others to the concerns expressed by aging individuals are only commiseration, condescension, empty reassurances, or quick changes of subject to "spare their feelings," aging individuals will be denied the counsel they so much need to best order what's left of their lives.

REASON ENOUGH?

Most readers will probably think that what's been said so far just isn't enough to raise the question of preemptive suicide in a serious way. There's

a rather standard cultural view of suicide as prompted by fear of intellectual
decline. Suicide is seen as romantically fitting when dedicated artists take
their lives because of despondency about flagging creativity, or, as in the
case of Virginia Woolf, because the very sensitivity that's made them
artistically productive leaves them unable to cope with depression over
diminishment. The feeling likely will be that ordinary people don't have
the same stake in intellectuality, and that they're being presumptuous if
they think their lives are forfeit for the sorts of reasons discussed above. It'll
seem to many that consideration of suicide isn't generally warranted by
what's been said about the imperilment of what seems to be a fairly high
level of intellectuality. This view can be articulated in terms of the concern
with the maintenance of intellectuality being less the prizing of something
possessed than a too-demanding requirement that certain standards always
be met.[25] That requirement discounts the value of other, if more passive,
aspects of life. Many people have to deal with the debilitating consequences
of illness or accident, and learn not to demand more of themselves than is
consistent with reduced capacities. Some learn that the desire to be
something is often a drive to do something, and that not being able to
achieve some things doesn't mean their lives offer no satisfaction.

Perhaps, then, the changes discussed shouldn't prompt thoughts of
suicide but, rather, inspire reassessment and resignation. In this view, the
need to retain intellectuality, which I've presented as centrally constitutive
of self for some, is really only a desire to continue to meet self-imposed
standards of performance. It may be more appropriate to acknowledge and
tolerate some diminishment of intellectuality as decline in a less-than-self-
defining performative aspect of our lives, than to see it as absolute lessening.
In that way, aging individuals can live for what life might still offer, such
as rewarding relations with family, rather than for what they might accomplish.

It's true that we can imagine ourselves reaching a time in life when
intellectual achievement must be forgone but different satisfactions can
still be had. It's also true that concern about endangered intellectuality may
have more to do with feared loss of achievement than with maintenance
of a capacity that defines the self. Life does have a great deal to offer, beyond
what we might accomplish, that is of real value. However, the validity of
at least consideration of preemptive suicide ultimately depends on what
particular individuals most value and what they're willing to bear. Their
valuations may be reoriented by understanding of new limitations and of
how what they most prize may not be as essential as they think; they also
may remain steadfast in their views. If so, their consideration of preemptive

suicide is perfectly in order, even if their reasons turn out not to warrant self-destruction in others', and even in their own, eyes. The hard question is the proper weighting of fear of personal diminishment in preemptive suicidal deliberation. Answering that question is in part the burden of the rest of the book, but it's worth preparing the way for later discussion by saying a little here about the notion of intellectuality most relevant to consideration of preemptive suicide.

In this chapter the point has been to say how preemptive suicide arises as an option for reflective aging individuals whose intellectuality is threatened by deterioration in reasoning and interpretive capacities. The thrust of the foregoing is that unlike physical suffering, which might prompt a person to escape punishing circumstances, threatened loss of intellectuality may prompt a person to relinquish life before being diminished and becoming someone else. The sense of this is that deterioration in reasoning and interpretive capacities doesn't just impair individuals; it isn't a matter of individuals experiencing even severe limitations on their thought and action. The deterioration in question destroys essential traits that make individuals the persons they are; it terminates the characters or personalities of individuals. What is left aren't individuals who find themselves unable to do what they used to do; what is left are new, reduced individuals who have little recollection not only of what they used to do, but of who they were. For reflective aging individuals, then, deterioration in reasoning and interpretive capacities constitutes death of themselves, rather than even massive crippling of their abilities.

Anticipation of intellectual diminishment has been put forward as sufficient to raise the question of whether one might not be better off dead than living on in a reduced manner. The main objection to all this is that there's more to life than intellectuality, and that even highly reflective persons may enjoy a reasonably happy old age despite serious intellectual diminishment, and though retaining little or no memory or appreciation of what they've lost. Higher-level thought and perspicacious self-reflection, it's argued, aren't the highest values in human life, much less the only ones, and their threatened loss doesn't justify suicide. There's a tendency for those who raise this objection to conceive of intellectuality too narrowly, as a less-than-necessary capacity for problematically useful abstract thought. There's an attendant tendency to think of self-reflection as intrusive self-consciousness—even as a Kierkegaardian bar to authenticity.

I'm not arguing that threatened loss of intellectuality and self-reflection so conceived justifies preemptive suicide. The point is that what's most central to our being is that we are self-aware, reasoning entities. We not only reason in means-to-ends fashion, we assess and reflect on what we do and what happens to us. Through reflection we achieve an intentional distance that enables us to be and act in the world in an intelligently responsive way, as opposed to merely reacting to things and events around us.[26] Some hone their reflective ability to a high degree, and value their resulting capacity to live aware not only of what affects them directly, but also of historical trends and influences, the subtleties of human behavior, and our increasingly deep understanding of the universe we inhabit. But a time comes when reflective persons anticipate the loss of what defines them as intelligently reflective participants in human life; they fear that their aging bodies can no longer support their reflective awareness. This is enough reason for some to wonder if further life might not be best forgone to avoid the agony of experiencing even the beginnings of intellectual death in advance of physical extinction. Those who press the objection that intellectuality is being overrated see the changes taking place as just that: changes. They can imagine acknowledging fundamental changes in themselves, changes that the personal histories of millions strongly suggest are never for the better, with equanimity, and hope for still-attainable value. But to others, the changes in question amount to the end of the persons they are, even though those changes don't mark their end as living organisms.

Reflective aging individuals may acknowledge the beginning of funda-mental change in themselves with some optimism that they'll be able to cope with that change—and, ironically, if deterioration moves apace, they'll never be disappointed. Or they might be more realistic and only hope there'll be some compensating value in expected decline. But they may cast a cooler eye on remaining life and be prepared to forgo it; their values and priorities may be such that they don't want to continue living as others, as diminished people very different from who they've been in youth and middle age. They may not want to live wholly immersed in the events that constitute their lives, lacking too much of the reflective awareness that raises human experience above what animals enjoy.

If reflective aging individuals take this cooler view of life, they'll see preemptive suicide as their last fully deliberate choice, as the last respon-sible act of specific persons whose existence is ending despite their lives continuing. Nor is this cooler view of remaining life in advanced age prompted only by intellectual loss. Reflective individuals also understand that because of grosser physical changes, they're reaching the end of their lives as autonomous persons. Soon they'll no longer be able to do largely as they choose. Soon constraints on them will cease to be only social and moral, and become personal in a way that they may wholly reject. They'll grow increasingly dependent on others; they'll begin to lose control not only of their activities but also of their own bodies.

Fortunately, recognition of threatened intellectual decline usually comes when individuals are still able to make and enact tough decisions about their futures. By the time physical deterioration has advanced to a point where it hampers individuals and makes them dependent on others, it's likely too late for them to take decisive action regarding their lives. Reflective aging individuals therefore face a last choice upon realizing that their existence as intellectual entities is jeopardized or is already being eroded by advanced age, and that eventually personal diminishment will destroy them well before physical death. The choice they must make isn't so much whether to live or die; rather, it's whether or not to allow emerging versions of themselves to continue living. They may make the hard decision that the emerging versions of themselves—intellectually crippled, socially powerless, wholly dependent, and predisposed to illness—don't merit life.

A NEW FACTOR

There's little or nothing in the foregoing sections of this chapter that Seneca or Hume wouldn't understand and likely endorse. But at the close of the twentieth century, reflective aging individuals must contend with something new regarding their choices to live or die. A sea change is taking place in societal attitudes toward life and death, a change manifest in the ongoing debate on assisted suicide. Chief Justice William Rehnquist acknowledged this change in saying that we're "engaged in an earnest and profound debate about the morality, legality and practicality of physician-assisted suicide."[27] In a historically significant reassertion of personal autonomy,[28] much is being said and claimed about individuals' "right to die"[29] when their lives cease to be blessings and become intolerable burdens because of suffering and demeaning dependency on others. It appears that we're achieving a social and cultural maturity about the value of blighted life, but as with most developments in human history, appearances are incomplete, if not deceptive. It isn't just that we've focused on what Rehnquist describes as the question of "whether a mentally competent person who is experiencing great suffering has a constitutionally cognizable interest in controlling the circumstances of his or her imminent death."[30] Assertion of autonomy with respect to one's own death entails a great deal about the bases for autonomous action. Those bases are discussed almost exclusively in terms of "great suffering," but there's inevitably reference beyond physical suffering to "loss of dignity." The latter accommodates a lot, and it's the clue to the fact that the new realism about life's value in desperate circumstances involves a more fundamental reevaluation of dependent life, of life that isn't viable in itself and the maintenance of which requires the help of others. The result is that reflective aging individuals now need to weigh a new factor in their assessments of whether they're willing to risk or endure personal diminishment. They have to give careful consideration to how the increasingly dependent aged are coming to be viewed by their society.

Debate of the right to die is structured in terms of a new need to assert and protect personal autonomy through legislation permitting assistance in commission of suicide.[31] Right-to-die activism looks to be a result of modern medicine's capacity to sustain highly problematic life and what many regard as abuse of that capacity. It's been claimed that we soon "will be able to keep virtually everyone alive indefinitely,"[32] so we face the question of "whether medicine is to remain a humanitarian . . . profession or [become] a new but depersonalized science in the service of prolonging life rather than diminishing human suffering."[33] Physicians now have the ability to keep their patients alive beyond the point at which survival ceases to be in patients' interests and even is contrary to their wishes. Supposedly, medicine's governing mandate to heal and to preserve life, and to above all do no harm, too often drives physicians to use newly available technology to maintain life at great cost, even if doing so is counterproductive in terms of human suffering. There is, then, a perceived need to extend patients' right to refuse treatment by legislatively establishing their right to assistance in commission of suicide when they're hospitalized or can't manage it on their own.

But as suggested, there's considerably more going on. Underlying the historically new concern about counterproductive maintenance of life is a more fundamental reconception of life as a valued but discretionary possession, instead of its being an unrenounceable gift entailing obligations regarding its preservation.[34] More liberal contemporary moral and religious views have greatly weakened the traditional—basically religious—idea that our lives aren't our own to take. But attrition of that idea, whether ownership is thought to be divine or communal, isn't due only to greater liberality and secularization. A number of recent developments have played specific and significant roles in reshaping public attitudes. One of the most important of these developments is the broader social impact of feminist thinking regarding abortion. Legislative recognition that women's bodies are their own to control had an important enhancing effect on attitudes regarding personal autonomy.[35] The way this worked is that while changing social attitudes drive legislative innovation, it's enacted legislation that crystallizes those often inchoate new attitudes, reinforcing and legitimizing them. In this way, legislation "bring[s] changes in the way we understand ourselves."[36] Abortion-enabling legislation had a profound effect we're only beginning to understand. It not only established autonomy as a key principle and reference point in social and legal debate,[37] it acknowledged and legitimized historically unprecedented social valuation of autonomy. That valuation of autonomy is clearly operant in right-to-die activism. Growing social acceptance of assisted suicide and death-hastening medical practices is driven by our culture's high valuation of autonomy. The basic idea is that individuals' autonomy gives them the right to "control . . . the circumstances of . . . imminent death." This is installation of autonomy as an important enough principle to override present legal, moral, and religious prohibitions against ending one's own life. But this prioritizing of autonomy carries the clear implication that given the value of autonomy, once people lose their capacity to be autonomous, their remaining life is irrevocably devalued.

While the Supreme Court ruled that assistance in suicide "is not a fundamental liberty interest protected by the due-process clause,"[38] by upholding two state laws prohibiting assisted suicide, it left the door open for states to legalize assisted suicide. The assisted-suicide debate was essentially unaffected by the decision, and will certainly continue.[39] There's little question that we'll soon see more legislation enabling assisted suicide. And just as legislation enabling abortion had profound effects on our society by crystallizing and legitimizing new attitudes, so legislation enabling assisted suicide will do the same. There are very good reasons to allow assisted suicide, but legalizing it, and thereby validating and codifying new social attitudes, carries a price. Legislation permitting suicide directly or indirectly places a higher value on "life that can be lived autonomously" and thereby depreciates "life that is dependent."[40] Such legislation will "heighten the prestige we accord autonomous, independent lives and depreciate the claims of those seen to be dependent."[41] Some of this depreciation is already evident. While there's no doubt that medical technology is sometimes unwisely used to keep people alive to no good purpose, there's been a decided shift in the opposite direction.

Assisted suicide and voluntary euthanasia may not be widely practiced, but some feel that "nowadays many, if not most, Americans die because someone—doctors, family members or they themselves—has decided that it is time for them to go."[42] Widespread use of practices no more intrusive than simple lack of "aggressive" treatment or compassionately generous sedation means that "[w]hat might be called managed deaths . . . are now the norm."[43] Physicians and nurses have always understood that conforming to medicine's principles occasionally means helping someone to die to alleviate hopeless and pointless torment, but traditionally they've been inclined—for both professional and legal reasons—to err on the side of preserving life. Now they're more and more inclined to act in accord with that understanding rather than adhering strictly to legal and professional requirements.[44] Certainly the larger part of what underlies the new facilitation—or at least nonobstruction—of death is compassion for the dying who are enduring needless and pointless suffering. However, another part is the growing conviction that some lives aren't worth living, and not only because of untreatable pain. Some lives are seen as not worth living because they are wholly dependent and allow only what can be done with the help and cooperation of others.

The upshot here is that while it may seem that new attitudes toward blighted life are very much in line with what I've said about preemptive suicide, and that right-to-die activism serves the interests of reflective aging individuals considering preemptive suicide, the fact is that the new social attitudes may unduly influence their decisions, and thereby render them less than rational. Our time's emphasis on personal autonomy regarding elective death is a bit too coincidentally convenient. An aging population is putting increasingly onerous pressure on our health-care system, and there's a good chance that the sea change in society's attitudes is more pragmatic than altruistic. Some regard the change as an ominous turn. They worry about "where we're headed as a society with respect to health care," and fear "that assisted suicide is not going to be the option of last resort—it's going to be the attractive solution of first resort."[45] What this means for reflective aging individuals, in practical terms, is that they will be less tolerated in society and they'll face growing expectations that they "should do the responsible thing"[46] and end their lives before becoming costly burdens.[47] Reflective aging individuals now have to take into account how continued life likely will be more unattractive than previously because of societal disapprobation of dependency. Deliberation of preemptive suicide must be qualified by how living dependent lives will be harder. Life in advanced age will include not just the deterioration and afflictions that may make life less than worth living, but increasingly grudging societal support, more difficult access to health care, and the stigma of appearing to deprive others of scarce resources simply by being old and continuing to live.[48]

NOTES

1. Prado 1983, 1986.

2. Cowley 1982:5.

3. As will be evident to many, much of what follows relies on Michel Foucault's work, which he describes as aimed at producing "a history of the different modes by which . . . human beings are made subjects." Foucault 1983:208. see also Prado 1995.

4. See Prado 1995: chapter 4; see also Foucault 1983:212.

5. Arthur Caplan notes the danger of "where we're headed as a society with respect to health care" because of an aging population:

People think now they're facing a system that's trying to ration. That is a mere hint of what is to come. . . . I worry that . . . suicide is not going to be the option of last resort—it's going to be the attractive solution of first resort. Not that we're going to have a government dictating, you must die, [but] that suddenly within the society, the notion will come that the older and disabled who are expensive should do the responsible thing. (Caplan 1996)

6. See, e.g., Tierney 1982; Henig 1981; Denny 1979; Hoffmeister 1979; Jarvik 1979; Birren and Schaie 1977; Birren 1968a, 1968b; Siegler 1976; Baltes and Schaie 1974; Bromley 1974; Botwinick 1967.

7. Prado 1986.

8. Ibid.:132–37.

9. Prado 1983.

10. See Levin and Levin 1980.

11. McKee 1988:133.

12. Ibid.

13. McKee 1988.

14. Most of us have had the experience of hearing someone try to smooth over an ill-advised racist or sexist remark, and just make things worse by revealing the depth of his or her prejudice.

15. MacIntyre 1977:454.

16. Ibid.

17. Ibid.

18. Kastenbaum 1964:321.

19. Blythe 1979:5.

20. Kastenbaum 1964:321.

21. Levin and Levin 1980:ix.

22. Ibid.

23. Salmon 1985:41.

24. Prado 1986; Levin and Levin 1980; Palmore 1971.

25. I owe the point to Chris Beeman.

26. See Edwards 1967:201–4.

27. From the June 27, 1997, Supreme Court decision on assisted suicide; quoted in Garrow 1997.

28. But see Glick 1997.

29. See Rosen 1996.

30. From the June 27, 1997, Supreme Court decision on assisted suicide; quoted in Garrow 1997.

31. The right to refuse treatment is already protected by law, and suicide itself isn't illegal in most North American and European jurisdictions. Germany decriminalized suicide in 1751; Canada, as late as 1972. Battin 1992b:46. *Assisted* suicide is widely illegal and is the focus of right-to-die activism. See Greenhouse 1997b.

32. Marshall Perron, author of Australia's Northern Territories' short-lived assisted suicide and euthanasia legislation, which was in force from July 1996 to March 1997. Quoted in Mydans 1997. Only four people availed themselves of the law while it was in force. See "Australia Strikes Down . . ." 1997.

33. Kübler-Ross 1969; chapter 2.

34. See Sandel 1997.

35. See Rosen 1997.

36. Sandel 1997. Quoted in Steinfels 1997b.

37. The popular label "pro-choice" asserts autonomy against the "pro-life" label, which asserts obligation.

38. The decision was handed down June 27, 1997; Chief Justice William Rehnquist, quoted in Scott 1997.

39. It's only a matter of time before the Court has to deal with the issue again. See Garrow 1997.

40. Steinfels 1997b. As Sandel puts it, "existing laws against assisted suicide reflect and entrench certain views about what gives life meaning. But the same would be true were the Court to declare, in the name of autonomy, a right to assisted suicide." Sandel 1997.

41. Sandel 1997.

42. Kolata 1997e.

43. Ibid.; see also Kolata 1996a; Cox 1997b.

44. See, e.g., Kolata 1996a.

45. Caplan 1996.

46. Caplan 1996.

47. See "Its Young vs. Old" 1997.

48. No one nearing retirement age in an academic setting will think this last point exaggerated.

3

SUICIDE AND RATIONALITY

The weariest and most loathed worldly life
. . . is a paradise
To what we fear of death.
Shakespeare, *Measure for Measure*

Despite the recent beginnings of change, our culture's prevalent view still is that life is the ultimate value, and that life is worth preserving, at all costs, for its own sake. A more sophisticated but almost as uncompromising view is that as the precondition of all other values, life is to be preserved unless and until other values become irrevocably unattainable.[1] What makes this view as nearly uncompromising as the first is the resistance to admitting that other values have indeed become irrevocably unattainable. In line with the conception of life as the ultimate value or the condition of all other values, is the currently dominant view that suicide is almost always pathological: "We now tend to treat suicide as the product of mental illness, or as a desperate dangerous 'cry for help' used by someone who does not really want to die."[2] These resolute views persist in spite of the sea change taking place in societal attitudes toward assisted suicide. The reason is that the change focuses on suicide in hopeless cases, where death is in any case imminent and survival is punishing.[3] Self-destruction remains something to be considered as a voluntary option, that is, one that isn't contextually coerced, only in the most extreme circumstances.

Even in cases where there's no hope of improvement in terminal conditions, desires expressed by individuals under medical care to be helped to die still are often dismissed as insufficient to justify cessation of treatment, much less more intrusive aid in dying. This is in spite of judicial support for the right to forgo life-sustaining treatment. In cases where patients are comatose or otherwise incapacitated, previously expressed wishes, such as in "living wills" and do-not-resuscitate orders, are sometimes, if not often, overruled. In a typical instance, a judge rejected a family's appeal to stop artificially sustaining the life of an elderly stroke-damaged relative by dismissing the patient's own explicitly and repeatedly expressed wishes not to be kept alive. The judgment was that the individual's earlier statements couldn't be "held to be clear and convincing proof of a general intent to decline . . . treatment once incompetency [set] in."[4] While the judge made an important point about too-ready acceptance of remarks made well before an actual condition, expressed willingness to abandon life even in hopeless circumstances isn't yet decisive in the event. The working assumption in such cases usually is that what's actually sought isn't death but help, reassurance, and comfort. It's too often assumed that no one can actually want to die, so that to reject life-sustaining treatment must be only to express horror at harsh realities. The problematic nature of how attempts to relinquish life in desperate circumstances are dealt with highlights how, in the common view, elective death isn't acceptable unless prompted by utter hopelessness.

What's important for my purposes is that suicide is largely perceived as justifiable only in cases where individuals are under extraordinary pressures of maximally negative sorts. Whether or not many are now concerned to defend the right to die—that is, to hasten death—in terminal situations, most are still unwilling to countenance cool, reflective suicide done because one decides it's the most sensible thing to do *prior* to serious and personally diminishing deterioration.[5] There's a broadly held and strong conviction that self-inflicted death could never be the most sensible option, that it could never really be a warranted option at all, for anyone not in an extreme situation. Suicide is deemed to be a driven act. It's thought to be an act driven by maximum desperation, utter confusion, or the need to make the consummate sacrifice: to lay down one's life for the sake of others, for moral principle, or for religious or political commitments. Recent changes haven't made a great difference to this view. Present attitudes are still against an individual committing suicide in anticipation of suffering or decline. This is even more true regarding individuals' committing suicide in anticipation of what is taken as "natural" age-related deterioration. These attitudes not only block preemptive suicide and threaten unwelcome intervention; they obstruct the counsel and support necessary for the making of sound preemptive suicidal decisions.

The first step toward countering present attitudes regarding suicide in less-than-desperate circumstances is to rebut the most basic philosophical objection to suicide generally. Objections grounded in ethical and religious beliefs can be dealt with in turn, and in any case require specification and consideration of particular moral codes and religious doctrines. Philosophical objections are more fundamental because they are conceptual, and the most basic of these has to do with denial of the intelligibility or coherence of elective death in less-than-desperate circumstances. The objection articulates perception of such suicide as invariably pathological, thus never rational, because not warranted by immediate and pressing states of affairs. Choosing to die in the absence of disastrous circumstances is seen as unthinkable in the absence of self-deception, bewilderment, or compulsion. Suicide is characterized as pathological, and its nondesperate instances as products of one or another form of derangement. This characterization of suicide extends to thinking that cases of self-inflicted death prompted by extreme and irremediable circumstances in some sense aren't really cases of suicide at all, precisely because in those cases it's thought intelligible and warranted to choose to die. This tendentious redefinition of suicide is evident in the common discomfort with description of self-destruction in circumstances of heroic sacrifice or great agony as "suicide." Suicide, then, can't be rational, and objections to its being held so receive their most pointed philosophical articulation in the "lack of contrast" argument, which attempts to establish as a matter of conceptual truth that suicide is irrational. Whatever one may think of the argument in the end, it's necessary to consider it, because if it's sound, it would allow only surcease suicide as rational and quite simply would preclude most cases of preemptive suicide from being rational.

THE LACK-OF-CONTRAST ARGUMENT

Perhaps the potentially most powerful argument against suicide's being rational denies the coherence of choosing to die by attempting to establish the unintelligibility of having "being dead" as the desired objective of a course of action. The argument allows for cases of surcease suicide, and self-destruction for moral and altruistic reasons, by making the desired objective in such cases not being dead, but the cessation of pain, the avoidance of moral evil, and the benefit of others. Among those who make this argument is John Donnelly, who contends that "we know (as an article of commonsensism) that suicide is not rational."[6] In keeping with the above-mentioned exclusion of justifiable self-destruction as not really suicide, Donnelly's definition of suicide excludes self-inflicted death in terminal illness or similar circumstances, and where the alternative is some otherwise inescapable gross moral wrong.[7] Donnelly's definition of suicide conveniently removes acceptable cases of self-inflicted death from the category of suicide, which is described as "self-murder." In effect, suicide is isolated as a special, nonrational sort of self-destruction. This definitional maneuver is typical of direct and indirect denials of the rationality of suicide where it isn't contextually coerced. However, "suicide" simply means "self-killing," and need neither be self-murder nor carry the moral opprobrium the term is often made to bear. Attempts to define suicide as irrational are unworkable efforts to stipulate suicide's irrationality, or often its immorality, thus are transparent semantic ploys, and don't merit serious consideration.

As for the argument itself, its central claim is that no one can intelligibly evaluate being dead as an alternative to continuing to live. The argument's point is that in order to rationally commit suicide, people must be able to judge that being dead somehow is better for them than being alive, and allegedly they can't do that. The reason is that it's conceptually impossible to evaluatively contrast being dead, that is, not existing, with being alive or existing. What's denied, then, is the possibility of a coherent evaluatory basis on which to ground the choice to die where circumstances don't force the issue.[8] The argument specifically rejects the conceptual possibility of an evaluative, comparative contrast between experienced existence and inconceivable nonexistence, and thus the possibility of such a contrast serving as a basis for warranted suicidal decisions. The lack-of-contrast argument's putative force is that the decision to die can't follow as a consequence of sound deliberation because we can't meaningfully evaluate being dead, which is nothing at all, in consideration of suicide, so we can't rationally choose to *be* dead. If individuals do choose to commit suicide, they allegedly do so irrationally, or at least arationally, because what they confusedly have in mind as their intended objective isn't actually being dead, but some muddled state of posthumous existence. Choosing to die, then, can't be rational because it's rooted in confusion. Clearly this argument goes to the heart of preemptive suicide, since the pivotal judgment of preemptive suicide appears to be that one would be better off dead than diminished in the future.

The essential idea of the lack-of-contrast argument has an initial plausibility. It does seem that to contemplate suicide in a rational manner, potential suicidists would have to weigh the manifest value of being alive—even in whatever punishing circumstances prompt consideration of suicide—against the inconceivable value of being dead. The plausibility of this idea is evident in the points made earlier, about ceasing to exist being an odd objective of intentional action, and about the difficulty of saying how nonexistence could accord with suicidists' interests. The trouble supposedly is that one of the alternatives weighed, being dead, can't be assigned a value because it's not any form of being at all. Attempting to assign being dead a value would require confusedly treating an unthinkable nonstate as an assessable state.[9] Since being dead isn't a very special kind of being, it can't be compared in evaluative or any other terms with being alive. Putting the point in our own terms, the lack-of-contrast argument attempts to show that we can't have "vivid awareness" or adequate understanding of the consequences of suicide. If the argument works, it would preclude that choosing to die could be rational, because we can't make sound evaluative judgments about those consequences. The lack-of-contrast argument has one apparent strength in contrast to our consideration of vivid awareness of suicidal consequences. That apparent strength is that rather than raising difficult questions about our capacities to conceive and understand the consequences of suicide, the argument straightforwardly denies the logical possibility of assigning a value to what one allegedly must prefer in choosing to die. Since it's a nonstate, being dead simply can't be a proper object of preference, and so can't be a proper objective of rational action.

To make out a case for preemptive suicide, the lack-of-contrast argument must be defeated both in the particular form considered and as representative of a priori arguments against rational suicide. According to the lack-of-contrast argument, the only way self-destruction may pass rational muster is if it's driven by unbearable agony, great moral threat, or possibly life-sacrificing altruism. But it's central to preemptive suicide that it can be rational to choose to die before being in circumstances that make self-destruction the only alternative to unbearable suffering. Therefore, the argument must be rebutted if preemptive suicide in advanced age is to be a rational alternative to anticipated dissipation of personality through loss of intellectuality and inevitable grievous loss of autonomy. Hume's claim that "suicide may often be consistent with interest and with our duty to our selves"[10] must be established against the view that it can't make sense to willingly choose to die, in the sense that individuals may opt to end their lives without being contextually coerced to do so. And it should be recalled here that we can't simply escalate rejection of anticipated diminishment to the level of coercive psychological torment without illegitimately turning preemptive suicide into surcease suicide. I need to show that the lack-of-contrast argument fails, and that's best done by showing that the argument only appears to work by manufacturing a conveniently inconceivable intentional object for suicidal deliberation.

CHOOSING TO DIE

The basic issue about preemptive suicide and the lack-of-contrast argument is whether it's conceptually possible for someone to judge that death is preferable to a life that soon will be lived as a diminished and essentially different person. What this comes to is that there must be a form of suicide that is a rationally justifiable ending of life after cool, well-reasoned reflection and consultation, and in anticipation of unacceptable circumstances rather than because of their unbearable actuality. For this sort of suicide to be rational, it has to be coherent to prefer and choose to die, and in that sense to have being dead or nonexistence as an intentional objective. Preemptive suicide isn't prompted by desperate physical or ethical dilemmas, so it can't be one of the exceptions that the lack-of-contrast argument allows. Instead, preemptive suicide is prompted by the realization that the quality of life left to one is seriously and irrevocably jeopardized by the inevitable consequences of the sheer accumulation of years. Preemptive suicide in advanced age is an act in accord with Hume's belief that there's a crucial duty to oneself not to allow life-despoiling personal diminishment to occur. Preemptive suicide is intended to prevent, not to escape, the kind of diminishment of self that age-related deterioration brings about. The basic presupposition is that such expected diminishment of self warrants self-inflicted death as much as does being tormented by dreadful physical suffering or being forced to irrevocably violate one's most deeply held moral convictions. But as such, preemptive suicide fails the rationality test set up by the lack-of-contrast argument.

Dealing with the lack-of-contrast argument requires noting that the allowed exceptions, self-destruction in extreme circumstances, are of secondary philosophical importance because contextual coercion in effect rules out alternative courses of action. Questions about the soundness of reasoning and motivation really don't come up in the tolerated cases, because the warrants for self-destruction are evident in the postulated situations. The matter of rationality doesn't really arise with respect to these putative exceptions to the irrationality of suicide, because the cases in question are precisely of the sort where *not* killing oneself makes even less sense than doing so. But what's important about the allowed exceptions is that the reason they are exceptions is that what individuals prefer, choose, and then act to achieve, isn't death or being dead per se. Rather, it's escape from hopeless agony, avoidance of moral compromise, or possibly altruistic provision of benefit to others. In other words, what contextual coercion does is provide a coherent intentional objective for self-destruction in place of the inconceivable one of judging being dead more desirable than remaining alive. Warranted self-destruction in extreme circumstances can then be understood in one of two ways: either as rational because preferable to remaining alive in torment or morally debased, or as simply not raising the issue of rationality because suicide is forced by circumstances. When we put things this way, we begin to see the artificiality of what the lack-of-contrast argument rules out as irrational suicide. That seems to be a matter of thinking that one is better off being dead than being alive *simpliciter*. What's obviously missing is why that supposedly impossible judgment might be attempted. Like so many a priori arguments, what the lack-of-contrast argument rules out seems to be hopelessly abstract judgments and decisions. If there's any force to the argument, it has to be that those considering self-destruction in less-than-desperate circumstances, like those considering preemptive suicide, *are* judging themselves better off dead than alive, in the allegedly incoherent way, because their circumstances provide no compelling reasons for them to disvalue being alive. Once this is clear, we see that what's actually going on is that hypothetical reasoning about self-destruction is being summarily dismissed as incoherent.

The lack-of-contrast argument fails, but before saying just how it does so, it's important to acknowledge that the argument does capture something that is intuitively compelling, which is that choosing to die seems senseless because of death's irrevocable nature. The lines from Shakespeare at the beginning of this chapter very effectively state the idea that however bad life may get, while one still lives, life could become endurable, whereas choosing to die is an utterly irreversible abandonment of all possibility. But it isn't just the irrevocable nature of death that's caught by the lack-of-contrast argument, and that gives it a measure of power it doesn't really merit. If vivid awareness of consequences is required for rational suicide, then those considering suicide have to acknowledge not only that death is irreversible, but that it's likely personal annihilation. Shakespeare's words, then, are doubly forceful, for the evaluative contrast has to be between even tormented life and possible, if not likely, total nonexistence. This is why contextual coercion plays so important a role in the alleged exceptions to the irrationality of self-destruction, because such coercion turns even likely nonexistence into a preferable alternative to wholly unbearable agony. We also see why the nature of contextual coercion is thought by so many to have to be of a consummate sort to justify self-destruction. The underlying truth in all this is that—pace the argument—in assessing whether they'd be better off dead than surviving in certain circumstances, people just can't know whether what suicide enables them to avoid would in fact prove intolerable, or whether it might not be alleviated by compensating values, and so whether it isn't preferable to dying and likely ceasing to exist. It would seem, then, that choosing to die must always be at least a precipitous, and hence less than rational, decision. Another way of saying this is that it looks as if there can never be a final moment when we can conclusively judge that it's better to die than to live.

To return to the argument, it may seem that the way to answer it, at least with respect to preemptive suicide, is to counter that there are cases where, even if the consequence of suicide is personal annihilation, dying is preferable to anticipated diminishment of self amounting to destruction of the person one is. This would be, in effect, to try to fit preemptive suicide into the class of self-destructive acts warranted by contextual coercion. But the claim needn't involve raising anticipation of dreaded future diminishment to the level of present psychological torment in order to justify self-destruction. That is, it wouldn't be an ill-conceived attempt to turn preemptive suicide into a special sort of surcease suicide. The claim would be that feared loss of personal identity, which by its very nature must occur prior to actual loss, is itself as compelling a reason for self-destruction as is great pain or moral threat. This sounds plausible initially, and there is some truth to the idea, but the maneuver won't work. The exceptions won't admit cases in which dying now is justified by something anticipated but not even immediately imminent, and, what's more, something certain neither in its occurrence nor in its expected virulence. In other words, fear of threatened personal diminishment isn't enough to constitute contextual coercion comparable to immediate great pain or moral danger. Not only can't we know beforehand that the feared diminishment in fact will take place and be as destructive as feared, but we can't predict with certainty that it might not be compensated for in some way. For instance, some diminishment might make individuals more open to the simple satisfactions still available to them in advanced age and that they otherwise would disdain. What would need to be established is that the anticipated diminishment would be unendurable in simply occurring, to *any* extent, and that appears unworkable.

What needs to be done about the lack-of-contrast argument is to clarify what is already implicit in the nature of the exceptions it allows. The point of the lack-of-contrast argument is that being dead can't be assessed in suicidal deliberation, and so can't be judged preferable to continuing to live, since we can't assign nonexistence a value because it's a nonstate. The exceptions the argument allows don't involve having being dead either as the preferred objective or as the end of intentional action. The cases allowed are ones where contextual coercion in effect provides a coherent object of assessment in consideration of self-destruction, that is, escape from torment or avoidance of moral debasement. Being dead is the consequence of choosing not to endure something, not itself an objective. But preemptive suicide precisely fits this scheme. Preemptive suicide isn't committed because being dead is considered preferable to living in a diminished way; being dead is the consequence of not allowing personal diminishment. Preemptive suicidists don't try to evaluate whether being dead or not existing is better than being diminished. They are unwilling to be diminished, and the only way they can avoid being diminished is by taking their own lives. Dying, ceasing to exist, is the result of the action they take, but that action has as its primary objective prevention of diminishment. Death isn't what's judged preferable. The comparative evaluation, then, is of the relative values of bearing something or not bearing something, where not bearing that something entails dying.

It appears, then, that if the lack-of-contrast argument raises a problem about preemptive suicide, it's one about time. It may be that feared personal diminishment in the future isn't acceptable as a pressing enough consideration to warrant rational self-destruction. But before considering this, it's important to see that whether or not it raises this temporal question about preemptive suicide, the lack-of-contrast argument fails to establish that suicide is irrational. It does so because it allows as exceptions all of the instances of suicide that are of significance with respect to rationality. In other words, the stipulative definition of suicide, which excludes contextually coerced self-destruction as not really suicide, empties the class of suicides that might be assessed as rational or not rational. What the argument precludes, if it precludes anything, is instances of suicide that are already irrational or arational, because we can readily admit that suicide committed on the basis that being dead is a desirable state of affairs is irrational or at least arational. But the concession is worthless, because the cases of suicide that raise the issue of rationality are those where the question is whether relinquishing life is warranted by avoidance of something, and where death is the consequence of that avoidance and not the primary objective. These cases can't be shown to be irrational or even arational merely by pointing out that being dead is a nonassessable nonstate, since being dead isn't what's assessed or preferred in the cases at issue.

The crucial evaluative assessment in consideration of preemptive suicide is whether or not one is willing to endure certain circumstances. In this, it's essentially like surcease suicide, but the difference is significant. In consideration of preemptive suicide, what potential suicidists are unwilling to bear is both in the future and not known to be unbearable, whereas immediate agony or moral threat is. But the nature of what they're unwilling to bear requires that preemptive suicidists commit suicide significantly ahead of the feared diminishment. Once that diminishment is evident, it becomes highly problematic whether preemptive suicide can still be committed rationally, or at all. The need to time preemptive suicide before the onset of what could otherwise serve as contextual coercion warranting self-destruction again raises the question of coherence. Though the lack-of-contrast argument doesn't rule out preemptive suicide a priori, it does raise the question of whether it can make sense to forfeit life on the basis of anticipated personal diminishment that not only is in the future, but also is of an importantly indeterminate nature. However, this question can't be tackled directly, at least not in a general way. As I indicated earlier, my strategy is criterial. I don't think it can be straightforwardly established that preemptive suicide is or can be rational, or that its timing can be accommodated in sound deliberation and be shown to be in accord with individuals' interests. What can be done is to say, carefully, under what conditions suicide and preemptive suicide would be judged rational. If those conditions are met, we can say, with Margaret Battin, that in "the absence of any compelling evidence to the contrary," the cases in question are cases where people rationally choose to die "on the basis of reasoning which is by all usual standards adequate."[11] We can proceed, then, on the understanding that the lack-of-contrast argument fails so long as it's coherent to choose to die, not because of a preference to be dead but because of a willingness to accept death as the price of avoiding what one deems unbearable. What's been gained is that suicide can't be shown to be irrational merely by making the logical point that being dead is a nonstate that defies evaluation, and so can't be the objective of rational suicidal deliberation and choice. We've also clarified the significance of the temporal element in preemptive suicide. We now need to articulate the conditions under which suicide and preemptive suicide may be rational.

INITIAL CRITERIA FOR RATIONAL SUICIDE

Part of what's needed to establish the rationality of suicide is captured by Jacques Choron. He explains that for suicide to be rational, not only must there be "no psychiatric disorder," and suicidists' reasoning must be "in no way impaired," but rationality further requires that "motives would seem justifiable, or at least 'understandable,' to the majority of . . . contemporaries in the same culture or social group."[12] This latter is a crucial point, but unfortunately Choron pairs it with a nonimpairment requirement that presupposes rather too much. While he's quite right to require that reasoning be unimpaired by either error or pathology, Choron seems simply to take it that potential suicidists' unimpaired reasoning includes the necessary vivid awareness of the consequences of what they're considering. This needn't be so, as we saw earlier. Furthermore, with respect to his central contribution regarding the accessibility of motivation, Choron's problematic addition of the phrase "or social group" to his specification of suicidists' peers tends to relativize the acceptability of motivation. Nonetheless, Choron's is a pivotal requirement, and clearly the accessibility of suicidists' motives to others, so they may judge them cogent or otherwise, is key to suicide's rationality. Suicidal motivation can't be only subjectively adequate if suicide is to be rational. Nor is it enough that it be deemed adequate only by a small group on the basis of possibly idiosyncratic standards. Potential suicidists' peers have to find that self-destruction is elected for cogent reasons, and do so on the basis of broad societal or cultural standards.

Choron may be optimistic in thinking that the majority of people in our culture are ready to earnestly attempt to understand suicidists' motives, and possibly judge them cogent, since suicide is still generally seen as inherently irrational. But this readiness used to be much more rare than it is now; people are increasingly taking suicide seriously as an option in certain circumstances. This is crucial to Choron's well-taken point about accessibility. Suicidists' peers must be prepared to assess suicidal motivation as possibly cogent. They must be ready to consider some motives as possibly justifying suicide, rather than dismiss all suicidal motivation as rationalization of compulsion or confusion. Not only is this necessary to establishing the rationality of suicide, but just as we can't allow the cogency of suicidal motivation to depend on a small group, so we can't allow suicidal motivation to be deemed adequate if merely consistent with individuals' own values and preferences. Even though standards for rationality aren't ahistorical, the soundness of suicidal motivation isn't relative to particular individuals or small groups. We don't need to embrace some form of objectivism to acknowledge that the main point of assessing whether motives are rational or otherwise usually is to test for idiosyncratic judgments made solely on the basis of personal values and preferences, even if shared by some like-minded others. Despite the foregoing qualification about groups, the insightfulness and importance of Choron's insistence on the accessibility of suicidal motivation to others is that suicidal motivation must have the same force for others as for the suicidist, even though those others might not themselves reach the same conclusion. Accessibility to the cogency of motivation, then, is our first specific criterial element.

Battin addresses the issue of the rationality of suicide by offering more formally articulated criteria than does Choron. Her criteria fall into two broad groups:

> The first three, ability to reason, realistic world view, and adequacy of information, are . . . the "nonimpairment" criteria. The final two, avoidance of harm and accordance with fundamental interests, are . . . the "satisfaction of interests" criteria. . . . We typically speak of a decision as "rational" . . . if it's made in an unimpaired way; we also speak of a decision as "rational" . . . if it satisfies [the agent's] interests.[13]

Comparing these criteria with Choron's requirements, one should note that while there's an absence of reference to accessibility, there's reference to interests. Battin may well be assuming that accessibility goes along with nonimpairment, but this sort of gloss, and resulting diversities, are exactly why we have to be eclectic in putting together a workable set of criteria for rational suicide.

While Battin's is the most satisfactory criterial treatment I've found, she, like Choron, seems to take the coherency of choosing to die as entailed by unimpaired reasoning and satisfaction of the other criteria. Her first nonimpairment requirement, the ability to reason, may look as if it covers the coherency issue in a more specific way, but it doesn't do quite that. The first criterion is really a methodological or procedural one. What it says is that potential suicidists must be able to engage in rational deliberation that is unimpaired by extraneous factors, such as disruptive emotions or neurotic or pathological obsession. In fact, the second and third nonimpairment criteria can be considered only special cases of the first. That is, potential suicidists' reasoning mustn't be impaired by significantly unrealistic world-views or lack information relevant to their deliberation. But all three "nonimpairment" criteria assume the coherency of choosing to die, since they're designed to ensure that forming the decision to die proceeds in accordance with sound reason, and forming that decision presupposes understanding what one might do. Battin isn't unaware of the coherency problem, but she sees it as a purely psychological one, saying that while death is clearly a certain consequence of suicide, still "this is precisely what a great many suicides do not accurately foresee."[14]

In clarifying this, however, she makes a point that actually shows why the coherency problem isn't only a psychological one. Battin tells us that suicidists' failing to appreciate the consequences of their self-destructive acts isn't as bizarre as it may seem at first, because "Freud claims that this is true of all people, insofar as the human unconsciousness 'believes itself immortal.' "[15] Unfortunately, Freud's claim doesn't raise a purely psychological problem. The claim has the serious cognitive implication noted earlier. If we're in fact incapable of believing that our deaths are, or at least may be, our own annihilation, then choosing to die can't be coherent because the choice, no matter how sound prior to enactment, is always vitiated in the event of its enactment by a reflexive blunting of vivid awareness of consequences. What this comes to is that a psychological incapacity may nullify well-reasoned decisions by distorting their enactments, and thereby constitutes a cognitive limitation on us. In short, we may be capable of understanding our own death only in the abstract. If this is the case, while deliberation of suicide may be rational, commission of suicide might never be so, which means we'd have to answer our fundamental coherency question in the negative.

However, Battin is right in a qualified way. It's not quite that the coherency issue is merely a psychological one, but that the possible existence of a distorting psychological mechanism isn't sufficient to preclude the rationality of suicide. Once we understand that a psychological incapacity may limit our cognitive ability to retain vivid awareness of consequences in the act of self-destruction, we can appreciate that whatever may be the case at the moment of enacting a sound decision to take one's life, it must suffice that potential suicidists accept the finality of death in their deliberations and intentions. There's a parallel here with the Kantian requirement that right moral action be done for duty and not for self-interest. Kant must allow that in fact people don't act purely from duty. In fact, it's conceivable that nobody's ever managed to perform a truly moral action because self-interest always intrudes in the event. But if this possibility were taken as preclusive of right moral action, deontological ethics would be impossible. It has to be enough that people consider their actions and act in good faith. In the same way, it has to be enough that people deliberate suicide rationally and act in good faith on the basis of their sound deliberations. We *are* capable of reasoning effectively and validly despite—theoretical—contrary unconscious inclinations. Moreover, our assessments of whether actions are rational are basically behavioristic: what matters is if actions are in accord with sound deliberation and reasoning. This is why consultation is so important with respect to establishing the rationality of suicide. It's the only way we can determine, over a period of time, that suicide may be rational regardless of whatever may cross suicidists' minds at the last minute. The rationality of action isn't entirely determined by the contents of thought and imagination in the moment of acting.

However, disbelief in one's own annihilation doesn't pose a problem only as a last-minute Freudian intrusion into the enactment of otherwise rational suicide, and it's in this connection that Battin's second or realistic-worldview criterion comes into its own. In discussing vivid awareness of consequences, I've allowed for the common—and rational—belief in an afterlife by requiring only that the *possibility* of personal annihilation be given due weight in suicidal deliberation. Regardless of deep faith, there's no conclusive evidence that anyone survives death in any form; therefore, it's at least possible that death is personal annihilation. To be rational, suicidal deliberation must take that possibility into account, or fail to include vivid awareness of consequences. The trouble is that some may not be capable of suspending their belief in an afterlife enough to meet the requirement that personal annihilation be considered a possible consequence of suicide.[16] But Battin is right about rational suicide requiring a "realistic world view," and that must include acknowledgment of the possibility that death is personal annihilation. The point of her second nonimpairment criterion is that for suicide to be rational, potential suicidists mustn't be under any illusions about the consequences of their acts. That means they can't rely on unsupported beliefs that they'll survive their own deaths. The notion that we survive our own deaths is problematic enough that the onus is on those who accept the notion to establish that acknowledgment of possible annihilation *isn't* necessary for rational suicide. What's at issue here is no less than what Albert Camus perceptively maintained was the fundamental philosophical issue: our capacity deliberately to cease to exist.[17] Nonetheless, so long as death *may* be personal annihilation, suicidal deliberation must take account of that possibility in order to be rational.

Battin's third nonimpairment criterion, adequacy of information, isn't of particular importance in the present context. It has to do with potential suicidists not being misinformed or ignorant of relevant information, such as thinking they've a terminal disease when in fact they're suffering from a nonfatal ailment. However, the criterion does raise questions about what counts as diligent enough efforts to gather relevant information, establish the reliability of diagnoses, and so on. These questions are particularly pressing with respect to preemptive suicide, where much of what's considered is less determinate than, say, a terminal diagnosis. Potential preemptive suicidists must take special care to determine, as best they can, how their parents and grandparents, and close relatives of the same generations, fared in old age. Here again we see the importance of effective consultation to rational deliberation of suicide and preemptive suicide. Nonetheless, to proceed, we'll take it that reflective aging individuals will readily appreciate the necessity of being sure of their ground when considering preemptive suicide.

Of considerably greater concern are the satisfaction-of-interests criteria: avoidance of harm and congruence with fundamental interests. These criteria are intended to meet arguments against the rationality of suicide claiming that since suicide is the worst possible self-inflicted harm, it can't be in the interests of potential suicidists, and so never rational. Suicidists admittedly do irremediable harm to themselves. They violate their own most basic interest, the interest in survival. Therefore, if suicide is to be rational, and somehow be in suicidists' interests, it can be so only if it causes less harm than does continuing to live. Battin makes the pivotal point that in assessing whether individuals do themselves unwarranted harm by committing suicide to avoid something deemed unbearable, we have to look at "the amount of other experience permitted . . . and whether this other experience is of intrinsic value."[18] For Battin, assessing whether suicide is the greatest self-inflicted harm, and hence irreversibly against individuals' interests, is a matter of assessing the degree of harm borne in continuing to live, and whether its being borne is made worthwhile by "important experience during the pain-free intervals."[19] By allowing relative weighting of the interest in survival against suffering in this way, Battin's position is contrary to the more unyielding popular view that because suicide is the worst self-inflicted harm, it can be justified only when people are in the position of, in effect, no longer having interests because of immediately pressing, intolerable, and hopeless circumstances.[20] Battin's approach allows comparative judgments to be made to the effect that life doesn't hold enough compensating value to outweigh harm being borne. But what matters most here is that those judgments may be made prior to harm's becoming overwhelming.

What Battin is after in arguing as she does is basically the point made earlier against the lack-of-contrast argument: that the evaluative comparison in suicidal deliberation is between the relative merits of continuing to live under certain conditions, and avoiding those conditions at the cost of dying. Battin's satisfaction-of-interests criteria test judgments about whether the bad in life outweighs the good, and whether abandoning lives in which bad outweighs good accords with people's interests. Battin's interests criteria, then, allow both for assessments about what one can't bear, which are relevant to surcease suicide, and about what one is unwilling to bear, which are relevant to preemptive suicide. However, things aren't as clear as they might be. Deciding whether or not to bear the sort of personal diminishment preemptive suicide is intended to avoid isn't a matter of weighing anticipated good and bad in life. To suffer personal diminishment is to be made into a lesser person, one whose thought is significantly reduced and whose sensitivities are greatly blunted. In this way personal diminishment is a kind of death, and whatever good may be anticipated in life won't be experienced by the person diminished. In this way, preemptive suicide shares an important similarity with surcease suicide. The greater their expectations of personal diminishment, the closer reflective aging individuals are in their circumstances to people who are in hopeless situations and essentially have lost their interests in survival. This aspect of preemptive suicide isn't adequately addressed by the interests criteria, so, like the others, they require further work.

DISBELIEF IN MORTALITY AND COHERENCE

Because we're dealing with life-and-death questions, we can't afford to gloss over conceptual matters that, if left unresolved, will undermine any conclusions we may reach at more practical levels. For that reason we need to pursue consideration of last-moment blunting of vivid awareness of suicide's consequences. Battin and Choron treat lack of vivid awareness of consequences as psychological impairment of reasoning, essentially discounting such impairment as peculiar to the states of mind of particular individuals. They don't see the possibility of such psychological impairment as a general obstacle to rational suicide. Above, I argued that we can reason soundly and effectively despite unconscious beliefs, and that intrusive last-minute conscious ideas that might blunt vivid awareness of consequences basically can be ignored in assessment of the rationality of suicide, if suicidal deliberation and intention meet the criteria for rationality. But the Freudian contention about deep-seated disbelief in our own mortality is a strong one. Freud's position is that it's "impossible to imagine our own death," and that "whenever we attempt to do so we . . . are in fact still present as spectators."[21] If it's true that "at bottom no one believes in his own death,"[22] then no one can commit suicide with the vivid awareness of consequences that rational choice requires.

My argument is that what matters is that suicidal deliberation and intention be rational. I then can concede that suicide may not be rational *in the event*. What the argument comes to is that Freud's claimed impossibility can be accepted as a psychological likelihood or even near-certainty, and rational suicide then can be reconceived as like issuing an advance directive to oneself and then fulfilling it. The parallel with advance directives is that while not comatose or unable to reason due to physical agony, suicidists are—ex hypothesi—rendered incapable of rational action at the time of death by intrusive disbelief in their mortality. Therefore, the structure of rational suicide is that while still capable of rational decision and action, suicidists initiate courses of action that result in their deaths, even though at the precise time of their deaths they're no longer capable of rational action. This shifts the locus of rationality from enactment to deliberation and decision, and that's perfectly proper, since, as noted above, the rationality of action isn't contingent on what occurs in the precise moment a soundly reasoned and cogently motivated act is performed. The role of criteria for rational suicide, then, would be to establish that everything leading up to the act of self-destruction meets applicable standards. Is this good enough?

The preclusive-reflex claim is that something always enters our consciousness at the last moment and alters the nature of self-destructive acts in a way that vitiates their rationality. If this is so, all self-destructive acts are in some way unwitting, and hence can't be rational. While not an a priori argument like the lack-of-contrast one, this is a holistic denial of the rationality of suicide on the grounds that it's impossible to maintain the vivid awareness of consequences necessary for rational suicide. The foregoing argument and restructuring may look insufficient because they seem to concede that all actual suicides may be irrational acts. However, the preclusive-reflex claim is odd with respect to its status. It purports to be an empirical claim; that is, one about human psychology, but the claim clearly can't be either confirmed or disconfirmed. Not even suicidists themselves can know whether or not their self-destructive acts are significantly skewed by some psychologically reflexive idea that they'll survive death. It's difficult to see how the preclusive-reflex claim can be empirical. On the other hand, it can't be an a priori claim because it *is* about human psychology. The claim is that even when we set out to take our lives on the basis of sound reasoning, and such action accords with our values and serves our interests, something always intervenes in our thought as we act, and vitiates our rational intention. So while the claim decidedly is about psychological mechanisms, if it can't be confirmed or disconfirmed, it lacks content as a general claim. This means that if the preclusive-reflex claim is to have any force, it must be about specific reasons for doubting that particular individuals are capable of rational suicide. This is Battin and Choron's basic stand.

Moreover, even if considered as general, the claim turns out to be fairly innocuous. The reason is that, as I've already argued, and contrary to appearances, we can accept—if only for argument's sake—that there's always some intention-skewing, self-protective reflex operant in enactment of self-destruction. The parallel drawn with advance directives shows that what needs to be done is to take into account, in deliberating suicide, that preclusive reflexes may, or likely will, intrude at the last moment. Individuals capable of rationally choosing to die are perfectly capable of understanding that in their final moments, their most carefully formed, warranted, and resolute intentions may be distorted by psychological factors. We're able to deal with situations where we know in advance that emotion—or medication—will alter our moods and perspectives, making previously intended actions look wrongheaded. We're also able to deal with situations where we understand that our own fallible nature may make the most careful deliberation and most focused intentions appear seriously flawed or misconceived when we actually set about enacting a decision. There's no compelling reason to concede the preclusive-reflex claim, if only because of its problematic status; but even if conceded, preclusive reflexes don't make rational suicide impossible. Given the complexity of human thought and action, and the fact that sound suicidal reasoning must involve careful reflection over a significant period of time, the rationality of suicide can't be made contingent on a postulated moment of confusion that occurs *after* sound reasoning and cogent motivation produced the decision being enacted, and that doesn't alter the outcome intended in that decision.[23]

It seems that satisfaction of criteria for rational suicide, such as Battin and Choron offer, exhausts the coherency issue of content. To proceed, then, we should concentrate on articulating the criteria for rational suicide as carefully and precisely as possible. Once specific requirements for rational suicide are spelled out, the coherency issue becomes a metaphysical question offering only a basis for skepticism. In other words, it suffices to show that suicide can be the most utile course of action in some circumstances, that its commission is well reasoned, that it would be chosen and enacted by others in similar circumstances, and that it's consistent with suicidists' values and interests.

ADDING AN ELEMENT AND TAKING STOCK

Jan Narveson provides an element that complements Battin's and Choron's criteria by arguing that suicide is rational if self-destructive action "is prescribed"[24] by rational values and desires. Narveson grants that saying "what it means to have rational desires and values is not easy," but contends that the crucial point is that "they pass the most basic tests of rationality if they are not founded on beliefs that are . . . false or illusory."[25] For Narveson, "to see whether suicide could ever be rational . . . we have only to ask whether it could be recommended by a scheme of [sound] values."[26] The well-groundedness of values is here made to bear the major weight of the rationality of ensuing behavior. In a manner similar to Choron's emphasis on cogent motivation, Narveson makes the reasoning and implementation of action that suicidists' values prescribe or "recommend" secondary to the soundness of the values determining that action. But, like Choron, Narveson has little to say about suicidists' interests, seeming to take it that well-grounded values will incorporate proper weighting of interests. In this way Battin's criteria are both more satisfactory in themselves and necessary additions to Choron's and Narveson's. On the other hand, Battin's requirement that suicide be in accord with suicidists' interests needs amplification as to the sound nature of those values.

What we have so far is that for suicide to be rational, the following three sets of conditions must be met. First, suicidists' deliberations must be sound according to established standards of discursive reasoning, and be unimpaired by error, correctable ignorance, or false belief (Battin, Narveson), uncoerced by pathological factors (Choron), and not distorted by unrealistic notions (Battin). Second, suicidists' motives must be accessible and cogent (Choron), the values operant in their motivation must be well grounded and not based on false beliefs (Narveson), and those values must prescribe suicide in the relevant circumstances (Narveson, Battin). Third, suicide must be judged, again by established standards, as best serving suicidists' interests and not harming them more than continuing to live would do (Battin).

To this point, there's no criterial differentiation among cases of suicide. The criteria govern self-destruction as surcease suicide to escape unbearable torment, self-destruction as altruistic sacrifice, self-destruction to avoid moral debasement, and self-destruction as preemptive avoidance of personal diminishment. Some of these forms of suicide may require further conditions, as we'll see is the case with preemptive suicide, but all must satisfy the basic criteria. It must be acknowledged, though, that satisfaction of particular criteria may be rather perfunctory in some cases. For example, in the most notable instances, those of surcease suicide considered in the most extreme circumstances, the requirement that suicide best serve suicidists' interests, and not harm them more than continuing to live would do, is more or less automatically met by the nature of the circumstances in which suicide is considered.

Now we need to consolidate and streamline the foregoing conditions for rational suicide, to be able to make some refinements and additions. To keep things manageable, I'll use the phrase "nonimpairment of reasoning" and its equivalents to refer to Battin's and Choron's requirements about sound reasoning by letting it cover exclusion of both impairment by procedural[27] error, false belief, ignorance, and confusion, and what Choron calls "psychiatric disorders" or pathological factors, compulsion, and clinical depression. All of these things impair deliberation in the sense of preventing it from meeting established standards for sound reasoning. Singly or combined, these factors would preclude our acceptance of affected decisions to commit suicide as sound. In like manner, I'll use "cogent motivation" and its equivalents to cover Choron's requirement that suicidists' motives for taking their lives be accessible to their peers, his related requirement that those motives be judged cogent by those peers, and Narveson's requirements that values not be based on false beliefs and that those well-grounded values prescribe suicide in the relevant circumstances. Finally, "consistency with interests" and its equivalents will cover Battin's requirement that suicide accord with suicidists' interests and not harm them more than would continuing to live. We can then restate the substance of the criteria given above in this more succinct way: *to be rational, suicide must follow on nonimpaired reasoning, be cogently motivated, and be consistent with suicidists' interests.*

With this tighter statement of the criteria in hand, we can close this chapter by briefly reviewing our tentative conclusion about the basic question of whether it's coherent to choose to die while understanding that death is almost certainly personal annihilation. Though we have to allow for the possibility of some sort of afterlife, since belief in an afterlife is itself rational, there is no evidence beyond matters of faith that we survive death in any way. The basic question, then, is whether suicide can be rational in the sense of its being intelligible to assess the cessation of existence as preferable to continued life. This is the question that finds its strongest formulation in the lack-of-contrast argument, which maintains, though unsuccessfully, as we saw, that suicide is irrational because no one can coherently prefer death to life. However, because the suicidal choice is not between being dead and being alive, but between bearing and not bearing something, where dying is the price of not bearing it, the coherency question either reduces to or is made redundant by the compound question of whether suicide satisfies the criteria for rational suicide we've considered, especially the requirement that suicidal reasoning be unimpaired. Given that we understand unimpaired suicidal deliberation to include vivid awareness of consequences, we saw that even last-minute distractive ideas regarding survival of death don't necessarily invalidate rational self-destructive action. Our conclusion, then, is that the coherency question doesn't really constitute a different question, and that to establish the rationality of suicide, it suffices to show that deliberation of suicide is unimpaired, in the comprehensive sense we've considered, that motivation for suicide is considered by others than the suicidist and found cogent and prescribed by well-grounded values, and that suicide doesn't cause suicidists more harm than would staying alive.

In Chapter 4 we need to consider an issue that is implicit in a certain tension between Choron and Narveson's concern with values and Battin's concern with interests. As we'll see, the possibility is quite real that these may conflict. The nature of that conflict must be dealt with before the criteria for rational suicide can be effective.

NOTES

1. Hook 1988.
2. Battin 1982a:297.
3. I'm including loss of autonomy in the idea of punishing survival, in line with my remarks in the last section of Chapter 2.
4. Chief Judge Sol Wachtler, in Shipp 1988:36.
5. After publication of the first edition of this book, I was contacted by a person who had read it and whom I later met. The person in question expressed agreement with my views and informed me of having chosen to commit preemptive suicide soon after turning sixty. The individual in question was at the time

fifty-eight and in excellent health. I was quite taken aback when I found myself seriously questioning the person's decision, thinking the reasons provided insufficient. I then appreciated the depth of the view that life should be abandoned only in the face of unacceptable deterioration or suffering. As will emerge, the timing of preemptive suicide is absolutely crucial to its rationality.

6. Donnelly 1978:89.

7. Ibid.:93.

8. Of course, contextually coerced suicide needn't be rational if circumstances are of the wrong sort, for instance, where the suicidist is driven by compulsion.

9. Donnelly 1978:96.

10. Hume 1963:595.

11. Battin 1982:301.

12. Choron 1972:96–97.

13. Battin, 1982a:298

14. Ibid.:299.

15. Ibid.

16. I don't know what else to say about belief that we survive death in some form or other. I find the notion of an afterlife incomprehensible. While at one time I believed that after death we were judged and allocated to one or another realm, I don't now understand what it was I believed—or thought I believed.

17. Camus 1955.

18. Battin 1982a:312.

19. Ibid.

20. Preservation of life is assumed to be a duty incumbent on everyone, and the law allows interference in attempted suicide, described as prevention of self-inflicted harm, as an available defense against charges arising from such interference. A passage in *Criminal Law Defenses* tells us that "society has nearly as strong an intangible interest in thwarting suicide as it does in thwarting murder." Robinson 1984:193; compare Shipp 1988.

21. Freud 1915:289.

22. Ibid.

23. It may be prudent to note that we're not concerned here with actual changes of mind. The preclusive-reflex claim is about distortions to the envisaged result of self-destruction, not about last-minute decisions to not commit suicide.

24. Narveson, 1986:106.

25. Ibid.:105.

26. Ibid.:106.

27. What I mean by "procedural" error is formal and informal logical errors, such as inconsistency, hasty generalization, and so on.

4

A QUESTION OF BALANCE

I hear only slow death preached,
and patience with everything "earthly."
Nietzsche, *Zarathustra*

Occasions for commission of rational suicide vary, including both times when surcease suicide provides release from immediately intolerable circumstances, and times when preemptive suicide offers the surest way of avoiding anticipated intolerable circumstances. But criterial conclusions about the rationality of surcease suicide needn't apply to preemptive suicide. The main reason they might not apply has to do with the fact that potential preemptive suicidists can't know with certainty that what they fear will in fact prove intolerable, whereas surcease suicidists take their lives to escape actually intolerable situations. Additionally, many argue that since there's always the possibility of committing surcease suicide if anticipated circumstances do prove intolerable, preemptive suicide is precipitous and isn't, or shouldn't be deemed, rational.

Our concern is with reflective aging individuals who determine that their very survival to an advanced age seriously threatens their valued intellectuality and their continuation as the reflective persons they are. Their hard realization is that their advanced age threatens to diminish them in ways they're unwilling to risk for the sake of a few more years of life. And it's part of their realization that at some not-too-distant point in time, they will probably lose the capacity to end their own lives. The deterioration they fear almost certainly will prevent unimpaired suicidal deliberation even of surcease suicide, and it may also prevent the physical enactment of suicidal decisions.

Preemptive suicide, then, needs to be deliberated and committed prior to the onset of incapacity, and this is where the trouble starts. The problem is resistance to the idea that it can make good sense to commit suicide prior to needing to do so in order to escape unbearable circumstances. Even when the various criteria we've looked at are met, some think there's something terribly wrong about relinquishing life—and most likely total existence— in anticipation of intolerable circumstances. Given what we've considered about the nature of the motivation for preemptive suicide being the expected eradication of persons well before their bodies' deaths, we can say that the key point in this resistance is a discrepancy between conceiving of age-related personal diminishment as hardship that befalls individuals, and conceiving of that diminishment as termination of the persons those individuals are. Unfortunately, while articulating this point clarifies the opposition of views, it does little to resolve the issue. To make some progress, we need to get clearer on the idea that gives bite to our original coherency question, which is that it doesn't seem to make sense to choose to die, if doing so most likely is utterly ceasing to exist, unless our reasons to do so are immediate, overwhelming, and irrevocable.

Many believe that death is personal annihilation, and for them, relinquishing life in anticipation of indeterminate personal diminishment doesn't make good sense. Nor are those who believe in an afterlife in a significantly different position. Belief in an afterlife is not only rational according to established standards, it's an extremely common belief. Nor is the belief only a product of religious or quasi-religious doctrines. Philosophers ranging from Plato to even so thoroughgoing a materialist as D. M. Armstrong have argued either for a full-blown immortal soul or that continued existence as an aware subject after the death of the body is coherent—that is, is logically possible.[1] However, despite biblical promises and philosophical conjecture regarding an afterlife, deliberation of suicide can allow no margin for error. In the absence of conclusive proof that we survive our deaths, suicide must be deliberated on the basis that we *don't*. Only then is it rational to take one's life, because only then is one vividly aware of the possibly annihilatory consequence of self-destruction. There- fore, even those who believe in an afterlife will see relinquishing life to avoid indeterminate diminishment as highly problematic. So while both believers and nonbelievers in an afterlife appreciate that surcease suicide may make good sense, both resist suicide committed for anything less than surcease of unendurable suffering. The basic reason is the view that it just doesn't make sense to trade still-viable life for possible nonexistence in order to avoid something as yet unrealized. This much is clear enough. My difficulty is relating this resistance to preemptive suicide, or suicide done for anticipatory reasons, more specifically to the criteria that we're in the process of articulating. There's little point in offering criteria for rational suicide if they will be applied only where they're largely redundant—that is, in cases where there's manifest warrant for suicide—and ignored in the cases that most concern us because of the conviction that their being met is insufficient to show anticipatory suicide is rational.

Battin thinks that the rationality of suicide is capable of being dealt with "as a compound issue: can suicide be chosen in a rational way, and can it be the rational thing for a particular person to do?"[2] The criteria Battin, Choron, and Narveson offer are primarily directed to answering the first part of this compound issue, and don't distinguish between surcease and preemptive suicide. That difference is one to be dealt with in assessing whether it's rational for particular individuals to commit suicide. At the particular level, Battin's assessorial question about the relative amounts of good and bad in individuals' lives may be posed in terms of immediately punishing circumstances and possible amelioration of or compensation for those circumstances, or in terms of anticipated punishing circumstances and possible amelioration and compensation. To Choron and Narveson, it makes no difference if the question is posed in terms of actual or potential suffering, because both give due weight to individuals' value-laden assessments of their own situations and prospects. In Narveson's terms, individuals' well-grounded values may prescribe or "recommend" suicide regardless of whether intolerable circumstances are actual or only potential. Battin's assessorial question about the good and bad in life is couched in terms of individuals' interests. However, though it's fairly obvious that Battin's use of "interests" covers most of what Narveson has in mind in discussing values, this apparently innocuous gloss or lapse brings out that in considering the rationality of suicide at the level of particular cases, we need to distinguish between values and interests. The reason is that, as was noted in Chapter 3, values and interests may conflict with one another. And while this possible conflict poses problems of its own, it enables us to understand the resistance to anticipatory suicide. That resistance is best characterized as perception of individuals' suicide-prescribing values as contravening those individuals' interests in survival.

Reservations about suicide making good sense are lowest with respect to surcease suicide, with suicide as release, and highest with respect to preemptive suicide, with suicide as anticipatory avoidance. For instance, we saw that adherents of the lack-of-contrast argument go so far as to redefine suicide to exclude surcease suicide or warranted self-destruction from what their argument rejects as irrational. The obvious reason for greater acceptance of surcease suicide is the immediacy and evident nature of the suffering that prompts self-destruction as escape. There's little room for doubt that individuals in great and hopeless agony are better off dying than living only to endure more pain. Choosing to die prior to circumstances becoming desperate is another matter, and a productive way of putting the point is to say that many doubt whether it can ever be reasonable to take one's own life except as release from unrelenting and irremediable suffering.

Despite common usage of the two terms as equivalent, there's an important difference between something's being rational and something's being reasonable. A judgment, a decision, or a conclusion drawn is rational if arrived at by reasoning that meets established standards for validity; an action is rational if it most efficiently achieves a desired end. "Rational" has to do with consistency and means-to-ends utility. However, despite the fact that we use "rational" also to describe the ends that rational action serves, in assessing ends, we don't usually speak of something's being rational or irrational, but of it's being reasonable or unreasonable. We usually resort to describing ends as rational or irrational when we want to emphasize either that they're perfectly reasonable, for instance, despite initial appearances, or that they're grossly unreasonable. The difference ultimately has to do with operant premises. Certain judgments, decisions, conclusions, and/or actions may be perfectly rational in terms of consistency and means-to-ends utility, *given operant premises*. But those same judgments, decisions, conclusions, and/or actions may be quite unreasonable because of flaws in those premises.[3] In particular, a course of action can be strictly rational, in the sense that it's prescribed by conclusions reached through valid inferences and be optimal to achieving an end, but still be quite unreasonable, or irrational in a broad sense, if the end the action serves is misconceived. The most telling examples of the difference in question are when we encounter rational reasoning and action serving ends that are quite mad. For instance, individuals convinced by mysterious dreams that everyone they know is conspiring against them may reason clearly about what they might best do, conclude that to protect themselves they have to kill everyone they know, and then plot out the most efficient means to kill their friends. Given their mad premises, their reasoning and behavior may be perfectly rational and at the same time be wildly unreasonable. What's important here is that action is rational *and reasonable* if it flows from valid reasoning, is the best means to achieve a desired end, *and* the end it serves is a good one. In other words, to be rational in a comprehensive sense that includes reasonableness, action not only has to be soundly reasoned and efficient with respect to its ends, but those ends must benefit the agent without harming others.

Reservations about criterially sanctioned preemptive suicide, then, can be put in terms of whether it's reasonable to avail oneself of a rational option, if doing so means giving up one's very life. In other words, even where suicide is deemed rational, some may judge it less than reasonable. That it is so judged will have to do with potential suicidists' values and premises, not with their reasoning. And the likeliest problems will be with how strictly values are interpreted and applied. Examples of suicide looking unreasonable, even if warranted by sound reasoning and well-grounded values, are most readily found where human adaptability is or appears to be underestimated. For instance, suicidists' values may prescribe suicide because of anticipated deterioration, but that deterioration may prove to be more tolerable than expected when it actually occurs. Individuals who totally rejected bearing certain sorts of deterioration, and rationally chose to commit suicide prior to that deterioration, may begin to accommodate themselves at least to the early stages of the dreaded deterioration. They may come to think it unreasonable to sacrifice their lives for circumstances that they find more tolerable than they anticipated.[4] This possibility is, of course, the idea common to the lack-of-contrast argument and reservations about criterially sanctioned preemptive suicide: merely anticipated circumstances fall short of justifying self-inflicted death, and likely annihilation, because we can't know that those circumstances will prove intolerable and/or that there won't be adequate compensation for tolerating them. This possibility isn't found in surcease suicide, because there self-inflicted death is release from circumstances that *are* intolerable and won't grow less so, regardless of adaptability. So long as the warrant for suicide is still in the future, many believe that suicide is unreasonable even if strictly rational.

The point about circumstances expected to be intolerable being adapted to in some measure, or perhaps being compensated for in some way, is a strong one. There's no denying that people may adapt to circumstances they thought would be unbearable before their occurrence, and it's also true that there may be compensation for all but the worst of those circumstances. The claim that preemptive suicide must be unreasonable, even if rational, is admittedly a powerful one. It's powerful enough that we have to carefully consider the possible conflict of values and interests, since the claim essentially contends that though rational self-destruction may serve preemptive suicidists' values, it contravenes their interests because their interests in survival are unduly outweighed by their suicide-prescribing values. But we also have to keep in mind that the possibility of adapting to deterioration is seen by some as more reason for preemptive suicide. The reason is that the deterioration preemptive suicide is intended to preclude is diminishment of the person, and reflective aging individuals fear adapting to or tolerating personal diminishment to a point where they'll neither understand why they should take their lives nor be able to do so.

To proceed, we need to restate the criteria for rational suicide, in order to enable a modification that will deal with the claim that suicide may be rational but still not be reasonable.

RESTATING THE CRITERIA

After considering Battin, Choron, and Narveson's various requirements for rational suicide, we restated the substance of those requirements, in Chapter 3, as rational suicide having to follow on nonimpaired reasoning, be cogently motivated, and be consistent with suicidists' interests. This was an admittedly tight articulation of a set of complex requirements, but the expectation was that the restated criteria would be read in the context of previous discussion. We now have once more to restate the criteria, again presupposing discussion of the various points. In this second restatement we need to make explicit mention of Narveson's contribution regarding values in order to facilitate a necessary modification. The criteria, then, are that suicide is rational if

1. Suicide follows on unimpaired deliberation, *and*
2. Suicidal motivation is accessible and cogent, *and*
3. Suicide is prescribed by well-grounded values, *and*
4. Suicide is in the agent's best interests.

The nonimpairment and accessibility criteria test whether consideration of suicide proceeds correctly according to established principles of reasoning, and isn't prompted by eccentric values or unduly influenced or distorted by emotional, psychological, or pathological factors. Essentially, the first two criteria test whether individuals' consideration and choice of suicide can be followed and appreciated by others, though not necessarily accepted or endorsed by them. The nonimpairment and accessibility criteria tend to come to the same practical test, because the force of saying that potential suicidists' reasoning and motivation must be sound and accessible to others is that both must be accepted by others as reasoning and motivation. Whatever else we may want to say about the standards for sound reasoning, they must be general: we must be able to see how potential suicidists' reasoning progresses discursively and would work for anyone in the same circumstances. As for accessibility of motivation, the point is to exclude serious idiosyncrasy and subjectivistic relativization of suicidal justification to individual judgments. Peers concerned to assess whether self-destruction is rational aren't prepared to consider it so if they, first, can't follow how potential suicidists move from perception of threatening situations to decisions to take their own lives or, second, can't understand how others with similar values and facing similar difficulties could make the same decisions.

The values and interests criteria test whether potential suicidists' values prescribe self-inflicted death, and whether their interests can intelligibly be said to be well served by self-destruction. The values criterion also tests whether the values prescribing suicide are themselves rational in terms of being well-grounded. But while the nonimpairment and accessibility criteria raise difficulties about whether reasoning or motivation is or isn't acceptable, the values and interests criteria raise difficulties of a rather different sort. These aren't just about determining whether something is or isn't acceptable; they are about whether something satisfies two possibly conflicting standards. The issues addressed by the values and interests criteria have to do with whether self-destruction does or doesn't accord with values and interests separately, and with whether accordance with values and with interests is adequate to both when there's a conflict.

Whereas assessment of whether reasoning or motivation does or doesn't meet criterial requirements can be independent of the other, assessments of suicide's accordance with values and with interests are inextricably tied together. Even if there's no direct conflict of values and interests regarding suicide, individuals' values color perception of their interests and vice versa. The values and interests criteria aren't independently satisfiable because first- and third-person assessments of what's consistent with potential suicidists' values must involve consideration of their interests, and assessment of what is consistent with their interests will be influenced by what they value. This is why the values and interests criteria have to do not only with the consistency of suicide with suicidists' values and suicidists' interests, but also with a proper balance in that dual consistency. Balance is of the essence, since we can't simply give values or interests undisputed priority. Values and interests are to an extent mutually determining. The intertwined roles of values and interests in assessment of the rationality of suicide may even complicate the application of the nonimpairment and accessibility criteria, since we may have difficulty in isolating cognitive or procedural factors in deliberation of suicide because of how values, and to a lesser extent interests, color perception of various factors in reasoning, such as the weight given to negative considerations that are still in the future. The basic point here is that if individuals value something enough, such as personal autonomy, their interests will accommodate greater sacrifice of good time left to them, because frustration of deeply rooted priorities or denial of what is highly prized devalues the life their interests protect. On the other hand, if the life left is reasonably substantial and promising despite growing dependency, the value they put on personal autonomy may have to be adjusted if its demands threaten their lives in unwarranted ways.

The importance of values' conditioning effects on interests is particularly relevant in our time, when reflective aging individuals face a new threat. Advanced age now not only threatens to diminish their intellectuality, but also forebodes reduced access and limited treatment in health care, palpable resentment of them by young people, and increasingly problematic financial security. When this new threat is added to others, reflective aging individuals' values may prescribe preemptive suicide despite their still having significant interest in continued life. Suicidal deliberation that even a decade or two ago would have delayed self-destruction, and so better accorded with their survival interests, may now advance self-destruction to satisfy more severely challenged values, and thereby contravene those interests.

Timing is crucial to rational preemptive suicide, because it's a trade of good time left for guaranteed avoidance of threatened diminishment. But it isn't only personal diminishment that enters the equation on the negative side. Feared dependency is also a major negative consideration. Newly prevalent social attitudes toward the aged may contribute to the unacceptability of dependence, if that dependence is seen as greatly resented and made more difficult to bear by grudging care. Even advanced age relatively free of diminishment and demeaning dependency can be made highly unattractive if one is ostracized for being old and socially expensive. And what's especially important is that new social attitudes won't just make the elderly victims of ageist resentment or prejudice; their more profound effect is that the elderly may share the view of themselves as unfairly clinging to life. Current debate of physician-assisted suicide has brought out that there's good reason to believe that if present views prevail, and assisted suicide is legalized and institutionalized, "people might feel that somehow it becomes a duty to die."[5] If the changes that are taking place in social attitudes toward old age are as broad and deep as they seem to be, elderly people will themselves come to think they've had their share of life and of society's resources. Not only will reflective aging individuals' values move them to reject living on at the risk of their intellectual identities, and at the risk of being treated as social pariahs, those values will be increasingly conditioned to make them perceive their own survival as unacceptably parasitic.[6] However, all of this is at least potentially at odds with elderly individuals' interests in survival. Value-driven decisions to commit preemptive suicide may well violate their interests in survival by unduly curtailing viable life left to them.

The values criterion has special importance to the rationality of preemptive suicide for two reasons. The more important reason is that preemptive suicide is self-destruction in less than desperate circumstances, and so is prompted more by value considerations than interest considerations. Reflective aging individuals considering preemptive suicide do so precisely because they're not yet in circumstances where surcease suicide is appropriate, and consider preemptive suicide precisely in order not to find themselves in such circumstances. Their primary motivation isn't release but not living on without what they most value: being the persons they are. Consideration and possible commission of preemptive suicide, then, is value-driven. The second reason for the values criterion's special importance is that our culture tends to subordinate interests to values in its moral teaching, if not in fact. There's a strong tendency to understand "interests" as personal, self-regarding, and even selfish, and "values" as communal and other-oriented. We applaud the sacrifice of personal interests for communal values, and condemn the reverse. Our culture teaches that we should be prepared to sacrifice our interests for our values, as in patriotic sacrifice of our lives. "Greater love hath no man than he lay down his life for his friends" is thought to capture the noblest of human capacities. Putting one's interests ahead of one's values is thought to be our basest tendency, and we're variously encouraged to subordinate interests to values in deliberation of any course of action. The result of both of these considerations is that there's a strong inclination to give priority to values in deliberation of preemptive suicide, and this is the source of reservations about the adequacy of criterial establishment of preemptive suicide as rational. In a word, preemptive suicide sometimes looks unreasonable, even if rational, because the weighting of suicidists' values is perceived as disproportionate to their interests.

RATIONAL BUT UNREASONABLE?

Battin rightly maintains that in "the absence of any compelling evidence to the contrary," we have to accept that someone may choose suicide "on the basis of reasoning which is by all usual standards adequate."[7] There are two key points here. First, as indicated earlier, we're not concerned to hammer out a philosophical theory about rationality. Our concern is with the "usual standards," with established canons. Whether those canons are objective and ahistorical or culture-relative isn't our concern. The question here isn't whether preemptive suicide might fail to be rational in some ultimate sense even though judged rational by operant standards. To consider whether preemptive suicide might be rational but unreasonable isn't to apply some transcendent sense of "rational" *or* "reasonable" in examining a puzzling sort of conflict. Second, we may not like suicidists' conclusions and decisions, but not be able to fault them in the sense of demonstrating that they follow on impaired reasoning, motives that aren't cogent or don't prescribe suicide, or violate interests. We may describe those conclusions and decisions as "unreasonable," but only be expressing our own disagreement rather than claiming demonstrable errors. What poses the problem is the case when suicidal conclusions and decisions pass communal standards for rational behavior, but still fail to gain communal acceptance. We need to consider in more detail how, in assessing preemptive suicide, we may find no impairment of reasoning, may understand the motivation and deem it well-grounded, be unable to show contravention of interests, and still feel that interests aren't well served by self-destruction.

It may look as if what's really at issue is Narveson's concern that values be well-grounded and prescribe suicide, and that reservations have to do with these requirements' only appearing to be met. Clearly the first way that preemptive suicide might be unacceptable, despite satisfaction of the nonimpairment criterion, is if operant values are irrational because based on false beliefs. Unfortunately, things aren't that simple. Cases where values are themselves irrational are rare. For instance, recall the 1997 Heaven's Gate suicides, where cult members killed themselves, believing that the Hale-Bopp comet would carry them to paradise, and the 1978 People's Temple suicides, where adult cult members followed the Reverend

Jim Jones in taking poison to avoid supposedly imminent persecution. These suicides were judged irrational because of the falseness of the beliefs underlying the operant values. There's little room for assessment of such suicides as unreasonable. The issue of reasonableness arises where operant values are well grounded but are interpreted in problematic ways or are too strictly applied.

The problem is that even rational values may function unacceptably in suicidal deliberation if their interpretation introduces priority errors. Individuals' interpretations of their values determine their decisions and actions, but while we have to concede that their interpretations are decisive with respect to their decisions and actions, that isn't to say we must accept those interpretations. We might well conclude that their values haven't been reasonably interpreted, and that however admirable their values and exemplary their subsequent reasoning, their suicides aren't acceptable if based on their particular interpretations of their admittedly well-grounded values. Our negative reasonableness judgments don't focus on out-and-out falsity underlying operant values, but on what we can best describe as lack of proportion in their application. The unacceptability is a matter of our perceiving undue exaggeration of values and consequent undue depreciation of interests. While we may accept and even appreciate the values in question, and acknowledge their rationality, we may think potential suicidists are being unreasonable, though not strictly irrational, in judging that, for example, a certain measure of deterioration or a certain level of dependence justifies violation of their interests in survival.

The fact is that values determine what we can call perceived interests, and values and perceived interests often clash with what are deemed to be suicidists' real interests.[8] Recourse to the admittedly somewhat fuzzy notion of reasonableness is basically resistance to letting suicidists' values and perceived interests overshadow their real interests. What underlies resistance to letting values and perceived interests prevail over real interests, and what prompts talk about real interests in the first place, is a strong tendency to rate continued life as the most important human interest, and as the one least readily overridden by value considerations. The fairly ready acceptance of surcease suicide can be understood as agreement that the individuals in question no longer have real interests in survival, in the sense that for them survival has become more curse than blessing. But the question arises whether, in judging some suicides unreasonable, we're genuinely trying to maintain a proper balance in the consideration of values and interests, or are only introducing a different set of values, one that assigns a higher place to continued life. This could lead to the rationality of suicide being regularly conceded in the abstract but never accepted in particular cases. We might be rejecting suicides, not because they're inconsistent with individuals' interests but because they don't accord with *our* values. We need to deal with the possibility that in the assessment of the consistency of suicide with values and interests, an appeal to reasonableness amounts to introduction of different values. The way to do so is to produce a new criterion for balance or reasonableness to complement the nonimpairment, accessibility, values, and interests criteria. It may be possible to say how values and interests must be balanced in suicidal deliberation, without injecting different values into the equation, by devising a criterial test for reasonableness.

Human beings, of whatever culture, are mortal entities, and so long as they are living, they have a basic interest in remaining alive. Some see this basic interest as absolute, and hence as not amenable to qualification by conflicting values or perceived interests. But besides being mortal, human beings are value-holding and value-seeking beings, so their interest in remaining alive isn't an interest in mere survival as organisms. This is the idea captured by the view that life's value isn't absolute but is as the precondition of all other value.[9] For self-aware beings like ourselves, the interest in survival is inextricably wrapped up with how we value our various experiences. Our interest in remaining alive isn't detachable from how we differentiate evaluatively among our experiences, so our putative real interest in survival isn't absolute and may be warrantedly superseded by our values and perceived interests. The question is, of course, how, when, and to what degree that interest may be properly qualified by values held. Minimally, the willing abandonment of irretrievable life for the sake of specific values needs to be supported with adequate evidence that suicide's according with those values outweighs the loss of all possible other value.[10] This is how the basic interest in survival may be overridden, because people have an interest in survival only to the extent that survival offers attainable value. If whatever still-attainable value is judged less important than the values served by suicide, then there's no violation of the interests criterion. This is usually the case in surcease suicide, but preemptive suicide calls for much more careful assessment of the relation between values motivating self-destruction and the interest in survival.

THE REASONABLENESS CRITERION

What the judgment that suicide is rational but unreasonable really comes to is that we feel that the rationality established by satisfaction of the nonimpairment, accessibility, values, and interests criteria may be rendered incomplete or inadequate by disproportionate weighting of operant values. This may look as if positive assessment of the consistency of suicide with interests actually is faulty, because the interest in survival is underestimated due to an imbalance in the weighting of values. The appeal to reasonableness would then appear not to differ from the claim that the criteria for rational suicide in fact haven't been met. But while reasonableness isn't a separate and mysterious dimension of assessment, judging suicide unreasonable does differ from judging that suicide fails to meet the relevant criteria for rationality. It does so because here we're dealing with matters of interpretive latitude, not with satisfaction of established standards. Assessing the reasonableness of suicide isn't a matter of separately assessing the consistency of suicide with values and with interests; it's a matter of jointly assessing the relative weighting of values and interests. What needs to be said goes something like this: we may feel there's significant imbalance in suicidists' own assessments of what their values dictate relative to what their interests are. Assuming that the nonimpairment and accessibility criteria are satisfied, we may assess suicide as in accord with suicidists' values, and also assess suicide as in their interests, *given suicidists' weighting of their values*.

However, we can't let the interests criterion collapse into the values one. That would be to fall into the subjectivist error regarding the acceptability of suicide: making interests wholly internal to individual perspectives. People do have interests that, though perhaps not objective, transcend their own perspectives, and people may deny, ignore, or underrate those interests because of the unwarranted importance they attach to their values. T. M. Scanlon quite rightly reminds us that in comparing competing interests, we don't limit consideration to "how strongly the people in question *feel* about these interests."[11] The point applies equally to consideration of competing values and interests. We aren't prepared to override significant interests in survival simply because of how strongly individuals feel about certain deeply held values. We can't allow the rationality and acceptability of self-destruction simply to follow from potential suicidists' preferences. We need to make room for real interests, where "real" means only that interests, particularly the interest in survival, aren't simply identical with individual preferences. Satisfaction of some interests may be crucial to well-being even if unacknowledged by some individuals. Some interests must be construed as grounded in basic human traits, and needn't be conceived in essentialist terms to be recognized as historically necessary to the well-being of creatures like us. Of these, the interest in survival is surely the least controversial. At the very least, the interest in survival can't be taken as unproblematically overridden by even the most strongly held values. How, then, can we ensure that proper weight is given to values and interests in suicidal deliberation?

Reflective aging individuals may be thought to be unreasonable in choosing to commit preemptive suicide because they're perceived as overestimating the importance of intellectuality, and of age-related danger to it, and as underestimating how much still-attainable value their lives offer. To deal with this perception, we could introduce a separate reasonableness criterion that would require that suicide satisfy the nonimpairment, accessibility, values, and interests criteria and, moreover, be consistent with the potential suicidist's values and interests in a balanced way. However, this would require clarification of what's meant by "balanced," which not only is what's at issue but is a daunting task. A better maneuver is to introduce consideration of balance in a more focused way, not in the form of a separate, wide-ranging criterion but as a specific qualification to the values criterion. The expanded values criterion would read:

> 3. Suicide is prescribed by well-grounded values, without
> unduly depreciating the interest in survival.

Admittedly, "unduly depreciating" is nearly as difficult to clarify as "well-balanced," but the qualification at least is specific in referring to a particular interest. This means that assessing undue depreciation requires only assessment of whether suicide-prescribing values contravene that interest. The assessment is also facilitated by how values and the interest in survival conflict. Consider that it may appear that having introduced a qualification to the values criterion, it's necessary to introduce a complementary qualification to the interests criterion, to the effect that interests shouldn't be so heavily weighted as to preclude suicidists' values from being duly weighted in suicidal deliberations. However, this further qualification isn't necessary. That's because there's a crucial lack of symmetry with respect to balancing values and the interest in survival. Exaggeration of values over the interest in survival is a serious problem in suicide, but exaggeration of the interest in survival at the expense of values doesn't pose a significant problem. The reason is that while it's problematic for suicidists' to give undue priority to their values, and so contravene their interest in survival, those same individuals' subordinating their values to their interest in survival isn't problematic. That's something individuals are free to do.

We may not think much of them for doing so, but people can and do adjust their values when those values threaten their survival; and though it may be degrading or even immoral for them to do so, it isn't irrational. The worrying counterpart to suicidists giving undue weight to their values over their interest in survival is others giving undue priority to suicidists' interest in survival to the detriment of their values. This is precisely what happens when others unwarrantedly intervene in suicide. But while others' unwarranted intervention in preemptive suicide is a problem, it's not one to be addressed by criteria for rational suicide.

We can clarify the idea of undue depreciation of the interest in survival by extending Choron's and Narveson's criterial insights. The nub of each is that suicidal motivation be cogent and that operant values be well grounded. Given these points, the qualification just introduced can be put in terms of assessment of suicidal decisions making sense to peers in that, first, the values driving the decision are values they themselves do or could endorse and, second, they themselves take the prescription of suicide by those values as warranted in the circumstances. Undue depreciation of the interest in survival would be present when the former condition is met but the latter isn't because suicide seems excessive in the circumstances. We're not concerned with cases where the first condition isn't met, that is, where peers don't find operant values cogent or accessible, because in those cases the issue of undue depreciation of the interest in survival doesn't arise, since values that are based on false beliefs or that are inaccessible can't outweigh the interest in survival. As Scanlon might add, we aren't willing to accept how people feel as sufficient to judge their self-destruction rational. Admittedly this introduces the worry that personal autonomy is being violated,[12] but recall that the issue here is whether we are prepared to judge suicide or preemptive suicide rational, not whether or not we should intervene in the commission of suicide. Pace Narveson, there may be cases where we shouldn't intervene in suicide even if we judge it irrational. My concern is to establish the criterial rationality of suicide in general and of preemptive suicide in particular, not to lay down rules for dealing with people considering self-destruction.

The sort of depreciation of interests that the balance qualification to the values criterion is designed to prevent is particularly likely in our time of increasingly costly health care. What the balance qualification is intended to ensure is that strong feelings about held values, and ready satisfaction of the values criterion, don't prompt insouciant treatment of the interests criterion. The qualified values criterion requires that full weight be given to suicidists' values but without corresponding reduction of the importance of their interest in survival. The sort of overweighting of values we've touched on is where reflective aging individuals put too much importance on their intellectuality and too little on what continued life might offer. A similar sort of overweighting is where the odium of dependency is exaggerated, with consequent depreciation of the rewards even dependent life may offer. But as indicated, we now have to add to diminishment of intellectuality and to dependence the additional burden of being old at a time when that's becoming synonymous with being a social burden. There's now a real danger that consideration of preemptive suicide may be seriously skewed by both the treatment reflective aging individuals may expect from others, and their own perception of their survival as justified only while they remain independent and their resources are adequate for their needs. If there are social changes taking place that are devaluing dependent life, that devaluation will be reflected in a lowering of tolerance on the part of the elderly for age-related hardships like enduring dependency and dealing with chronic health problems. It will simply seem less worthwhile to them to survive under such conditions, so the value they'll put on their intellectuality and independence will escalate, with a proportionate depreciation of their perceived interest in continued life. But that interest may remain unaffected; in fact, it may be greater now than before. Given modern medicine's new capacities, and the results of better nutrition and more health-conscious lifestyles, life in one's seventies and even eighties is considerably more rewarding now than ever before. The socially influenced overweighting of values prescribing preemptive suicide ironically comes just when the elderly's interests in survival are greatest.

There's a fairly clear sense in which negative aspects of the social environment are fully as important as negative aspects of the physical environment when it comes to considering if life is worth living. Coping with social opprobrium can be every bit as difficult as dealing with dependency or ill health. There's a sense, then, in which gains made in longer life are offset by untoward changes in the social context in which those lives are lived. One might argue that the problems the elderly face today are simply different from those they faced four or five decades ago, and not necessarily worse. Though certain physical conditions that were fatal fifty years ago are now controlled and no longer life-threatening, previously beneficent attitudes toward the elderly have been replaced with intolerance and resentment. Thus while the burden of age has been eased in one respect, it's been worsened in another. But as suggested above, the most disturbing aspect of the social changes we seem to be witnessing is how the aged are coming to see themselves. The old are being made complicitous in their own prejudicial objectification as costly social millstones. Too many of the elderly are accepting as their due the changes that run from restricted access to health care to growing public tolerance for humorous stigmatization of the old.[13]

The danger to the rationality of preemptive suicide posed by negative social attitudes toward the old is that aging individuals' suicide-prescribing values may be unduly strengthened by their fear of living on as social pariahs. Unwarranted strengthening of values prescribing self-destruction comes at the cost of equally unwarranted depreciation of interests in survival. But there's another danger to achieving a proper balance between values and the interest in survival in deliberation of preemptive suicide. Not only are social attitudes toward the aged changing for the worse, social attitudes toward suicide are undergoing an even greater transformation. The past six or eight years have seen a huge growth in the attention paid to physician-assisted suicide and a surprising increase in public support for it.[14] Despite the 1997 Supreme Court decision, legalized assisted suicide most likely isn't far off. Like abortion, assisted suicide is an immensely controversial practice, but one that seems to be gaining enough support to force some, if not most, jurisdictions to sanction it. But like greater intolerance of dependent life, growing acceptance of assisted suicide affects perception of the acceptability of unassisted preemptive suicide. Until recently, suicide was simply unthinkable for many. Now, arguments that support assisted suicide have eroded the taboo by showing how there may be good reasons to willingly relinquish life in punishing and hopeless circumstances. What concerns us is that the more acceptable self-destruction becomes in our society, the likelier it is that values prescribing suicide will gain undue precedence over interests in survival. While it's liberating to be able to consider self-destruction as a possible alternative to unacceptable situations, rather than its being an unspeakable course of action branded as cowardly and sinful, abandonment of the taboo has a decidedly negative effect on the value put on survival in problematic circumstances. The qualified values criterion, then, assumes a new importance in guarding against too facile dismissal of what continued life may offer.

A PRACTICAL CONSIDERATION AND A REMINDER

However difficult in practice, it seems the criterial approach to establishing the rationality of preemptive suicide can be satisfactory, though it's emerged that special care must be taken to give due weight to the interest in survival that deeply held values might otherwise unduly depreciate. Consideration of preemptive suicide is value-driven. It's mainly in cases of surcease suicide that interests, or rather their loss, prompt consideration of self-destruction. It's interests, then, that need protecting in deliberation of preemptive suicide, and it's recognition of this fact that drives reservations about the reasonableness of suicide despite its criterially established rationality. Potential preemptive suicidists' interests in continued life and its still-attainable value may be seriously at odds with their suicide-prescribing values. This means that the central issue about the balance of values and interests is just what most people would anticipate, namely, whether suicidists' value-generated reasons for committing preemptive suicide sufficiently outweigh their interests in continued life. We can put the reservation about the reasonableness of criterially rational suicide in this way: assuming that the unimpairment and accessibility criteria are satisfied, that is, that suicidal decisions are soundly deliberated and motivated, we find that satisfaction of the values criterion poses a special difficulty. Initially, the criterion requires only that suicide be prescribed by well-grounded values. However, it soon emerges that that isn't enough, because suicide could be motivated and prescribed by rational values but still appear to violate suicidists' interests in survival. Suicide may not seem reasonable, and this reservation simply is concern that the unqualified criterion might be met because of the importance given to suicide-prescribing values, but that the importance given those values may be significantly out of proportion to the importance of potential suicidists' interests in survival. The criterion therefore has to be amended to require that suicide be motivated and prescribed by well-grounded values without undue depreciation of the interest in survival.

The danger posed by the reasonableness reservation is that rather than giving due weight to suicidists' values and interests, what can happen in peer assessment of the rationality of suicide is that peers' own values are imposed during the assessment of suicidists' deliberations. The question then is whether the imposed values are valid communal values that do apply to suicidists' deliberations, or only values strongly held by the particular assessors. Fortunately, strongly held personal values—usually moral and religious ones—almost invariably are evident if they're being imposed in conducted assessments. What's much more likely is that differences in interpretation of values incline assessors to think that potential preemptive suicidists are giving undue importance to, say, their fear of personal diminishment, and giving too little importance to what life still has to offer. Unfortunately, at some point these interpretive differences may become intractable, but to say this isn't to admit serious weaknesses in the criterial approach. We have to keep firmly in mind just what it is that the criteria are intended to do, and that is to enable peer judgment of the rationality of suicide and preemptive suicide.

Our aim is neither in-depth psychological analysis of suicidists nor unattainable establishment of the absolute rationality of suicide. Our aim is to assess suicide and preemptive suicide as rational or otherwise on the basis of established standards, and this must allow for human fallibility in assessment. In judging preemptive suicide rational or otherwise, suicidists' peers play a role very like that of jurors. Their job is to assess the "evidence" and to render a "verdict" in the form of acceptance of suicide as rational or rejection of it as irrational. The key point is that what's assessed is the evidence, that is, what is evident and available to assessors. Discussion with potential suicidists can elicit rationality-affirming and -disconfirming factors, but no one can know another's mind fully; neither are we dealing with matters that admit of exactness or that are immutable once discerned. It's of course the case that even suicide judged fully rational might be blighted by deeply hidden confusion or false belief or obsessively held values. In the same way, suicide judged irrational in fact may not be so. Assessors, like jurors, may err or slant their judgments because of differences in their interpretations of communal values. That's why the jury system has the safeguards it has and, in particular, why it involves a number of people and requires in-depth debate. Assessment of suicide and preemptive suicide must also involve a number of people, thus ensuring diversity of perspectives, and involve in-depth debate. The criteria for rational suicide provide minimal, general conditions for acceptable suicide. Determining whether those conditions are actually met is a messy and unsure business involving much discussion, soul-searching, and compromises.

The important thing here is that in the messy and unsure business of deciding whether preemptive suicide is both rational and reasonable, our attention must focus on the relative weighting of suicide-prescribing values and real interests—that is, communally recognized interests. We can't let individuals' idiosyncratic evaluations simply override what the community sees as their interest in continued life. At the same time, we have to remember that the reasonableness reservation is contingent on the accessibility and well-groundedness of suicidal motivation. Suicide-prescribing values tend to be looked at very carefully, if it appears they're being unduly prioritized, but if in the end peers can't understand suicidal motivation, Choron's and possibly Narveson's requirements won't be met, and suicide will fail to be rational on that score. In other words, some cases of unreasonable suicide won't be cases where values are given unwarranted priority over the interest in survival, but failures of the accessibility or rational-motivation requirement. If the weight given some suicide-prescribing values, against the weight given the interest in survival, just doesn't make sense, as opposed to merely being excessive, peers must conclude that what's gone wrong is not that an intractable opposition of interpretations has been reached, but that suicidal motivation really isn't accessible.[15] The qualification to the values criterion is extremely important, but it remains a qualification. The qualification functions in two ways: first, its main job is to assess whether suicide-prescribing values are unduly overriding the interest in survival; second, if it appears that interest is being unduly overridden, it tests whether the favoring of values is intractable, and if it is, the judgment will be that suicidal motivation isn't accessible. In the latter case, the failure doesn't have to do with reasonableness, but with the intelligibility of suicidal motivation itself.

In this chapter I've tried to clarify reservations about judging suicide rational on the basis of the satisfaction of criteria. What surfaced is that a major difficulty with the criterial approach is that satisfaction of the values criterion and the interests criterion is complexly interrelated. What's required is a good balance between the force of suicide-prescribing values and the promise of remaining life. However, achieving that balance is obviously not only a difficult but also an ultimately imperfect exercise. The importance attached to values and interests can be regulated only to a point by communal standards. Incommensurable interpretations of values may be legitimate, producing intractable differences in judgments about the weighting of interests. In our time, two additional influences have been added to the balance equation: dependent life seems to be in the process of being devalued in our society, and there's an undoubtedly related increasing social tolerance of suicide and assisted suicide. Both of these influences are bound to strengthen suicide-prescribing values, and thereby weaken perceived interests in survival. This may or may not be acceptable. It may be that for the purpose of determining the rationality of suicide, the acceptability of reasoning, motives, and values stands or falls by established social or communal standards.[16] But it could be that interests in survival transcend social or communal standards. We need to look more closely at potential suicidists' interests, and at how the interests criterion works. We need to understand better how individuals' interests in survival either can be well served by their deaths or may fail to constitute a significant obstacle to value-driven suicide.

NOTES

1. See, e.g., Plato's *Phaedo* and *Meno*, see also Armstrong 1968.

2. Battin 1982a:298.

3. The parallel here is to arguments that may be valid, in that their conclusions follow from their premises, but not be sound, because one or more premises are false. As any first-year logic student knows, validity isn't enough; sound arguments require validity and true premises.

4. Consider how standard it is for people in their twenties to think they'd rather die young than bear even the benign age-related problems they see their parents and relatives enduring. When those people are in their fifties and sixties, those problems will be normal parts of their lives.

5. Drew Smith, analyst for the Public Policy Institute, quoted in Navarro 1997.

6. "Fifty percent of Medicare expenses is spent during the last six months of an elderly person's life." Michael A. Gross, Florida Asst. Attorney General. Quoted in Navarro 1997. See also Caplan 1996.

7. Battin 1982a:301.

8. I return to the question of real interests below.

9. Hook 1988.

10. Recall that cases where future value is no longer attainable are cases of surcease suicide, and our concern is with preemptive suicide.

11. Scanlon 1975:660.

12. See Fried et al. 1993; Glick 1997.

13. Comedy has changed noticeably in the last few years. Sexist and racist jokes have decreased markedly, but Alzheimer's and other age-related jokes have increased as markedly.

14. Berke 1997. A *Washington Post* survey yielded results running from a high of 54 percent to a low of 47 percent of people polled endorsing legalized physician-assisted suicide. The survey was related to political-party affiliation, with 54 percent of independents, 53 percent of Democrats, and 47 percent of Republicans agreeing that it should be legal for doctors to "help a terminally ill patient commit suicide." It's been claimed that "nearly two-thirds of Americans, including doctors," believe the terminally ill should be assisted in suicide if they request it. J. E. Brody, 1997. See also Steinfels, 1997a, 1997b, 1997c; Prado and Taylor 1998; and Media section of Bibliography.

15. Note that it will then be a further question whether or not to intervene in the suicide.

16. This is a difficult issue. I don't subscribe to cultural relativism, believing that basic principles of reasoning and basic values apply to human beings across all cultures. However, this tangled philosophical issue can't be settled here. To avoid it, I've accepted that the standards operant in assessment of suicide as rational, and so of reasoning, motivation, and values, are the established social standards and may vary from culture to culture. For a succinct account and critique of cultural relativism, see Bond 1996:21–47.

5

SUICIDISTS' INTERESTS

[T]here are . . . occasions on which
a man should leave life . . . for reasons . . .
not as pressing as they might be—
the reasons which restrain us
being not so pressing either.

Seneca, *Letters from a Stoic*

We can begin consideration of how preemptive suicide may be in reflective aging individuals' interests by filling in some details. As we've seen, preemptive suicide is value-driven. The value that individuals put on being the persons they are, means that they view old age not only as posing health and other difficulties but also as threatening to destroy their very selves. Reflective aging individuals in their late sixties and early seventies will probably have already outlived their parents, but unlike their parents, they face some harsh facts that are very much at odds with their values. Their longer survival means that they may have begun to notice some decline in their intellectuality. They're increasingly conscious of impending deterioration in health and face diseases of the very old that their parents may not have lived to contract. They've likely begun to notice levels of resentment on the part of younger people that their parents never encountered.[1] A crucial consideration is that the detected decline in intellectuality doesn't yet amount to impairment of reasoning or significant decrease of interpretive flexibility. The decline has more to do with a slight but markedly new difficulty with abstract ideas, with a general slowing of thought, with loss of some previous interests, with increasingly unreliable memory, and with an ominous intensification of sentimentality. Aging individuals find themselves less willing to tackle some of the issues and questions that so challenged them earlier. They find that it takes longer to reach conclusions and it's harder to feel confidence in those conclusions. They continuously feel pressed to check things that may have slipped their minds. They find that more often than they like, they get caught up in memories of the past. They're more and more drawn to passive entertainment. They find that their lives now include continuing loss as still-living friends have less to do with them or die, and younger family members move away.[2]

There are no doubt additional pressures, such as rising property taxes that make their homes less and less affordable, and growing difficulty in day-to-day dealings with younger people who seem to grow increasingly more impatient and less understanding. They envisage futures in which they'll be plagued not only by the ills and losses that threaten them but also by self-doubts and possibly by regret that they didn't end their lives before losing their autonomy. Finally, they realize that as friends and family members of their age decrease in number, and younger ones grow more independent or distant, their personal responsibilities to others are decreasing to a vanishing point. For all these reasons reflective aging individuals may begin to consider whether they should forgo what Hume describes as a "few years of infirmity" for the sake of dying on their own terms, in their own time, and before risking greater loss.

All of this may strike many as insufficient to compel serious consideration of suicide. While the foregoing inventory brings out the disconsolation that is our lot toward the end of life, those same many will think that there's still value to be attained and insufficient reason to forfeit life. Here we encounter again the deep-seated view that life should be relinquished only in the most desperate circumstances. In the view of those who think preemptive suicide unjustified, what's most called for aren't morbid thoughts about self-destruction but decisive moves to develop new interests, to explore novel possibilities, and to make the best of an admittedly burdensome but not hopeless situation.[3] In a word, preemptive suicide won't be seen as sufficiently in the interests of reflective aging individuals, because their interests in survival will be judged still too strong to allow their suicide-prescribing values to override those interests. Their lot just won't be considered bad enough to warrant suicide. The interests criterion, which requires that suicide serve individuals' interests more than staying alive does, that self-destruction at least not harm suicidists more than continuing to live would do, looks very hard to meet when the individuals in question aren't yet enduring actual great suffering. Some may argue that the psychological burden reflective aging individuals bear is intolerable, but that's in effect to try to turn preemptive suicide into surcease suicide by substituting psychological agony for physical agony. This won't do. First, it simply denies the possibility of rational preemptive suicide without adequate argument. Second, the maneuver distorts the cases in question by misrepresenting potential suicidists' circumstances. It's just not the case that most reflective aging individuals are suffering intolerable psychological torment. Many are simply considering whether the deterioration they've begun to experience, which is a harbinger of worse to come, warrants their taking their lives in order not to suffer personal diminishment and likely find themselves unable to take their own lives on their own terms.

The key issue here is the same as the one underlying questions about the coherency of choosing to die and a priori arguments—like the lack-of-contrast one—against the rationality of suicide: How can suicide, and likely personal annihilation, be better for someone than continued existence? As we've seen before, this issue is especially pressing when applied to preemptive suicide. Even granting that the life left to one looks ominous in terms of what it likely holds, the fact remains that what's feared is still anticipated. Many, many people feel that the only sensible options are to face what's coming and rely on adequate care, or to face what's coming in readiness to commit suicide if and when life in fact becomes unbearable. In contrast to this way of thinking, I'm arguing that preemptive suicide in fact can be the most rational and wisest thing to do for some people in advanced age. The basic reasons are, first, that age-related deterioration may result in personal diminishment that marks the end of who individuals are as surely as does physical death. Second, that age-related personal diminishment at some point precludes the possibility of rational suicide, thus leaving individuals prey to vegetative existence or death on the basis of someone else's decisions. The consequence is that reflective individuals may find themselves living on as other people, and in effect dooming those other people to live out lives of increasingly limited scope and growing dependency.[4]

But to make out my case, and despite what's been said in previous chapters, I still have to deal with the question of how willing, elective death can be in one's interests if it isn't escape from immediate, unbearable suffering. Put this way, the question acknowledges that it seems willing, elective death makes sense only as release, and that preemptive suicide seems to be always irrational in appearing to be a disproportionate response to unrealized threats. But things are worse still, because what potential preemptive suicidists find threatening are circumstances that they're only *unwilling* to bear, rather than circumstances they'll be *unable* to bear. The changes and developments prompting reflective aging individuals to consider preemptive suicide aren't agonizing in themselves, as are physical pain and extreme psychological duress. Personal diminishment doesn't hurt, and it needn't involve psychological anguish. In fact, one of the things that frightens reflective aging individuals is that diminishment of intellectuality and interpretive flexibility is gradual and may proceed unnoticed. The kind of personal diminishment reflective aging individuals reject is diminishment that many people unknowingly endure, or that some at most are vaguely aware of but consistently rationalize in reflex reduction of psychological dissonance.

Battin is right in acknowledging that "death is a harm," and adding that harm isn't just "injury or discomfort, but also . . . deprivation of pleasures, satisfactions, and other goods."[5] Preemptive suicidists harm themselves and act contrary to their interests. By taking their own lives, to avoid anticipated diminishment, they deprive themselves of pleasures, satisfactions, and other goods that life still holds for them. Their lives haven't yet gone from being the condition of all value to being the condition of *dis*value; they aren't yet suffering without adequate compensation. Preemptive suicide, then, seems inescapably self-inflicted harm of the worst sort. Clearly we need to better understand how the interests criterion might be satisfied in the case of preemptive suicide.

What prompts preemptive suicide is a deep unease, not actual suffering. The unease, though powerful and heartfelt, isn't concrete anguish like that of physical pain or intense mental torture. The unease itself doesn't justify forfeiture of life or make such forfeiture consistent with one's interests. Unlike surcease suicide, preemptive suicide isn't a forced choice. Instead, preemptive suicide is essentially a trade: some good time left to one is given up in order not to become something less than what one is. This may be a fair enough trade, but it still involves self-inflicted harm through deprivation of future benefit. The trick is to show that the self-inflicted harm is justified both by the values that prescribe suicide and by remaining life's offering too little benefit to compensate for what it threatens. In short, the argument has to be that what preemptive suicidists deprive themselves of doesn't outweigh the threat of diminishment. The decisive element in this argument is that reflective aging individuals don't see the diminishment they fear as only hardship they'll have to endure, and that could be compensated for by still-attainable value in the time remaining to them. Rather, they see that diminishment as causing their remaining life to be lived by someone other than themselves, by lessened versions of who they presently are. What they fear isn't hardship but profound changes to themselves, changes amounting to the end of the persons they are. They don't, therefore, see preemptive suicide as causing them harm by depriving them of "pleasures, satisfactions, and other goods," not just because the benefits that might be in store for them don't adequately compensate for personal diminishment, but also because it won't be them receiving those benefits. The way reflective aging individuals would indeed harm themselves, and violate their interests in survival, is by acting too soon. Preemptive suicide committed too soon would unduly contravene their interests in survival by sacrificing more good time than is necessary. But against this, these individuals understand that to wait too long is to risk being diminished beyond the point at which they can commit rational preemptive suicide.

It's central to understanding preemptive suicide that some individuals may judge that life no longer has the value it once did for them as particular persons, even if life still offers achievement of some pleasures, satisfactions, and goods. Their judgments don't have to do with what life still offers, but with precisely who will enjoy those pleasures, satisfactions, and goods. Far too much discussion of suicide simply assumes that life's value is value for the individual whose life it is. This may be an obvious thing to think, but like most obvious things, it's more complex than it appears. Human beings are remarkably stable throughout their lives as particular persons with particular traits and perspectives, or what we call "character" or "personality."[6] In fact, it's notoriously difficult to get people to change in fundamental ways, even if they want to do so. Some traumas can change people quite radically, but these are exceptional situations. Generally, we take it that once adulthood is reached, individuals have been formed as the persons they are and will be to the end of their lives.

While we make much of how children's growth to adulthood can be tragically altered by deprivation or abuse, and how they then may turn out different persons than they began to be, we see change in advanced age as inevitable deteriorative development in people's circumstances, not as fundamental transformation in who they are. It's seldom considered that some forms of intellectual and attitudinal change in advanced age are destructive of the person, as opposed to only impeding or distorting the person's abilities, traits, and perspectives. Changes for the worse in mental performance and outlook in advanced age are taken to be natural deterioration that individuals must contend with. Even in cases of advanced dementia, affected individuals are seen as sadly reduced, as mere shadows of their former selves, not as different selves. When people speak of those individuals as no longer being themselves, it's always metaphorically, it's always as recognition of great degeneration and decline. Our culture's traditional Platonic/Cartesian conception of the self inhibits our considering that someone who lives to eighty literally may not be the same person at eighty as at twenty or fifty. We're strongly inclined, because of our traditional philosophic and religious belief in the unique and autonomous self or soul, to think that persons and individuals are identical, and that they remain the same throughout their adult lives. We think that what may change disastrously isn't them but their attitudes, behavior, experience, and ability to exercise their mental capacities. However, some age-related changes, like some pathological changes, affect persons themselves; those changes in effect kill the person though not the individual. Reflective aging individuals understand this, and they may see preemptive suicide as in their interests because what they fear isn't so much what will *happen* to them, but what will happen to *them*.

"IN ONE'S INTERESTS . . ."

There are four important senses in which something's in one's interests.[7] The least significant of these—except to the extent that it's often confused with the other three—is the sense in which something's in one's interests if it simply satisfies a desire. That is, if one desires something, it's in one's interest to get that something. However, this sense is neutral on whether what we want is good for us. This sense is evident in how children notoriously have difficulty accepting that what they want may not be to their benefit. We can call this the "satisfaction of desire" or simply the "desire" sense of "in one's interests." A second sense of something's being in one's interests is that in which that something is acknowledged as desirable but isn't in fact desired. This sense is more sophisticated than the "desire" sense because it acknowledges a possible discrepancy between desire and benefit. For instance, whereas the "desire" sense is best illustrated by children who identify their desires with their interests, this second sense is best illustrated by adults who are well aware of the difference, such as smokers who don't want to stop smoking despite understanding that it would be good for them to do so. This second sense can be dubbed the "potential benefit" sense of "in one's interests." A third sense is when something is in one's interests in a given context or from a particular perspective. This sense is often central to disputes about interests, and is very close to being about values, since the perspective determining the interest is itself value-determined. Suicide, for instance, may be in individuals' interests from their perspective because, for instance, their moral code holds it's better for them to die honorable deaths than to live in shame. But suicide may not be in their interests from another or a broader perspective. This sense can be labeled the "perspective" sense of "in one's interests." The fourth sense of something's being in one's interests is the one that concerns us most directly, and that was anticipated above in contrasting perceived interests with real interests. We'll call this the "real benefit" sense. This is the sense in which something is in people's interests if it's in fact good for them, regardless of their individual preferences or perspectives. This sense is admittedly problematic because it appears to introduce objective interests.

Many argue that the idea of something's being in someone's interests regardless of preference or perspective—in effect, from any perspective, hence from no perspective—can't be coherently made out. As we saw, the reasonableness reservation about preemptive suicide has it that suicide in less than intolerable circumstances violates suicidists' interests because their values obscure what's really in their interests, which is continued life. The idea is that the interest in survival is a "real" interest in the sense that living beings have a basic interest in continuing to live that overrides their values and perspectives except in the most drastic circumstances. In the case of reflective aging individuals, we tend to be disinclined to accept the rationality of their suicides because we feel that their situations aren't yet unendurable, so that their values don't yet override their real interest in survival. Given the foregoing senses of "in one's interests," we can say that preemptive suicide apparently isn't in anyone's interests in the "real benefit" sense, though it may be so in the "perspective" and "desire" senses.[8]

The question here is what we can make of the "real benefit" sense of the interest in survival without embroiling ourselves in metaphysical discussions about objective interests. We don't want to have to argue for a Platonic heaven to house objective human interests. At the same time, we don't want to concede that reservations about violation of real interests in preemptive suicide amount to the tacit introduction of their own values by assessors of the rationality of suicide. But the appearance that there are only two alternatives is misleading; we don't have to opt for only unviable objective interests or our own value-determined understanding of others' interests. There's another alternative, touched on earlier, which is to understand the "real benefit" sense of something's being in one's interests as determined by the broadest communal consensus on conflicts of values and interests. In this view, incommensurable assessments of interests aren't due to a difference between what's objectively the case and what's only thought to be the case, but to how interpretations of the same values may vary enough to be irreconcilable. Recourse to real interests need be no more than attribution to human beings of a communally recognized prima facie interest in remaining alive. The ground of the attribution isn't something ahistorical, but rather the understanding that human beings are mortal, that life is irretrievable once lost, and that other things being equal, it's better to stay alive than to die willingly or unwillingly. Differently put, personal existence is the condition of all other value, so personal existence doesn't require justification for its continuance. On the contrary, it requires justification for its willful termination. The justifiability of surcease suicide illustrates the point, because there "real benefit" interests in continued life are overridden by intense suffering. Preemptive suicide poses problems precisely because "real benefit" interests in remaining alive aren't clearly overridden by punishing conditions.

The notion of a "real benefit" interest in continued existence, then, is only that of a given, of a default position, against which we must show adequate cause for self-inflicted death. "Real benefit" interests in survival don't have to derive from a sacrosanct human nature or divine will; they're minimally communal recognition that living beings don't need to justify continuing to live, but do need to justify willfully ceasing to live. The "real benefit" sense of survival's being in one's interests is at base a social community's requirement that its individual members be able to say why they're better advised to die than to continue living. What emerges, then, is that appeals to "real benefit" interests in assessment of the rationality of preemptive suicide, or of suicide generally, amount to recognition of life as the condition of all value, recognition that life is irretrievable when lost, and a consequent expectation of justification for life's willful forfeiture. What underlies the expectation for justification of willful forfeiture of life is communal understanding that people sometimes behave rashly, particularly when motivated by deeply held values, and so may harm themselves unduly.

INTERESTS AND PERCEPTIONS

The matter of real interests, or the "real benefit" sense of something's being in one's interests, can be further clarified by considering the sorts of factors that properly worry us about people taking their own lives, especially in circumstances that are less than intolerable. Battin offers a statement of what's important in considering an analogous situation. Speaking of depressed individuals' assessments of their options, Battin reminds us that their "judgment about probabilities may be seriously affected," and that they may overemphasize the likelihood of negative events, "subconsciously suppressing data which lead to a more optimistic prediction."[9] Nor is it only depressed individuals' perceptions of their future prospects that are distorted; it isn't only that "good things in the future tend to seem less significant than bad things occurring now." Their perceptions of the past are also affected, because "depression tends to warp our recollections about our preferences."[10] This means that long-held values and priorities may be equally skewed by depression and not allowed to play their proper role in individuals' deliberations. My concern isn't with the depressed, but reflective aging individuals are prey to similar difficulties. They may fixate on certain features of their situations. For instance, contact with friends who're in the early phase of Alzheimer's may make them lose perspective on their own small troubles with memory and prompt them to unduly depreciate their still significant interests in continued life. The danger is that their perceptions and assessments of their probable futures may be as much distorted by their values as memories and expectations may be distorted by depression. Friends and advisers counseling potential preemptive suicidists need recourse to the "real benefit" sense of interests, to enable them to contrast reflective aging individuals' assessments of their future prospects with something other than their own value-laden assessments. Preemptive suicidists must be able to see that discussion of self-destruction doesn't involve only their own perceptions and the particular perceptions of those whose advice they seek out.

Some, in arguing that suicide or preemptive suicide violates the interest in survival, try to present life itself as the ultimate particular value.[11] But by maintaining that life itself is the supreme value, what they do is stipulate a definition of the interest in continued life in a way that simply precludes preemptive suicide or possibly even surcease suicide. A more realistic approach to ensuring that potential suicidists fully appreciate the real interest they have in the lives they may decide to forfeit, is to take the alternative position that was described earlier as more sophisticated, that is, that life is the condition of value.[12] By doing so, the interest in continued life can be characterized not as a particular value but as an interest in continuing to be in a position to attain value; that is, pleasures, satisfactions, and other goods. Assuming that we can take it as unproblematic that value is desirable, it clearly follows that it's desirable to be in a position to attain value. This is the sense in which our society and culture recognize and acknowledge that human beings have a "real benefit" interest in continuing to live. Potential preemptive suicidists may need to be shown that they could be underestimating their "real benefit" interest in survival, and overestimating the threat to their continuing to live as the persons they are. This can't be achieved with dogged insistence that life per se is a gift too precious to relinquish for any reason.

SPECIAL REASONS

Given the nature of old age, there's a certain false optimism behind claims that preemptive suicide is precipitous forfeiture of life because of its anticipatory nature. The idea that even significant diminishment and deterioration in old age may be compensated for by still-attainable pleasures, satisfactions, and goods, promises the elderly rewards that in reality are extremely dubious with respect to their possible achievement, character, and actual worth. The hard fact is that Seneca is right that "the reasons which restrain us" from self-destruction in advanced age aren't as pressing as they might be. However, resistance to Seneca's point of view is considerable, and the core of that resistance seems to be the belief that if the reasons for suicide are a matter of individuals' perceptions, of how potential suicidists perceive their situations, as opposed to actual suffering evident to all, then those reasons aren't sufficient to forfeit life. This belief is a more epistemic version of the reasonableness reservation we considered. Its basic content is that preemptive suicide isn't adequately in one's interests if what prompts self-destruction is "intentional," or "in the minds" of individuals, rather than "material," or having to do with their physical circumstances. This is, in effect, still another instance of the limitation of justifiable suicide to surcease suicide. What underlies it is a clash between the "perspective" sense in which suicide is perceived to be in their interests by particular individuals, and the "potential benefit" sense in which suicide is seen by others as not in those individuals' interests. Perception of self-destruction as in one's interests seems to be standardly thought to be the product of depression or pessimism.[13] In short, individuals' "perspective" interests are given short shrift in favor of "real benefit" interests.

The "perspective" sense in which suicide may be perceived to be in someone's interests, or at least to not contravene those interests more than continuing to live does, is tested by the values criterion. The criterion is designed to establish whether individuals' values are rational, and whether those values prescribe suicide in the relevant circumstances. To say that suicide is consistent with suicidists' interests in the "perspective" sense, therefore, is to say that operant values are well grounded, and that given that they prescribe suicide under certain specific conditions, suicide is warranted to the extent that it's not outweighed by "real benefit" interests in survival. It seems, then, that "real benefit" interests in survival are decisive with respect to the rationality of suicide. This may be so in most cases, but we have to allow that sometimes individuals have good enough reasons for self-destruction regardless of what others think. That's just when the values criterion becomes most important. However, it's commonly assumed that "real benefit" and possibly "potential benefit" interests always outweigh individuals' "perspective" interests. The reason for this assumption that most concerns us is, once again, the anticipatory nature of preemptive suicide. We need to say how preemptive suicide may be deemed consistent with potential suicidists' "real benefit" interests prior to actual suffering befalling them. Additionally, we must do so without appearing to change the nature of preemptive suicide, that is, without looking as if we're turning preemptive suicide into surcease suicide by escalating potential suicidists' concerns about their futures to levels of punishment equivalent to surcease-justifying torment. Our only resources for performing this necessary task seem to be the nature of advanced age and age-related elimination of some individuals' personas.

So far, we've clarified a philosophically innocuous sense in which living human beings have a "real benefit" interest in continuing to live. We've also clarified how they may have perceived or value-determined "perspective" interests in dying. But we need to state even more plainly how "perspective" and "real benefit" interests relate to one another in the situations in which reflective aging individuals find themselves considering preemptive suicide. Once this is done, it should be clear how their concerns about intellectual diminishment and increasing interpretive rigidity, as well as loss of autonomy and the gamut of age-related difficulties, prompts them to consider ending their lives prior to those afflictions befalling them. If such suicide is to be rational, it has to be consistent with both "perspective" interests and "real benefit" interests. The first consistency doesn't pose a problem. Since consideration of preemptive suicide is value-driven, it automatically will be in accord with "perspective" interests. That is, preemptive suicide wouldn't arise as an option or be seriously considered if it wasn't thought to serve "perspective" interests. The second consistency is another matter. As mentioned more than once, preemptive suicide can't be made to accord with "real benefit" interests by in effect denying those interests and turning preemptive suicide into surcease suicide. We can't attempt to deny that potential preemptive suicidists have genuine "real benefit" interests in survival, because preemptive suicide is of an anticipatory nature and precisely a trade of good time left for avoidance of personal diminishment. So it looks as if for preemptive suicide to be consistent with still-existent "real benefit" interests, continued life as the condition of value-attainment must be significantly outweighed by potential suicidists' "perspective" interests. Unlike consideration of surcease suicide, where "real benefit" interests collapse into "perspective" interests,[14] what needs to be established in consideration of preemptive suicide is that "perspective" interests supersede "real benefit" ones. This is where the nature of age-related changes is crucial.

In consideration of preemptive suicide, continued life in advanced age is judged to no longer constitute a significant enough "real benefit" interest when the still-attainable value it offers will be available only to materially reduced versions of those reflective aging individuals contemplating preemptive self-destruction. Still-attainable value doesn't suffice to generate compelling "real benefit" interests in survival because the attainable value will benefit aging individuals only from others' perspectives; that is, from the perspectives of the diminished subjects whom old age produces and of third parties. The fact that reflective aging individuals will be the same individuals in the future isn't enough to make them the same persons. Value that accrues to those aging individuals in their impending diminished states won't be value that will accrue to them as the persons they are when considering preemptive suicide. Reflective aging individuals understand that their lives as themselves are drawing to an end well before the deaths of their bodies. If their fears about diminishment are realistic, their lives as the persons they value being simply don't offer enough future value, despite the fact that there likely is more value to be attained beyond their diminishment. Their only concern, then, is to commit suicide as late as possible in order to attain as much value as possible while still themselves. The catch is that they have to commit suicide early enough to avoid ceasing to be who they are and losing the capacity to rationally take their own lives. The key point, then, is that "real benefit" interests in continued life accrue to diminished reflective aging individuals only if we ignore who it is that benefits from what life still offers.

What would convince reflective aging individuals to postpone or forgo preemptive suicide isn't claims that their lives as individuals still offer much that is worthwhile. Rather, it would be that the changes they fear will destroy them as persons—before death destroys them as individuals—really aren't as malign as they fear. As they see it, reflective aging individuals' predicament is a matter of age inexorably changing them by diminishing their capacities to a point where they cease to exist as the persons they are. But if this is the central concern, and if the key question regarding the consistency of preemptive suicide with "real benefit" interests is *who* it is that will benefit from continued survival, then the obvious rejoinder is that the diminishment of reflective aging individuals is being exaggerated or is misconceived. The fundamental premise in the foregoing is that reflective aging individuals' real interests in continued life dissipate to the extent that age destroys them as persons. If age doesn't destroy them as persons, then their "real benefit" interests in survival aren't as readily outweighed by suicide-prescribing values and "perspective" interests.

THE NATURE OF THE CHANGE AND OF THE CHOICE

This may appear to be the place to inventory the varieties of age-related neurological deterioration, but that actually wouldn't get us very far, unless we turned to numerous particular cases to support an inductive generalization about age-caused diminishment. What's crucial here isn't detailed pathology, because the claim that age-related diminishment ends the lives of persons, before death ends the lives of individuals, isn't primarily a claim about the physical causes of mental changes. The claim is primarily about subjects, about how subjects are changed. Physical or neural deterioration doesn't change subjects directly, unless it's catastrophically pathological. Physical or neural deterioration changes the conditions of subjectivity: it changes the circumstances in which persons are subjects.

Consideration of preemptive suicide is consideration of suicide prior to diminishment and in less than desperate situations. However, it needn't be simply a matter of trying to determine whether or not life, as the condition of future value, is worth retaining in spite of some particular threatened or impending form of diminishment. This sort of choice is exemplified by the most straightforward sorts of preemptive suicide. For example, aging individuals, both of whose parents and all of whose grandparents were Alzheimer's victims, may consider preemptive suicide to preclude their falling victim to the disease. But reflective aging individuals may face more subtle choices. In surcease suicide, suicidists are assailed by conditions or situations that befall them, such as terrible illnesses or critical ethical choices forced on them by circumstance or malevolence. Their choices are whether to continue living lives inescapably blighted by the intrusive elements, or to forfeit those lives in order to escape their predicaments. Reflective aging individuals facing something like what they judge as a near certainty of contracting Alzheimer's are in a position similar to that of surcease suicidists. The significant difference is that their self-destruction would be anticipatory and preclusive of something rather than escape from something immediate. But in other cases reflective aging individuals don't so much fear particular though still future diseases or other misfortunes, as they fear themselves being changed in ways they can't abide.[15] I've stressed this point numerous times because it's initially one that many have difficulty taking seriously, due to our strong Platonic/Cartesian tradition of conceiving the self as a singular essence. However, the self is better understood more as a construct than as an unchanging ego.[16] Experience and our physical circumstances define us as subjects, and experience and those circumstances are quite capable of redefining us as different subjects. Some reflective aging individuals face the choice of whether or not to allow themselves to be redefined as subjects.

Reference was made above to how difficult it is for people to change in fundamental ways, and to how we strongly tend to perceive individuals as basically unchanging throughout their lives. To the degree that change in character or personality is difficult and rare, that may seem a function of the stability of some core self. But it isn't; it's mainly a function of the stability of the circumstances in which people are who they are. This is an amply recognized fact of human psychology; witness such things as the efforts made to ensure productive environments for growing children and teenagers, as well as to prevent old associates and practices from causing recidivism in lawbreakers. The subjects we are, who each of us is, is a complex experiential, social, neurophysiological, and anatomical product. Change any of these enabling conditions significantly, and the subject changes. What most threaten reflective aging individuals are changes that inhibit the reflection and interpretive capacities that define them as subjects, and those capacities are contingent on fine balances among their experiential, social, neurophysiological, and anatomical circumstances. Age affects all of these circumstances to a greater or lesser extent. This is what many deny in arguing that old age is itself a social construct. It's also what many more deny by default, in downplaying holistic change in old age by focusing on particular ailments and problems.

But reflective aging individuals understand that what's happening to them is holistic and inexorable. They understand, though perhaps only more or less clearly, that the subjects they are, their selves, are complex constructs, and that deterioration and other changes in the circumstances supporting those selves are reshaping them as diminished persons or are threatening to do so. What they consider, in considering preemptive suicide, is not allowing those changes to continue, not allowing the passing of time to make them over into persons they'll neither recognize nor want to be. Potential preemptive suicidists aren't really deciding whether to live and bear certain afflictions, or to cease to live to not bear them. Instead, they're considering whether or not to continue to live as different, lessened people, because they have no choice about continuing to live as themselves. That's the key to preemptive suicide in advanced age. The persons reflective aging individuals are, and value being, are beginning to disappear. They're evaporating and being gradually replaced by others, albeit at varying rates in different individuals; they're dying well before their bodies' biological deaths.

I said above that reflective aging individuals may decide that the persons into whom age is turning them aren't ones they think should live. That very tough judgment is the heart of the decision to commit preemptive suicide in advanced age. It isn't that reflective aging individuals can't or won't bear being diminished in the sense of being limited in various ways; it's that they refuse to bear not being themselves. They then see no good reason why reduced and dependent versions of themselves should continue to survive. As we've seen, this means that still-attainable value plays a different role in deliberation of preemptive suicide than in deliberation of other sorts of self-destruction. Reflective aging individuals realize that the value their lives still offer is value only for their diminished selves. Still-attainable value can't compensate *them* for their diminishment; at best it can compensate their diminished successors for whatever those successors must endure. Potential preemptive suicidists therefore assess still-attainable value more negatively than do third parties, and this makes for conflicts between their assessments of their own "perspective" interests and their peers' assessments of their "real benefit" interests. Still-attainable value becomes an important consideration for potential preemptive suicidists only to the extent that diminishment may not be destructive of the persons they are and prize being. If diminishment were judged likely to be less malign than feared, then still-attainable future value would gain significance and "real benefit" interests in survival would be enhanced. Short of that, the fact is that still-attainable value just isn't good enough to deter preemptive suicide, if the bulk of it comes after notable diminishment. What this means is that reflective aging individuals see their preemptive suicides less as choosing to die rather than endure diminishment, than as final affirmations of who and what they are at the moment of their self-destructive acts. The essential decision they make in choosing to commit preemptive suicide is that they no longer have an interest in continued life, regardless of still-attainable value, because they recognize that the persons they are have come to the end of their existence, even if as individuals they've not come to the end of their physical being.

A common argument against preemptive suicide in advanced age is to the effect that by continuing to live, and struggling with the diminishment age brings, individuals may become better persons, not just in the moral assessment of others but in their own experience as well. Allegedly, adversity in advanced age provides the occasion for fortitude, tolerance, and other virtues, and so contributes to its own alleviation. The compensation promised is a mix of virtue as its own reward and satisfaction gained through effort and acceptance. But the picture painted is at best naïve and at worst condescendingly pernicious. For one thing, it ignores the point I've been stressing about diminishment destroying persons well before individuals' actual deaths. But even if that point is waived for argument's sake, and we imagine diminished individuals benefiting by virtuously enduring deterioration, the argument still fails. It portrays elderly people heroically coping with degeneration and decline, somehow gaining satisfaction in their own forbearance, relishing ever-smaller pleasures, and enjoying the love and admiration of family and friends. This portrayal's promises are empty; the harsh evidence of that is most evident in any Alzheimer's ward, nursing home, or hospice.

What actually prompts this view is the commonly tacit idea that we have a moral obligation to bear and combat adversity,[17] and that suicide is cowardly avoidance of our lots. Unless individuals hold moral or religious beliefs that preclude suicide, nothing requires them to bear personal diminishment in advanced age, and whatever benefits attach to doing so are invariably of little worth compared with what must be endured. Moreover, though there's no question that dealing with adversity can be a rewarding experience, the character strengthening that doing so promotes is a forward-looking benefit. Bearing personal diminishment of the sort feared by reflective aging individuals has no long-term point. They're no longer in a position to benefit in the future from courage and forbearance in the present. All that accepting their diminishment would come to is living on as lessened individuals and those lessened individuals enduring more deterioration than they need to endure. The major component of reflective aging individuals' self-defining values and "perspective" interests is *being* the persons they are, and valuing everything else *as* the persons they are. Since it's who they are that's destroyed by diminishment, and diminishment is a consequence of surviving, they gain nothing by living on and allowing their own destruction. Reflective aging individuals' only meaningful choice is between dying as themselves, and enduring diminishment and dying as someone else.

THE NATURE OF WHAT'S LEFT

Once we understand the nature of the choice facing reflective aging individuals, we've half of what we need to appreciate the reduced nature of their "real benefit" interests in survival. We now understand that for them, continued life has become the condition of still-attainable value only in a Pickwickian sense, because value that may accrue to them as living beings won't accrue to them as the persons they are. The other half of what we need has to do with the nature of their remaining life. We can clarify this by recalling that reflective aging individuals considering preemptive suicide are in their late sixties or early seventies. What they may sacrifice in committing suicide is a relatively modest period of time, and time that is highly problematic with respect to its quality. However, the point here isn't primarily that the time left may be blighted by disease, dependency, and possibly dementia. The point has to do with the nature of that time itself. Average age at death is still in the low seventies in North America, so even if we take seventy-five as a more or less arbitrary reference point, people who are, say, seventy may be forfeiting some five years or less in committing preemptive suicide. Five years may sound like a substantial period of time, and too much to forfeit willingly, but it must be appreciated that the time in question is "terminal." The overwhelming majority of people in their seventies are living out periods of time that are equivalent in nature to periods of time allowed for in diagnoses of terminal illnesses. At that age, as in terminal illness, there's a predictable end point in sight. Death ceases to be a vague and indeterminate eventuality and becomes palpable closure. The harsh reality is that at seventy-five the vast majority of lives are almost over, and people that age recognize that reality. Aging individuals appreciate the "hard fact of having come to the end."[18] Ronald Blythe remarks that "when the old say . . . 'I simply can't go on,' they are stating their major frustration, not announcing a coming to terms with death."[19] The time left isn't just time, blighted or otherwise; it's limited duration, a kind of countdown.

The importance of this is that given that people in their early and mid-seventies appreciate that their lives are nearly over, and given the risk of diminishment, disease, and dependency, the finite handful of years at issue reasonably may be judged to be not promising survival but dangerous postponement. It's true that modern medicine and nutrition have made the quality of contemporary life in the eighth and ninth decades comparable with that of previous generations' sixth and seventh decades, and it's true that there are people who now live even into their nineties in relatively good health and with their intellectuality pretty much intact. But in spite of these facts, the realistic view is that most who live beyond their early seventies have predictably short futures. Assessment of aged individuals' "real benefit" interests in the time left to them, then, must be qualified both by the terminal nature of the time left and by the experience of closure attendant on that time's terminal nature. Once aged individuals' "real benefit" interests in survival are put in their proper perspective, there may be greater agreement with those who, like Robert Kastenbaum, believe that when we've changed present cultural attitudes toward suicide, and better understand the realities of the advanced ages more of us now attain, we won't need to justify suicide in advanced age.[20] The conflict between suicide-prescribing values or "perspective" interests and "real benefit" interests may dissipate, and preemptive suicide may become the preferred way to end one's life[21] because it enables us to die on our own terms and in our own time.

However, despite what's been said here, awareness of life's closure needn't be pervasive or paralyzing. Deterioration in advanced age is relatively slow, and some accommodation to it can be made. Moreover, there are specific values special enough to retain their worth and serve as important goals for those who've lost even a good measure of their capacities and may be enduring significant suffering. For instance, some may be willing to bear a good deal to witness an anticipated event before dying, such as the birth of a great-grandchild or some notable historical achievement. It's all very well to talk in the abstract about ceasing to be the persons we are, but quite another to believe in and reject diminishment deeply enough to kill ourselves. Battin reminds us that in old age "we will lose control not just over our pocketbooks and our bladders but over all the major circumstances of our lives," and that "[t]here will be no recovery from this condition."[22] Still, in practice we adjust as we age to what a year or two earlier we rejected as intolerable. People are immensely adaptable. This adaptability is, in fact, one of the things reflective aging individuals fear, because it may result in their making too many small adjustments and thereby losing their intellectual identities without realizing it. Nonetheless, we are highly adaptable; circumstances may make us value what we earlier disdained. "Real benefit" interests in continued life don't simply evaporate at the first sign of age-related trouble or even on realizing that we "can't go on."

We're back to suicide-prescribing values and "perspective" interests. While it's true that we're highly adaptable, not all of us *want* to adapt to what we consider demeaning, much less to diminishment of ourselves as persons. Once we understand the nature of the choices made in preemptive suicide, and the nature of the time that may be forfeited, we see that "real benefit" interests in survival need not be decisive, and that the pivotal difference is the role of reflective aging individuals' values. We can take it that there will be aging individuals whose values won't prescribe preemptive suicide, and others whose values will prescribe preemptive suicide. These latter cases are the ones that interest us, and it's with respect to them that it's important to appreciate the quality of life left to those of advanced age and the significance of the terminal nature of that life to their "real benefit" interests. Still, "perspective" and "real benefit" interests are at odds, so even if "real benefit" interests aren't necessarily decisive, it becomes even clearer than when first mentioned that the key question regarding the conflict of interests is that of the timing of preemptive suicide. Since it's rational to maximize one's benefits, even if reflective aging individuals' values strongly prescribe preemptive suicide, and their "real benefit" interests in survival don't preclude self-destruction, it wouldn't be rational for them to do anything too soon, thereby unjustifiably precluding achievement of still-attainable value.

The question of timing is a complicated one, and we'll consider it more thoroughly in the next chapter, but it's worth noting a couple of points here that are often neglected. The general requirement regarding timing is that preemptive suicide should be committed when individuals are advanced enough in age that discerned or threatened deterioration can be judged to be age-related rather than due to other, perhaps treatable, causes. Where no significant deterioration is discerned, there must be careful estimates made about its likelihood, based on such things as parents' circumstances at a similar age. Potential preemptive suicidists need authoritative information on their own mental and physical conditions, but they also need the best available evidence of how genetically close relatives fared in old age. Potential preemptive suicidists are considering trading time left to them for the avoidance of what that time likely will bring, so the bases for their decisions must be as solid as possible.

The other half of the general requirement is that potential preemptive suicidists shouldn't be so advanced in age that their deliberations are no longer reliable, or that they've lost the requisite autonomy to enact suicidal decisions. Given this general requirement and the difficulties it raises, two matters tend to be overlooked because they appear peripheral. First, people's natural optimism and pessimism play key roles in preemptive suicidal deliberation. Optimism may tend to unduly delay, and pessimism to unduly advance, the timing of preemptive suicide. Consultation with friends and professionals is crucial to allow for the appraisal-distorting effects of these opposed outlooks, and those counseling preemptive suicidists shouldn't underestimate the importance of these attitudinal factors. Second, romanticizing old age can have a quite negative impact on preemptive suicidal deliberation. Robert Browning's invitation to grow old because "the best is yet to be" is, if not a lie, an unintentionally cruel false promise.[23] There's abundant evidence that beyond a certain point, survival becomes mere survival in the sense that the lives of very elderly persons come to be a series of worsening trials, lessening autonomy, and decreasing understanding and awareness. And as Battin notes, things aren't going to get better for aging individuals. What may be forfeited in hastening death, therefore, should be realistically understood as a number of relatively stable periods of minimal difficulty that may afford opportunities to attain the value suicide would preclude. The compensation a later, natural death offers, for the risk it entails, isn't a continuation of normal life interrupted by difficulties, but the chance for periods of time during which life may still be relished despite escalating hardship. If we understand "pain" to encompass significant diminishment of oneself, preemptive suicide must be weighed not against life going pretty much as before for a little longer but against what Battin describes as "important experience during . . . pain-free intervals."[24]

We've made some progress in gaining better understanding of the sort of choice faced by reflective aging individuals, and how "real benefit" interests in survival aren't decisively preclusive of preemptive suicide in advanced age. However, as just indicated, the key question of timing is a difficult one and needs further consideration.

A RECAPITULATION

To close this chapter, it's useful to pull together the salient points made above. First, there's an important sense in which reflective aging individuals' interests in continued life aren't identical with their interest in continued existence as human beings. The great majority of us don't survive quite as long as our bodies. As persons who are subjects of experience in determinate ways, we're products of delicate and complex neurophysiological processes and structures, and no little social influence. For most of our lives our existence as persons is adequately supported by our underlying neurophysiology and social circumstances. But as our bodies begin to deteriorate toward the end of their functional life spans, and as we come to be different social entities because of our society's classifications, our existence as persons is no longer as reliably supported or as stable as before. Reflective aging individuals realize this, and understand that they will almost certainly cease to exist as the persons they are some time before their bodies actually die. The choice they face, as we saw, isn't between dying by their own hand and dying naturally. They face a choice between dying as themselves and eventually dying as others less than themselves. Their "real benefit" interests in continued life are therefore complex and qualified, and needn't preclude self-destruction. For instance, it might appear likely that certain aging individuals will live for a number of years that afford the attainability of value, and therefore have significant "real benefit" interests in survival. But there may be good evidence that their projected lives as the persons they are amount to only a fraction of their estimated life spans, due to deteriorative changes projected on the basis of family histories and careful examinations. It would be wrong, then, to judge that their suicides would unduly contravene their interests, because assessments of their "real benefit" interests in survival are based on their bodies' projected life spans. Their suicide-prescribing values and "perspective" interests in dying could be decisive, despite contravention of "real benefit" interests in survival.

The requirement that preemptive suicide accord with reflective aging suicidists' interests, and not harm them more than continuing to live, is basically a matter of establishing whether there exist significant possibilities of their realizing still-attainable value *as the persons they are*. As human beings age, their "real benefit" interests in survival change from interests in existence per se, to interests in existence as more and more qualified by both identity considerations and value requirements. The value of life is a dynamically changing function of identity, quantity, and quality. In the early stages of life, the promise of time available reduces the importance of immediate and short-term quality, because poor quality is compensated for by the possibility of significant improvement. But with advancing age, life becomes more and more a qualitative asset; the lessening of time left intensifies the importance of quality. The "real benefit" interest in continued life isn't an interest in sheer duration. As living beings we clearly have a real interest in remaining alive. But we aren't only living beings: we're self-aware, thinking, feeling, and valuing beings. Continued existence is of worth to us only if it includes levels of satisfaction and gratification in keeping with our values.

We seem to end up where we might have anticipated, namely, judging that the consistency of suicide with interests depends on the nature of those interests. This should not surprise us or make us feel we've labored too hard for too little return. As always in philosophy, pace Marx, nothing's changed and we end up where we started, but with better understanding. In considering the consistency of preemptive suicide with potential suicidists' interests, we begin with a given: the "real benefit" interests that living beings have in remaining alive and that prima facie preclude willful self-destruction. But interests in survival have to be qualified by the likely quantity and quality of continued life. That much may be obvious. What's not so obvious is that there's another dimension to assessment of "real benefit" interests that has to do with whose interests they are. If significant deterioration of persons is likely, those persons' "real benefit" interests in continued life may be radically out of line with their "real benefit" interests in survival as living beings. The greater the threat of diminishment or extinction to individuals as the persons they are, the less real interest those persons have in survival, regardless of how much life is left to them, because it isn't *they* who will live on. Our conclusion must be that preemptive suicide in advanced age may be rational despite the existence of "real benefit" interests in survival. Contravention of interests in survival by value-prescribed self-destruction may well be rational if timed to violate those interests to the smallest extent possible. We now need to consider the matter of timing in more detail.

NOTES

1. My own experience confirms what other older people have told me about repeated expression by the young of their view that those presently in their sixties and seventies are most likely the last to enjoy financial security in old age.

2. Tolchin 1989.

3. Compare J. Brody 1997.

4. The classic example is someone who might be diagnosed as in the early stages of some form of senile dementia; who at that point is capable of suicide but chooses to live on; and who then, for the sake of a very short time of reasonably aware life, spends a decade existing as a mindless organism requiring constant care.

5. Battin 1982a:308; compare Feinberg 1984:79–83.

6. I return to clarify this point.

7. Bond 1988:279.

8. Others also may feel that suicide is or isn't in his/her interests in the "potential benefit" sense. This sense is largely immaterial to him/her, since he/she thinks suicide *is* in his/her interests.

9. Battin 1982a:304.

10. Ibid.

11. Ibid.:309.

12. Hook 1988:22.

13. See J. Brody 1997.

14. Assuming, of course, that the individuals understand what others understand, which is that they have lost their "real benefit" interests in survival.

15. Of course they also fear becoming victims of illnesses and other problems related to their age.

16. The concept is Michel Foucault's. See Prado 1995 for an account of my understanding of this concept.

17. See Hamel and DuBose 1996.

18. Blythe 1979:5.

19. Ibid.

20. Kastenbaum 1967.

21. Ibid.

22. Battin 1987:162.

23. Robert Browning, "Rabbi Ben Ezra."

24. Battin 1982a:312.

6

A MATTER OF TIME

Judging whether life is . . . worth living
amounts to answering
the fundamental question of philosophy.
Camus, *The Myth of Sisyphus*

The aim in the last chapter was to show that in advanced age, individuals'
interests in continued life are qualified by still-future but inescapable
deterioration. Those interests, therefore, needn't preclude preemptive
suicide even if they are still significant. The deterioration in question is
usually thought of as physical, but the main consideration for us is that the
importance of "real benefit" interests in continued life declines in proportion to the likelihood that individuals won't live the time left to them as
the persons they are, instead surviving as diminished versions of themselves. However, precisely because deterioration, regardless of how inevitable, is still future, the timing of preemptive suicide poses unique
difficulties. Preemptive suicide is a trade of at least some good life left to
ensure that one doesn't end up surviving as a diminished other. We have
no way of establishing with any degree of certainty just when age-related
changes may begin to diminish us. Preemptive suicide must be timed when
suicidists' and their peers' best judgments are that it's late enough to allow

individuals as much still-attainable value as possible, but early enough not to risk diminishment and the erosion of autonomy it entails.

Assuming that what was said in the last chapter establishes that contravention of qualified "real benefit" interests in survival can be rational, we need a way of articulating the condition that preemptive suicide must contravene those interests to an acceptably minimal degree. There are, of course, all sorts of practical limitations on determining when that is. The best we can hope for is to establish a narrow temporal range within which commission of preemptive suicide is judged to result in minimal contravention of suicidists' interests in continued life and still-attainable value. Regardless of what other criteria may be satisfied, preemptive suicide wouldn't be rational if committed too soon, for that would be to sacrifice more life than necessary and to contravene one's interests excessively by robbing oneself of still-attainable value. Preemptive suicide also wouldn't be rational if self-destruction occurs late enough that suicidists aren't capable of sound deliberation and fully intentional action. We might paraphrase Camus and say that the fundamental question in the present context is determining *when* life is no longer worth living. There's a need, then, to formulate a temporal criterion or a temporal qualification to one of the criteria for rational suicide.

An additional aspect of the timing question has to do not with interests but with self-assertion. The idea is Nietzsche's moot intention to "convert the stupid physiological fact [of death] into a moral necessity."[1] The readiness for death that Seneca and Hume exhibited is best described as a weariness of life, especially of life that has become burdensome. But thinking of readiness for death as weariness with life underestimates the degree to which some aged persons may not be reacting to their long lives' negative aspects but rather asserting themselves and their values in choosing to abandon those lives. Understanding readiness for death as weariness denies the extent to which some aged individuals' suicidal decisions are positive affirmations of their wills regarding their present circumstances and future prospects. It's difficult for many people to imagine choosing to die, so they construe elderly persons' readiness to die as a kind of profound fatigue or even despair. But some elderly persons may appreciate and share Nietzsche's idea about self-assertively turning the inevitable event of death into an act of will. This idea not only introduces an element of ultimate self-definition to the end of life, it also contributes importantly to justifying the contravention of remaining "real benefit" interests in survival by adding value and meaning to the sacrifice of those interests. Readiness to commit preemptive suicide can be a last positive, self-defining act rather than only a hurrying of the inevitable.

The timing of preemptive suicide, then, is even less closely related to reflective aging individuals' physical conditions than might be thought. We can't tie any temporal criterion or qualification too tightly to particular considerations, such as threatened or impending terminal illness, because not only must preemptive suicide be committed in anticipation of deterioration but its timing may be in part dictated by intensely personal factors. We have to keep in mind, as we proceed, that age itself is the basic reason for preemptive suicide, and that therefore its timing is considerably more problematic than self-destruction prompted by specific, and thus temporally definite, pressures. Preemptive suicide is an essentially discretionary act. Its timing must be more a matter of choice than of circumstantial prescriptions. Nonetheless, in order to have only warranted contravention of "real benefit" interests in survival, commission of preemptive suicide must be timed as late as possible. Of course, if self-destruction in advanced age is to be preemptive rather than surcease suicide, self-destruction can't come so late that there's compelling pressure from discerned diminishment or deterioration. For one thing, if diminishment or deterioration is discernible, it's likely advanced enough to make sound deliberation and action problematic, and thus is likely to preclude rational preemptive suicide.

The timing of preemptive suicide, then, involves an intentional aspect that outweighs the material aspect. That is, potential preemptive suicidists must first consider not their physical conditions and prospects, but their mental preparedness to end their lives. The special significance of the intentional aspect is due to the fact that potential preemptive suicidists can't establish with certainty precisely when their suicides actually are best timed to allow them to live as long as possible but still to die before the onset of personal diminishment. Reflective aging individuals aren't able to determine the optimum time for suicide purely on the basis of their physical circumstances and prospects. They need to decide when to die, within the time frames established by their material conditions and their and others' best assessments of their prospects. Those time frames are established by advanced age, and are bounded, on the one hand, by good enough health to rule out impairment of reasoning and action, and, on the other hand, by indications that deterioration is imminent or may have begun. This is why preemptive suicide inevitably contravenes "real benefit" interests in survival to some degree. As stressed above, preemptive suicide requires sacrifice of enough good time still left to one to safeguard against the onset of preclusive diminishment and its attendant impairment of faculties.

Preemptive suicidists must relinquish more of their remaining lives than they actually would need to relinquish if information about their futures could be perfectly complete. They appreciate that they must make personal judgments about precisely when to take their lives, fully aware that they're likely sacrificing more life than is ideally necessary.

Unfortunately, the very centrality and the discretionary role of the intentional in the timing of preemptive suicide can be obtrusive. The intentional can be an obstacle to both consideration and commission of preemptive suicide in cases where elderly individuals are enjoying good health and are immersed in their activities and relationships. Even though reflective, these people may be rendered psychologically incapable of considering, much less committing, preemptive suicide by a lack of distance from their involvements. Everything in their lives may militate against their thinking of practicing—and their wanting to practice—Nietzsche's "difficult art of leaving at the right time." It takes serious and concentrated reflection over weeks or months to consider whether preemptive suicide is one's best advised course of action. That sort of reflection is difficult to achieve if one's own diminishment is pushed to the back of one's mind by busyness and engagement with others. Active, full lives are highly desirable at any age, but in advanced age they're at odds with effective reflection and pose the danger that individuals will suddenly find themselves trapped by gradual deterioration and no longer be able to commit rational preemptive suicide. The trouble is that since its purpose is to preserve the identities of reflective aging individuals from diminishment, preemptive suicide tragically is most indicated when those individuals are most themselves, when they still possess all their intellectuality and interpretive perspicacity. That's when those individuals are getting a great deal out of life, which means reflective aging individuals should take their lives just when they'll feel they have the most to lose. The point here is what was said above: that preemptive suicide requires trading good time left for judicious avoidance of diminishment. Potential preemptive suicidists face a tremendous challenge that pits their satisfaction and pleasure against their cool reason.

Unlike surcease suicide, the timing of which is imposed on people by circumstance, the timing of preemptive suicide must be decided on; hence reflective aging individuals' states of mind take priority over their physical conditions. As Chapter 2 established, the very age of reflective aging individuals is the prime reason for consideration of preemptive suicide. Most people tend to think suicide in advanced age is prompted by imminent terminal illness, but individuals' anticipated health problems are actually secondary to age with respect to determining the timing of preemptive suicide. What needs to be done with respect to the material aspect of the conditions for rational preemptive suicide is relatively straightforward. Potential preemptive suicidists must establish as accurately as possible that their physical conditions neither impede sound reasoning nor distort their motives.[2] They also must assess their prospects with respect to what age likely will bring.[3] But once the material conditions are adequately dealt with, the considerably more difficult task is establishing potential preemptive suicidists' readiness to die. That requires focusing the most intensive assessorial efforts, by potential suicidists themselves and their advisers, on the intentional aspect. Assuming that there is readiness to die, and that it's soundly reasoned and cogently motivated, a temporal criterion or qualification to the articulated criteria must provide guidance as to when that readiness to die may be justifiably enacted.

AN UNSURPRISING CONVERGENCE

What we have so far is that reflective aging individuals who choose to end their lives, rather than risk personal diminishment, must approximate as closely as possible the time when they most likely have gotten as much out of life as they can before the danger of diminishment grows too great. Exactitude can't be attained, but as little viable time should be relinquished as is reasonably possible, given the limitations on information about their futures that is available to potential preemptive suicidists. The basic equation is a balance of the likely onset of age-related diminishment against continued worthwhile life. But while there must be sound assessment of material conditions and prospects to justify its commission, preemptive suicide is an essentially discretionary act. Potential preemptive suicidists must appreciate that there's an unavoidable measure of arbitrariness in the timing of their deaths. Given advanced age and unwillingness to risk diminishment, the temporal boundaries of preemptive suicide are fairly flexible. Preemptive suicide must be timed early enough that reasoning and motivation remain unproblematic, but not so early that "real benefit" interests are unwarrantedly contravened. However, those boundaries encompass a considerable period that may stretch to many months. The precise timing of self-destruction, then, requires a degree of intuitive decisiveness. Enactment of preemptive suicidal decisions is always underdetermined by suicidists' material circumstances in the sense that nothing compels commission of suicide at a particular time.[4] Therefore, so long as impairment isn't risked and the interest in survival isn't unduly violated, that enactment is ultimately a matter of personal choice. This is why the criteria for rational preemptive suicide must incorporate temporal conditions. The proper timing of preemptive suicide is made uncertain enough by its material underdetermination; effective temporal guidance is necessary to ensure that its commission is rational.

To proceed with the formulation of a temporal criterion, or a criterial qualification, certain material circumstances need to be excluded that might otherwise confuse the issue. It's necessary to make the exclusions because the sort of preemptive suicide at issue is self-destruction in anticipation of age-related personal diminishment. The problem is that the notion of preemptive suicide may be taken by many to relate to the suffering of terminal illness. Reflective aging individuals may choose to commit preemptive suicide to avoid terminal conditions,[5] but the focus of concern here is preemptive suicide done to avoid reduction of the self through age-related loss of the faculties, traits, values, and interests that make us the persons we are. Preemptive suicide done for reasons having to do with impending terminal illness shades off into surcease suicide, and thus can't serve as our paradigm. If preemptive suicide to avoid personal diminishment can be shown to be rational, preemptive suicide done to avoid the pain and debilitation of terminal illness will emerge as that much more warranted. Our focus must be on cases where reflective aging individuals consider preemptive suicide with reasonable expectation that they'll live a minimum of two or three years[6] free of diagnosable terminal illness. Individuals in these circumstances are our paradigmatic preemptive suicidists, because they feel no compulsion to end their lives for reasons other than their unwillingness to be diminished by age.

Given the foregoing, the criteria articulated thus far are in need of review. The criteria for rational suicide that Battin, Choron, and Narveson offer are broadly conceived and intended to apply to suicide in the most general terms. In practice, the three sets of criteria are very much in line with philosophical polemics and with popular debate about suicide, both of which focus on suicide that's contextually coerced and done in exigent circumstances. But the criteria are less in line with consideration of preemptive suicide. The need to qualify the values criterion, regarding undue depreciation of interests, in my amalgamation of Battin's, Choron's, and Narveson's lists, indicates how their criteria fall somewhat short of adequacy for assessment of preemptive suicide. That qualification was the first emendation of the combined and restated criteria, but it isn't the only one necessary. Now I need to make criterially explicit the temporal conditions discussed above. Doing so productively means slightly reformulating the criteria; they need to be made more succinct and more narrowly applicable to preemptive suicide. The first formulation of the amalgamated and restated criteria was that suicide is rational if

1. Suicide follows on unimpaired deliberation, *and*
2. Suicidal motivation is accessible and cogent, *and*
3. Suicide is prescribed by well-grounded values, *and*
4. Suicide is in the agent's best interests.

Consideration of the "real benefit" interest in survival yielded a new version of the third criterion, that is, that rationality requires that preemptive suicide be

3a. Prescribed by well-grounded values without undue depreciation of the interest in survival.

For brevity's sake it can be taken that sound deliberation must be unimpaired, and that to be cogent, motivation must be accessible. The criteria can then be restated in a preliminary way as follows: to be rational, preemptive suicide must be

1. Soundly deliberated, *and*
2. Cogently motivated, *and*
3. Prescribed by well-grounded values without undue depreciation of the interest in survival, *and*
4. In the agent's best interests.

A preliminary restatement is called for to bring out the slight tension between the third and fourth criteria. Using the distinctions drawn in the last chapter, the operant contrast is describable as being between value-prescribed suicide unwarrantedly contravening the "real benefit" interest in survival, and suicide serving the "desire," "potential benefit," and "perspective" interests of suicidists, as well as their "real benefit" interests exclusive of the interest in survival.[7] This tension can be resolved by couching the third criterion not in terms of ("real benefit") survival interests but in terms of due evaluation of survival. This change highlights that the original emendation of the third criterion was designed to guard against suicidists' not properly valuing their own survival, and thus being too ready to contravene their "real benefit" interests for the sake of their suicide-prescribing values.[8] As we've seen, "real benefit" interests in survival are inevitably contravened in preemptive suicide. The third criterion ensures that those interests are contravened to a warranted degree. And what makes warranted contravention possible is that "real benefit" interests in survival are qualified by advanced age.

What should now be evident is that the interests referred to in the fourth criterion don't include the "real benefit" interest in survival. This is hardly worrying or puzzling, since no form of suicide can be in suicidists' interests in the sense of serving their interests in survival. Suicide being in the agent's interests, as required by the fourth criterion, can't mean that the agent's "real benefit" interest in survival must be served; hence serving that interest can't be a condition for rational suicide. In the case of surcease suicide the agent has no "real benefit" interest in survival, or only a vestigial one, and in preemptive suicide the interest in survival is seriously or even occlusively qualified by advanced age. Once this point is clear—that preemptive suicide must be in the agent's "desire," "potential benefit," and "perspective" interests, but in the agent's "real benefit" interests exclusive of the interest in survival—it emerges that the temporal concern or condition is simply the other side of the values qualification. The thrust of the temporal considerations we reviewed is that preemptive suicide shouldn't contravene "real benefit" interest in survival more than is warranted by their age-related qualification. Those considerations parallel the ones reviewed in connection with suicide-prescribing values' being given undue priority over the same "real benefit" interest in survival. Both necessary emendations to the criteria, therefore, focus on protecting the "real benefit" interest in survival. One protects that interest from undue weighting of other values, and the other must protect that interest from precipitous self-destructive action. It makes the best sense, then, to combine the necessary qualifications. This can be done by producing yet another version of the third criterion. To be rational, preemptive suicide must be

> 3b. Prescribed by well-grounded values without undue depreciation or untimely contravention of survival's value.

In their final form, with the values and temporal conditions incorporated, the criteria require that to be rational, preemptive suicide must be

> 1. Soundly deliberated, *and*
>
> 2. Cogently motivated, *and*
>
> 3. Prescribed by well-grounded values without undue depreciation or untimely contravention of survival's value, *and*

4. In the agent's best interests.

A JAMESIAN LIVE OPTION

The timing of rational preemptive suicide is clearly a difficult issue, but there's a further complication that, though not itself a temporal matter, nonetheless is one integral to the issue of preemptive suicide's commission in a way that directly affects timing. In assessing when to commit preemptive suicide, individuals need to ask themselves when they would commit suicide if they had all the information relevant to their decisions.[9] In other words, they must review the data available to them regarding their concerns about their prospects, as well as what they still hope to accomplish at their age, in order to establish when they might have the least amount of ambivalence toward taking their own lives and the least reason not to do so.[10] Potential suicidists can avail themselves of various resources: medical and other technical information about how advanced age affects human beings, family histories, and personal observations, both of others and of inclinations in themselves. Perhaps the most important of these resources will be information on how close relatives, especially parents and grandparents, fared in old age. They may also have recourse to literary material. A fictional work like *The Stone Angel*[11] may prove as useful as any set of statistics or the most complete family history, by providing vicarious experience that may play a decisive role in suicidal deliberation. But all of this may remain at an abstract level; it may constitute no more than a hypothetical exercise. What underlies and enables effective deliberation regarding the timing of preemptive suicide is suicide's presenting itself as a real option, rather than as an abstract possibility.

If we think of individuals' intellectual lives as asymptotic progress toward an ideal of self-knowledge and perspicacious self-understanding,[12] it seems fairly clear that at some point age slows that progress and soon begins to impede and then reverse it. While age-related changes are the subject of much contemporary discussion,[13] some think those changes are manufactured products of cultural constructivism, some think of them as at least exaggerated, and others acknowledge them only with euphemistic technical descriptions like "decreased adaptiveness" or "disengagement." But it's extremely difficult to maintain plausibly that age doesn't blinker and slow us mentally, as it dulls our senses and checks our mobility. Preemptive suicide is intended to prevent mental blinkers and sluggishness from inhibiting and reversing progress toward self-realization, because inhibition and reversal of that progress amount to undoing of the persons we are and value being. Preemptive suicide's rationale is that it's better to die as oneself than to live on as a lesser version of oneself. However, few are capable of deciding, purely on the basis of cool reflection, "This is the best I can be; living longer can only diminish me, so I choose to die now." Most of us require stronger prompting.[14] In connection with understanding preemptive suicide's proper timing, we need to grasp how it becomes a real option for reflective aging individuals.

If reason alone sufficed to prompt them, preemptive suicidal deliberation, decision, and enactment would constitute an Aristotelian practical syllogism. Abstract acknowledgment of the preferability of death to personal diminishment would serve as the major premise, acceptance of oneself as in danger of personal diminishment due to advanced age would serve as the minor premise, and the suicidal act would be the practical conclusion. In this rationalistic construal of preemptive suicide, reason "recommends" self-destruction, as Narveson would put it. Reason presents preemptive suicide as in our "potential benefit" interests, but reason alone can't make preemptive suicide a compelling option. As Hume would remind us, reason alone can't move an agent, especially if what's at stake is that agent's very life. In addition to reason's "recommendations," suicide must present itself as what William James called a "live option."[15] This means that suicide must be an option that's immediate and pressing in the sense that there's a strongly felt need to choose or reject it, as opposed to suicide only being intellectually recognized as an advisable course of action.[16]

Preemptive suicide's anticipatory nature would seem to preclude its presenting itself as a pressing choice, as surcease suicide does. If the onset of diminishment is still only anticipated, it's at least unclear what turns an abstract preference for death over personal diminishment into a "live option." The likely expectation that what's needed over and above reason's "recommendations" is sufficiently strong anticipatory distress only blurs the important difference between preemptive and surcease suicide. We can't require that reflective aging individuals be tormented by fear of diminishment because preemptive suicide isn't a driven act. What, then, complements and completes rational considerations and makes preemptive suicide a live option? The obvious answer is *motivating values*. For preemptive suicide to present itself as a Jamesian live option, negative valuation of a threatened kind of existence must reduce the importance of survival and make death actually preferable rather than only abstractly preferable. To see preemptive suicide as an immediate and pressing option, reflective aging individuals must strongly value living only in certain ways and strongly eschew surviving in other ways.[17] Suicide is, after all, expression of the ultimate negative valuation of a mode of life forced on one by circumstances.

But most people take survival to be the ultimate value; for them, death is outside the realm of the elective; death is an event that befalls one, it's something that happens. Even the most reflective individuals share our biologically rooted survival instinct. How, then, do some individuals' values come to prescribe anticipatory forfeiture of life? The first step is when survival is objectified by some threat and there's deep recognition of one's own mortality. This happens most commonly when serious health issues arise, but it also happens when sheer accumulation of years forces acknowledgment that one is running out of time. Life then is pushed to conceptual arm's length, and it becomes an object of appraisal in that it has begun to end. The next step is further recognition that one's existence transpires in a certain manner, and that it may cease to do so, just as it eventually ceases altogether. There's comprehension that deteriorative changes in how one's life proceeds run the gamut from mobility-inhibiting illnesses to identity-eradicating dementia, and that worthwhile life and bare survival are different things. The third step is reflection on the inadequacy of sheer survival, and that brings suicide-prescribing values into play.

For preemptive suicide to become a real option, reflective aging individuals must consider survival as desirable only if it includes elements they deem essential to retaining and enjoying their identities as the persons they are. These elements will include their intellectuality, interpretive perspicacity, and their autonomy, as well as adequate measures of satisfaction and gratification, and reasonable levels of emotional, physical, and financial comfort. Most, if not all, of these elements may be compromised to greater or lesser degrees without disastrous consequences, but they separately and jointly have levels below which their erosion or loss becomes intolerable. However, these elements aren't actually necessary for individuals' bare survival as organisms. What these elements do, to greater and lesser extents, is define the persons whose experience they condition and enrich. Therefore, when age-related diminishment threatens significant erosion or loss of these person-defining elements, what is threatened is the lives of the persons defined, even if the lives of their bodies aren't yet endangered. This is because for reflective aging individuals, survival as diminished versions of themselves is tantamount to death. Our conclusion, then, is that a precondition of preemptive suicide becoming a Jamesian live option for reflective aging individuals is realization on their part that age-related diminishment doesn't just weaken or impede their capacities, but dissipates and eventually obliterates who they are and value being. The key point that reflective individuals must grasp is that what they face isn't hampered life, but *no* life as themselves. Once that point is grasped, preemptive or anticipatory self-destruction looks quite different to those considering it. Instead of appearing to be self-destruction done when death is still substantially distant, preemptive suicide is self-destruction done only shortly before the end of one's existence as a particular person. Preemptive suicide presents itself forcibly, to persons about to be diminished to extinction, as the only way to avoid the demeaning, protracted deaths entailed by their bodies' longer life spans.

NIETZSCHEAN APPROPRIATION, TIMING, AND RATIONALITY

Preemptive suicide's becoming a Jamesian live option is closely tied to self-assertion as a determinant of the timing of suicide's commission. Reflective aging individuals aware of preemptive suicide as an abstract option may be moved to consider it as a Jamesian live option, not only because of the threat of personal diminishment but also because of how it enables attainment of meaningfulness. There may be value-driven realization that self-destruction can enhance lives as well as end them. What may happen is that self-inflicted death comes to be perceived as capable of conferring a measure of meaningfulness on life that it otherwise would lack. The key to understanding this is appreciation that suicide needn't be only a way of avoiding something; it also can be the ultimate assertion of who one is. Suicide may come to be seen as the best and most fitting way to end life, especially when continued survival is clouded by impending diminishment. Everyone must eventually die, and suicide offers an opportunity to precipitate the inevitable in a way that makes death add meaning to life, rather than simply being the event that ends life. This is the point of Nietzsche's remark about turning death into a moral necessity.[18] In committing suicide, reflective aging individuals may be less concerned with avoiding diminishment than with rejecting diminishment as an assertion of the value they put on who they are and can't continue to be. Their main concern may be to confirm everything they've lived for and valued. By committing preemptive suicide, they take their deaths out of the realm of occurrences and make them intentional, value-prescribed, life-affirming acts. In self-destruction, reflective aging individuals may appropriate their own deaths, and enable those deaths to bear a significance they wouldn't have as mere events.

Abstract awareness of the possibility of preemptive suicide may become a live option with realization that self-inflicted death not only is advisable for preventive reasons, but also can be given self-affirming value in itself. Preemptive suicide also may become a live option with realization that diminishment constitutes the end of the person one is, regardless of the body's continued life and its support of a lessened version of oneself. These realizations are mutually supportive and may be jointly compelling. However, the self-destructive action they prompt must be rational in order not to violate the insight and significance they provide. It wouldn't be rational to commit preemptive suicide as ultimate self-affirmation if doing so unwarrantedly contravenes "real benefit" interests in survival. Making death an act *in* life rather than letting it be only the end *to* life may be desirable, but not at the cost of sacrificing too much good time and still-attainable value. In like manner, avoidance of personal diminishment might be desirable, but wouldn't be rational if suicide is committed too far in advance of diminishment's likely onset. Seeing self-inflicted death as a fitting act of closure and/or avoidance of self-lessening can't be allowed to endanger the rationality of suicide.

The judgment surcease suicidists make is: "Let *this* end, even if everything else must end." Preemptive suicidists' judgments are quite different. The judgment they make is: "Better that everything end now, than that I be diminished and live on as a lessened other." But diminishment is still a relatively distant eventuality. Reference to diminishment in preemptive suicidists' judgments isn't reference to ostensible, pressing evil comparable with the "*this*" in surcease suicidists' judgments. In the preemptive case, the content and force of what prompts suicidal deliberation are wholly functions of value-laden and predictive envisagement of developments that, though perhaps extremely likely, aren't wholly certain with respect to their occurrence or their malignancy. Therefore, the question that haunts the notion of preemptive suicide, and that we've noted in several forms, is whether an unacceptable but only anticipated condition can suffice as the negative evaluative counterpoint in appraisal of life's worth. Can a condition that is only anticipated warrant self-destruction?

In the context of the question of suicide's timing, the question is whether an anticipated condition is enough for sound appraisal of when preemptive suicide is best done. The general concern is that decisions about preemptive suicide's timing may be too arbitrary, that they may not be arrived at through careful enough assessment of when self-destruction is most prudent and least contravenes interests. The lack of pressing reasons to die may make reflective aging individuals rely too much on impulse or symbolism in determining when to commit suicide, and thereby cheat themselves of worthwhile time and still-attainable value. For instance, there's nothing properly compelling about a seventy-fifth birthday as a time to commit suicide, if the person planning self-destruction on that date can reasonably expect to enjoy another year or two of undiminished existence. Given that expectation, it would be irrational to commit preemptive suicide on a date made special only by the calendar. This sort of consideration is particularly relevant where preemptive suicidists see their deaths as decisive acts that add value to the lives they finish.[19] But despite the need to time preemptive suicide in line with reason's demands, its timing must be arbitrary to a certain extent. Commission of preemptive suicide isn't determined by particular, immediate circumstances, so its timing must be discretionary within the practical limits established by minimal contravention of "real benefit" interests in survival. Picking one's seventy-fifth birthday to commit preemptive suicide may be unacceptable if doing so sacrifices a year or two of worthwhile life, but not if the time relinquished is estimated to be considerably shorter and there are no other compelling reasons to act sooner or later. So long as "real benefit" interests in survival aren't excessively contravened, preemptive suicidists are free to pick a time that has some significance for them and that they feel is appropriate for their self-destruction.[20]

COHERENCY AGAIN

The matter of preemptive suicide's timing seems to raise again the initial question about the coherency of choosing to die. We put aside that question because it appeared to be emptied of content by satisfaction of the various criterial requirements considered. There doesn't seem to be anything left to the question once the criteria for rational preemptive suicide are met, and it's understood what's involved in meeting the conditions regarding unimpaired reasoning, accessible and cogent motivation, sound values, and well-served interests. However, the question may resurface when suicide's timing is considered, because of doubts that individuals really can set a time for their unforced self-inflicted deaths with vivid awareness of the consequences of their planned acts. But it's difficult to establish the precise grounds for and nature of such doubts. We've assembled and restated the initially eclectic criteria for rational suicide and have added two crucial qualifications. We've considered how preemptive suicide may present itself as a Jamesian live option. We've considered how value-prescribed preemptive suicide can be fitting appropriation of death and ultimate affirmation of who one is and what one values. If doubts persist that preemptive suicidists fully understand what they're doing, it begins to look as if we're dealing not with genuine concerns but with a deep-seated, though ultimately unfounded, resistance to the acceptability of suicide.

Consider what it would be to wonder if potential preemptive suicidists can meet the criteria for rational preemptive suicide, see suicide as a live option, intend their self-inflicted deaths as affirmation of their identities and values, and still somehow not fully understand the consequences of self-destruction. If this is to be a general doubt or question, it must apply not only to problematic cases, such as where potential suicidists exhibit confusion, but also to "best case" instances where we have every reason to believe that preemptive suicide has been soundly deliberated and elected. But precisely what would it be to ask, about these latter cases, whether potential suicidists understand the consequences of self-destruction? There seem to be only two answers here. One is that it would be to make a theoretical claim, like Freud's, that human beings can't rationally commit suicide because they're psychologically incapable of believing in their own deaths. The other answer is that it would be to make a philosophical claim, like the one underlying the lack-of-contrast argument, that it's conceptually impossible to prefer death and likely annihilation to continued life. Both answers turn on potential suicidists' somehow lacking vivid awareness of what they're doing. However, what would it be to meet either claim, what would it be for suicidists "truly" to have vivid awareness of consequences in the manner both claims require? If the various factors we've reviewed are somehow insufficient to establish the rationality of suicide, what more could there be that would satisfy either the psychological or the philosophical claim or both? Wouldn't it be for suicidists somehow to succeed in imagining what it's like to be dead? This is, of course, quite absurd, and is the grain of truth in Freud's view: when we try to imagine being dead, we can't, because we're always there as spectators.

Descartes taught us centuries ago that there's a difference between imagination and conception.[21] The criteria for rational preemptive suicide require vivid awareness of consequences, but that doesn't mean suicidists have to imagine the consequences of self-destruction. They need only conceive them in the sense of understanding that death is the end of life and likely the end of personal existence. When put this way, the point is clear enough: once we've said what needs to be said about satisfaction of the criteria for rationality, about the reality of the suicidal option, and about intentions to appropriate death, there's no more to be said about the coherency of preferring to die. At that point we have to agree with Battin that in "the absence of any compelling evidence to the contrary," individuals can choose to die not only "on the basis of reasoning which is by all usual standards adequate,"[22] but also on the basis of the specific standards we've assembled, reformulated, and developed. Neither psychological nor philosophical demands can successfully require that a state of mind be achieved and discerned that "truly" is vivid awareness of the consequences of suicide. Having mapped out how preemptive suicide may be rational, we've dealt with the general question about the coherency of choosing to die. What remains is a very lengthy series of empirical questions about individual cases, but that's not something we need to—or can—undertake here.

The timing of preemptive suicide must be early enough to avoid diminishment but late enough to at least contravene "real benefit" interests in survival. There aren't precise determinants for either of these conditions. The timing of preemptive suicide is discretionary within the boundaries established, on the one hand, by sound assessments of how long suicidists have before their decisions and actions become problematic and, on the other hand, by the need and desire to allow as much time as is prudent and as much achievement of still-attainable value as is possible. Productive consultation will be necessary with respect to meeting both conditions. Neither can be met without reliance on others, not only to provide required information but also to counsel potential preemptive suicidists and to help them avoid the obvious pitfalls posed by (nonclinical) depression and its opposite, unwarranted optimism. Despite the discretionary nature of the timing of preemptive suicide, the choice of just when to take one's life for anticipatory reasons can't be left entirely to the suicidist.

Beyond providing necessary information and counseling, others may be involved in individuals' preemptive suicides in another way. Self-inflicted death is hard enough without being made harder by painful or uncertain means of self-destruction.[23] Others could involve themselves in preemptive suicide by supplying humane and effective means for people to take their lives when doing so is warranted. It's at this point that discussion of preemptive suicide overlaps with physician-assisted suicide. The fact is that the means of taking one's own life presently available to ordinary people are unacceptably distressing and/or unreliable. Overdoses may not work, or may fail but do enough damage to leave individuals in vegetative states. Starvation is a slow way to die, and takes a level of resolve that most people don't have. Recourse to devices like plastic bags can make death more harrowing than it need be. And any emergency-room nurse or doctor can tell horror stories about bungled gunshot attempts at suicide. Killing oneself takes a certain ability, as well as great courage,[24] and can go wrong in numerous ways.[25] Humane but lethal prescriptions should be available to those who want them for good reason. However, their availability requires that growing social acceptance of physician-assisted suicide extend to preemptive suicide. Unfortunately, while legalization of physician-assisted suicide appears more or less inevitable, though delayed by various judicial developments,[26] it's much more problematic that society is prepared to countenance preemptive suicide. In fact, the very proposal that preemptive suicide be facilitated could militate against acceptance of physician-assisted suicide. The reason is that many who fear that acceptance and legalization of physician-assisted suicide is a step onto a "slippery slope" leading to unwarranted taking of human life, will see acceptance and facilitation of suicide done for anticipatory reasons as compounding the problem.

At present, physician-assisted suicide is practiced in jurisdictions where it's prohibited by law.[27] Many feel that's as it should be. They believe that assisted suicide sometimes should be done for compassionate reasons, but also believe that it ought not to be formally acknowledged by either avowed acceptance or legalization. The reasoning is that a practice as dangerous as helping others to take their lives is best controlled if it remains legally proscribed. When it needs to be done, in exceptional circumstances calling for extraordinary compassionate action, it should be left to the courts to deal with particular cases, and juries and judges should be trusted to allow for mitigating circumstances in their verdicts and sentences. This isn't the place to assess this line of reasoning, but we do need to consider whether supporting preemptive suicide, even if only by providing a criterial basis for its consideration and possible commission, is a step onto a "slippery slope."

NOTES

1. Nietzsche 1967:484.
2. E.g., as in the case of clinical depression.
3. For instance, persons in their late sixties, whose parents and near relatives are known to have lived into their eighties with no sign of diminishment and only moderate physical decline, needn't consider preemptive suicide for some time unless there are special circumstances. On the other hand, those whose parents suffered very sudden onsets of dementia early in their advanced age will need to consider their situation well before they otherwise might do so.
4. The contrast here is with surcease suicide, the timing of which is determined by material circumstances.

5. For example, personal diminishment may be a secondary consideration if there's good reason to fear the onset of a catastrophic terminal illness.

6. Note that while two or three years may seem a short time to someone younger, that can be a large percentage of an aged individual's remaining life span. The period of two or three years also allows for significant personal diminishment.

7. For instance, being released from great pain is a "real benefit" interest that might be served by hastening death.

8. Basically, the value most directly served would be that of one's own selfness.

9. See Brandt 1975.

10. Motto 1972.

11. Laurence 1964.

12. Rorty 1989:23–43.

13. Thorton and Winkler 1988.

14. This truth is, of course, part and parcel of the view that suicide is justified only in the most immediately exigent circumstances and the unwillingness to countenance anything but surcease suicide.

15. Note that James was speaking of religious belief as a "live" option. James 1956:9, 11.

16. Even if individuals have a reasoned preference for death over personal diminishment, the instinctive resistance to deliberately terminating their own lives will make circumstances that seem intolerable and demanding of death in the abstract seem considerably more benign as the moment for self-destruction approaches.

17. Note that we can't simply say that what turns abstract possibility of preemptive suicide into a real option is motivating values, because that gives values too decisive a role and would be to adopt the untenable relativistic view that suicide is "rational" merely if consistent with suicidists' values.

18. Nietzsche 1967:484.

19. It's just this perception, though possibly distorted by false belief, that enables martyrs to give their lives for religious and political causes.

20. Their choices, though, will have as much to do with others as with themselves. For instance, it would be unforgivably unthinking, even cruel, to kill oneself on a day of special importance to someone close.

21. As is pointed out in *The Meditations*, we can't imagine a thousand-sided figure, but we can certainly understand or conceive of a thousand-sided figure.

22. Battin 1982a:301.

23. See Stolberg 1997b; Kolata 1997c.

24. Recall that we're not concerned here with suicide committed out of desperation.

25. See Humphry 1994, 1992a.

26. See Scott 1997; Navarro 1997; Garrow 1997; Rosen 1997; Prado and Taylor 1998.

27. Kolata 1997e; Prado and Taylor 1998.

7

INCLINING TOWARD SUICIDE

[T]he notion will come
that the older . . . who are expensive
should do the responsible thing.

Arthur Caplan

Growing social acceptance[1] of assisted suicide as sometimes justified appears to many to be a calamitous development. They feel that we invite disaster if we qualify categorical prohibition of help in self-destruction, even though we know it's occasionally done for good reason. The fear is that some last-resort practices are best left unspoken and proscribed, lest acknowledgment and even tacit approbation result in their radical misuse. Acceptance of any form of suicide looks to a lot of people like erosion of a fundamental protective cultural taboo. Acceptance of assisted suicide appears especially dangerous due to the potential for coercive influencing of those who because of age, illness, or incapacity are dependent on others for their survival. Current efforts to legalize physician-assisted suicide, growing professional and public toleration of it,[2] and "right to die" activism look to opponents of assisted suicide like significant depreciation of dependent life. Few of those who oppose it deny that physician-assisted suicide occurs, but they see legalization of the practice as leading to expedient pressuring of the elderly, the terminally ill, and the severely handicapped into self-destruction. Those opposed to assisted suicide[3] would see acceptance of preemptive suicide in advanced age as equally hazardous and as encouraging damaging attitudes on the part of the elderly toward themselves, and on the part of the young toward the elderly.

Concern that acceptance of assisted suicide invites its abuse is embodied in the "slippery slope" argument. Though moral and religious arguments against assisted suicide abound, the "slippery slope" one is especially popular because it captures a profound but hard to articulate unease about condoning suicide, an unease that has more to do with human psychology than with moral or religious prohibitions. Additionally, the argument is "nondenominational," invoking no particular moral or religious code. What it tries to establish is that acknowledging and condoning practice of even warranted assisted suicide is a first step down a steep incline to coerced suicide and eventually to involuntary euthanasia. The argument has it that "[p]ermitting physicians to assist in suicide, even in sympathetic cases, would lead to situations in which patients were killed against their will."[4] The contention basically is that if assisted suicide becomes a routine practice, as opposed to one hedged about with social, legal, and professional prohibitions, it inevitably will be abused by being often resorted to for expediency, rather than rarely for compassion.

Our present interest isn't in assisted suicide, but the charge that its acceptance sets us on the path to abuse of self-destruction raises a question that applies equally to preemptive suicide. That question is whether facilitation of preemptive suicide, even if only by provision of criteria for its rationality, contributes significantly to people's manipulating themselves, or being manipulated by others, into contravening their "real benefit" interests in survival. The "slippery slope" argument against social acceptance and legalization of physician-assisted suicide must be of real concern, if my project is to better enable preemptive suicide by providing criteria for assessing its rationality. The reason is that though the criteria are intended to ensure the rationality of preemptive suicide, it may be that something about the present social environment vitiates their proper employment. If current social acceptance of assisted suicide is driven by problematic factors, and establishes or reflects a milieu in which people will too readily avail themselves of that option, or induce others to do so, then facilitation of preemptive suicide may induce aging individuals to too readily contravene their interests in survival. Just as routine preparedness to assist suicide may develop into a coercive influence on patients assessing their terminal circumstances, so criterial enabling of preemptive suicide may have a coercive effect on reflective aging individuals concerned about personal diminishment. For preemptive suicide to be rational, it can't be prompted by coercion of any sort, beyond the contextual coercion resulting from threatening age-related diminishment of self.

How might facilitation of preemptive suicide constitute a coercive influence on reflective aging individuals? The short answer has to do less with personal than with socially prevalent values and attitudes. It's a real possibility that what will eventually prove to be voguish values will distort the application of the criteria for rational preemptive suicide. The most serious threat is to the third criterion. Prevailing but historically circumscribed social values that depreciate dependent life could prompt individuals deliberating preemptive suicide consistently to underrate their "real benefit" interests in continued life. The third criterion could be regularly but wrongly perceived as satisfied, despite contravention of interests, in an atmosphere of lessened regard for dependent life. Problematic[5] societal values exalting youth and personal independence may cause individuals fatally to depreciate their interests in survival.[6] This danger is particularly acute at the present time. Contemporary circumstances provide genuine grounds for worry that the elderly are coming to be seen, and to see themselves, in a negative light due to their dependency and the greater demands they make on others and on the hard-pressed health-care system. As the North American population ages, the number of people drawing more heavily on health-care resources than contributing to them is increasingly disproportionate to the number contributing more to those resources than drawing on them.[7] There are now more old people living than ever before, the old need more care, and that care is increasingly expensive. "Fifty percent of Medicare expenses is spent during the last six months of an elderly person's life."[8] Nor is it just a matter of private and public costs; it's also a matter of time and effort. As health-care programs are cut back, and health-management organizations reduce coverage, the old are forced to rely more and more on help and housing from family members. Younger members of society are being increasingly encumbered with the difficult and time-consuming care and accommodation of aged parents and grandparents.[9] The young are ending up paying higher insurance premiums and taxes while assuming a bigger share of caring for the old. At the same time, they're seeing a marked decline in the level of care they can expect for themselves.

Given these trends, there's a real danger of a broad change in traditional values, change detrimental to the interests of the old, the terminally ill, and the severely handicapped. Though it's perhaps not yet an actual problem, it's possible and even likely that many will adopt the view that the old have had their share of life and of society's benefits, and that they should do "the responsible thing" and end their lives before becoming burdens. The fact is that "*suicide is cheap,*"[10] and significant savings would be realized if even a small percentage of elderly people took their lives prior to using up that second half of their Medicare. It's already the case that "[p]eople 65 and older have the highest rate of suicide among any age group in [the] United States."[11] There could be a precipitous and unjustified increase in the number of suicides among the elderly if they're made to believe that they're unfairly clinging to lives already forfeited by their age and dependency, and "that somehow it becomes a duty to die."[12] General acceptance of this idea would contribute to pushing the old into suicide. Values could be widely adopted that not only give a low priority to the preservation of dependent life but also that encourage resentment of its cost. The resulting social atmosphere would not only put peer pressure on the old to do "the right thing," it would greatly worsen people's last years by making survival *feel* wrong and disgraceful. If there's any likelihood that such social circumstances may be in the offing, provision of criteria for rational preemptive suicide, and endorsement of preemptive suicide as affirmation of identity, would be less empowering than coercive. Such provision and endorsement then wouldn't enhance autonomous choice regarding elective death, but would put still more pressure on the elderly to do "the responsible thing."

We have to remember that the more numerous and longer lives that pose the health-care and social-support problems we now face are, after all, of value to those whose lives they are. People shouldn't be pushed into self-destruction because of their age. Nor is it enough that they not be pointedly forced into committing suicide. We can't allow a social milieu to form in which the old are made complicitous in their manipulation into suicide by values that make them reluctant to live out their lives.

Of course, suicide-prescribing values that now appear unduly depreciative of dependent life eventually may be accepted as well grounded, and so would come not to contravene "real benefit" interests in prompting self-destruction. A consensual rather than objectivist conception of rationality requires we accept that what initially seem to be unsound suicide-prescribing values could come to be accepted as sound. The only viable assessment basis for consensual rationality is history. Nonetheless, the values we see operant and being developed in current efforts to legalize assisted suicide are suspect, less because they seem to depreciate dependent life than because they appear to be the result of economic causes. There's something quite problematic about the coincidence of a hard-pressed health-care system, an aging population, and a suddenly vocal movement to legalize assisted suicide. It's quite possible that in time, rather than being accepted as well grounded, values that depreciate the old's interests in survival—as well as the interests of the terminally ill and the severely disabled—will be judged an excessive reaction to temporary demographic and economic imbalances. A decade or two in the future it may be thought that the 1990s' view of dependent life was too permissive or encouraging of unjustified self-destruction. That's why we have to take the "slippery slope" argument seriously. We need to consider whether facilitating and endorsing assisted or preemptive suicide, at this time, is unwitting complicity in a transient but deplorable social phenomenon.

THE "SLIPPERY SLOPE" ARGUMENT

The "slippery slope" argument's point is that legalization of assisted suicide will turn currently proscribed but occasionally warranted assisted suicide into routine expedient euthanasia.[13] The argument doesn't assume malice or even mere indifference toward the interests of the elderly, the terminally ill, and the severely disabled. Its pivotal point is that sanctioned practice of assisted suicide will produce insensitivity to the "real benefit" interests of the dependent. The claim is that it'll get easier and easier to justify helping people to die, until the "helping" becomes coercive. The fear is that if we legalize assisted suicide, we'll be taking a big step toward inexorably devaluing the remaining life of those who are very sick or very old or wholly unable to care for themselves. Expedient euthanasia, masked as compassionate assistance in suicide, then would become not the solution of last resort but what Arthur Caplan calls "the attractive solution of first resort."[14]

However, few opponents of legalization of assisted suicide think the danger is that health-care practitioners and family members will start to callously kill off the aged, the terminally ill, and the severely disabled. Arguing against legalization of physician-assisted suicide, Herbert Hendin best articulates what concerns opponents of legalized assisted suicide. Hendin argues that consideration of assisted suicide by patients, in consultation with their physicians and their families, is too fluid and emotionally charged a process to be adequately controlled.[15] The unpredictability of how diverse and usually conflicting feelings and attitudes shape the decisions reached makes the process ungovernable, and hence renders it too vulnerable to what should remain extraneous emotional and practical factors. Overly expedient decisions may be made because of a desire for closure or concern about the cost of continued care and treatment.

Charles Rosenberg graphically summarizes Hendin's point as being that legalizing assisted suicide "would necessarily shape a new gradient in decision-making," and result in "steepening the incline of innumerable slippery slides toward premature death."[16] Rosenberg remarks that the focus of Hendin's argument is "[t]he linked system of clinician, patient, family and friends," and that the particular and highly variable "emotional dynamics" of this linked system "will inevitably determine individual outcomes." What is crucial are the various predispositions at work. "The patient is often depressed . . . , relatives are guilt ridden and ambivalent, [and] the physician is often driven by a need for closure and control when available technical tools are no longer relevant."[17] The combination of vulnerable patients, irresolute relatives, and frustrated physicians is one that too often could result in less-than-rational self-destruction. By making assisted suicide an available alternative to unpromising and costly treatment, legalization makes permissible a previously proscribed solution[18] to intractable medical situations. But by the same token, legalization of assisted suicide introduces a major complication into the already complex situations in which treatment of the dying and the hopelessly dependent is considered and determined. The real threat captured by the "slippery slope" argument is that the availability of assisted suicide as a relatively simple alternative to difficult, costly, and often unavailing treatment options could be so inviting a course of action that too many people would be subtly and not so subtly coerced into self-destruction.

The danger of steepening the incline to assisted suicide applies equally to deliberation of preemptive suicide by reflective aging individuals. Social acceptance of preemptive suicide could result in too many premature self-inflicted deaths among the elderly by unduly influencing assessments made by both suicidists and those counseling them. However, steepening the incline to preemptive suicide may have less to do with others' coercive roles in counseling self-destruction than with imbalances in suicidists' own assessments of their interests. The main operant mechanism may not be so much the active participation of others as the personal values at work in deliberation. The biggest danger is that "real benefit" interests in survival won't be given their due weight in consideration of preemptive suicide. There's always a risk that reflective aging individuals will act immoderately on the basis of overly pessimistic assessments of their prospects, and that they'll unduly contravene their interests in survival by committing suicide too soon or perhaps at all. That risk is unavoidable because it's a function of how our perceptions and judgments are inevitably colored by our values.[19] However, if this risk is augmented by compelling modish values that depreciate the old's interests in survival, preemptive suicidists' "real benefit" interests may be systematically contravened. If exaggerated worth is given to personal autonomy, consequent misplaced guilt for being a social and familial burden will be generated and will add significantly to fear of personal diminishment. Reflective aging individuals' values and "perspective" interests then could regularly but wrongly prevail over their interests in survival. An added negative influence would be the nature of the context in which deliberation of preemptive suicide takes place. Modish values that depreciate the old's interests in survival will inevitably occasion resentment of the old. Experience of that resentment by the aged would further jeopardize their assessment of their interests in living out their lives. The upshot is that in a social milieu where it's widely thought that the dependent have only a qualified right to live, the criteria for rational preemptive suicide could be consistently vitiated in their application, despite appearing to be properly satisfied.

Above, I said that the question for us is whether facilitation and endorsement of preemptive suicide will contribute to contravention of "real benefit" interests in survival. The "slippery slope" argument has it that legalization of assisted suicide would lead to such contravention, and there seems to be no reason why even criterial facilitation of preemptive suicide might not have the same effect. Unfortunately, we don't have an adequate basis on which to predict whether we can have assisted suicide as a sanctioned practice without significant and possibly escalating abuse. Our culture's experience with sanctioned assisted suicide is extremely limited, going back only some two or three decades and consisting largely of Holland's quasi-legal practice of physician-assisted suicide.[20] Australia's brief experiment with legalized assisted suicide and voluntary euthanasia lasted only nine months before the legislation was overturned, and only four people availed themselves of the law.[21] The American experiment, initiated by attempts to legalize assisted suicide in Oregon, Washington, and Florida, has provided little or no grounds for extrapolation, since the legislation has been either overturned or stalled by court challenges.[22] Moreover, in July 1997 the Supreme Court upheld New York and Washington States' lower-court bans on assisted suicide, declining to recognize assisted suicide as "a fundamental liberty interest protected by the due-process clause."[23] The ruling wasn't preclusive, since it leaves the issue to individual states,[24] but it hasn't prompted a groundswell of support for legalization of assisted suicide in any state,[25] with the possible exception of continuing efforts in Oregon and perhaps Florida.

It seems we won't soon have adequate data to determine the longer-term impact of legalized assisted suicide. In the absence of reliable historical evidence to the contrary, the fear is that if we legalize assisted suicide, we'll grow lax about protecting people's interests in survival, and individuals will unduly depreciate their own interests because of social pressure to quit life before the onset of burdensome dependency. The "slippery slope" argument represents a consensus that in the absence of convincing data that we can permit assisted suicide without abusing it, we're best advised to keep it controlled by maintaining its illegality and social proscription.

The situation is analogous with respect to preemptive suicide, and prompts a similar consensus, that is, that preemptive suicide is best left unspoken and unsupported, lest acknowledgment and facilitation of it constitute a malignant influence on the elderly. It's possible, if not probable, that social acceptance of preemptive suicide could result in significant abuse because prevailing values would prescribe suicide contrary to "real benefit" interests. Worse still, it's also possible that prevailing values would mask contravention of "real benefit" interests in application of the criteria for rational suicide. The criteria can't ensure their own proper application, and strong enough "perceived" interests and values could obscure the importance of preemptive suicidists' "real benefit" interests in survival.

However, once we understand the steepening danger, it's important to note that efforts to preserve the illegality of assisted suicide have little to do with denying either the rationality of suicide or the soundness of criteria for establishing that rationality. Neither of these is the "slippery slope" argument's actual target. The argument is about what's described in legal phraseology as "flowing from" legalization of assisted suicide: whether or not individual cases of assisted suicide are rational and well-advised. What drives the argument is the idea that it's better for society at large if assisted suicide is proscribed, than if warranted instances are accommodated at the cost of enabling greater abuse of the practice than there is under present proscription. The question the "slippery slope" argument raises for us doesn't bear directly on the criteria for rational preemptive suicide or on the reasons for preemptive suicide. Possible misuse of the criteria and abuse of assisted or preemptive suicide don't impugn either the soundness of the criteria or the rationality of suicide; they impugn the practical wisdom of legalization of the one and social acceptance of both. The question the argument raises can be put in this way: Can the criteria, especially the third, be effectively applied on a broad basis? The issue is whether individuals can properly employ the criteria as a regular practice, or whether their attempts to do so may be persistently vitiated by the power of prevailing social propensities. If individuals are too inclined to accept the third criterion as met because of the commanding but possibly unsound predilections of the day, then the criteria won't ensure the rationality of preemptive suicide, regardless of their intrinsic soundness.[26]

For us, the core of the "slippery slope" issue has to do with the role played by values in the deliberation of preemptive suicide. Prevalent social values[27] may not allow enough latitude for reasoned assessment of interests they depreciate. That's why it's the third criterion that's most directly challenged by the "slippery slope" argument. If the result of social conditioning is that values consistently and unduly override individuals' "real benefit" interests in their deliberations of suicide, the third criterion wouldn't be met in the majority of cases. The trouble is that it would *seem* to be met because of the dominance of the relevant values. However sound the criteria, if their application is regularly vitiated by strong values depreciative of interests in survival,[28] they would be ineffective in establishing the rationality of suicide because violation of the third criterion would go unrecognized by both suicidists and their counselors.[29] Provision of criteria for rational preemptive suicide then would be at best useless and at worst harmful, not because of flaws in the criteria but because human beings are too much the products of their social milieu to use them effectively. "Slippery slope" adherents could be right; legalization of assisted suicide and acceptance of preemptive suicide could result in large-scale contravention of "real benefit" interests in survival. Human psychology may be such that sanctioning assisted suicide and facilitating preemptive suicide puts us on a path to excessive misuse of both.

SOCIALLY SHAPED SUBJECTS

The last decades of the twentieth century have seen three major developments that have contributed directly and indirectly to more tolerant attitudes toward suicide.[30] First, the importance of personal autonomy or self-determination has been greatly enhanced. Since the seventeenth century our culture has been increasingly concerned with individuals' rights, of which the right of self-determination, in all its forms, has received the greatest attention.[31] Second, modern medicine has gained the capacity to sustain life, or to protract the process of dying, to a high degree. Third, the 1960s and 1970s saw a rise in the standard of living that evoked heightened awareness of the importance of the quality of life. Because of the first and third of these developments, perception of the suicide issue has been structured in terms of individuals' right to refuse to be kept alive under conditions they find abhorrent. And because of this structuring and the second development, the focus of debate about suicide has been technological treatment of terminal illness. It therefore looks to many as if the issue of whether society should condone assisted suicide is about the prolongation of life in terminal illness. But this is misconceived. Where life is being technologically prolonged, patients are free and legally empowered to refuse further treatment.[32] The real issue is whether society should sanction assisted suicide where incapacitated individuals are dying slow and agonizing deaths *without* life-sustaining treatment that they might rightfully refuse.[33] The contentious cases are those where people whose lives aren't being prolonged want help to hasten their deaths. These are the cases that most worry "slippery slope" adherents, and those that are closest in kind to preemptive suicide.

The choice we're facing is whether to legalize assisted suicide, as distinguished from already legal requested cessation or noninitiation of life-sustaining treatment. It isn't patients kept alive on ventilators who pose the central question, but people who don't want to die the slow, often painful, and degrading deaths entailed by many terminal illnesses. Legalization of assisted suicide would enable many more people than do now to end their lives rather than suffer naturally slow deaths.[34] The choice bears on preemptive suicide because if assisted suicide is legalized, preemptive suicide in advanced age almost certainly will become more acceptable and be resorted to more often. Good arguments for dying rather than enduring the suffering and degradation of a protracted death, are good arguments for dying rather than enduring self-destroying personal diminishment. If the arguments for assisted suicide prevail, their application to preemptive suicide will follow.[35] However, legalization wouldn't be just a matter of enacting some new statutes. Legalization of assisted suicide would reflect and compound a profound change in social values, and so would influence the life-and-death decisions it enables. "Slippery slope" adherents fear that the change would make helping people to die too easy, and degrade into coercion, but the deeper question is whether the change might make people too ready to die. Just as we've learned that the capacity to prolong life—or to protract death—is a mixed blessing, so we need to learn that gaining discretion over the timing of our own death poses its own problems. Whenever we gain the power to choose among new alternatives, or old ones previously denied us, we need to understand what shapes our inclinations to choose one way or another.

Right-to-die activists portray legalization of assisted suicide as empowering, as enhancing personal autonomy. Their view is that the important thing is to enable people to exercise their autonomy, even if it means helping them take their lives. But it's naïve to think that our choices are all or even mostly truly autonomous. Myriad influences color our desires and direct our actions, and these influences work at different levels. At one level, they're discernible by individuals and their counselors. At another level, they're transparent because they in part constitute what it is to be a subject[36] in a particular social milieu. This deeper level is where we find the cumulative perspective-defining effects of society's practices. As mentioned in Chapter 2, those practices determine what individual members of society assimilate through enculturation, and so define what they consider "normal." This is what Foucault saw so clearly: a society shapes its members' subjectivity and controls their behavior by imposing on them the discipline of normalcy.[37] The shaping is achieved through the mechanisms of peer example, expectation, and pressure, as well as by statutory regulation and formal education. The result is that the sum of others' actions governs individuals' behavior, and repeated behavior of specific sorts imbues individuals with certain values that, in being internalized, further direct and control behavior.[38] Societal practices establish what individuals prize and eschew, and what they do and don't do, and so determine *who they are* as subjects. The import of this for us is that a social environment in which health-care resources are tight, in which the population's average age is disproportionately high, and in which assisted suicide is available as an alternative to treatment, is an environment that will shape people as subjects who think self-destruction is a normal response to onerous age-related dependency.

One way to see current growing toleration of physician-assisted suicide is as widespread realization that dragging out the process of dying is usually counterproductive. In this favored view, tolerance toward physician-assisted suicide looks essentially unrelated to such things as pressure exerted on the health-care system by the "baby boomer" generation reaching its fifties. The scenario is one in which what's going on is concerned entirely with terminal conditions, and is a matter of empowering patients to end their lives rather than suffer slow deaths or be kept alive just because contemporary medicine has the means to do so. In this scenario, social acceptance of preemptive suicide in advanced age would be a natural extension of acceptance of physician-assisted suicide. Both practices would be perceived as having the common objective of reducing needless suffering and degradation. However, while there are plenty of physicians who strive to preserve the lives of their patients at all costs, including patient unwillingness, far fewer patients are kept alive with heroic effort—much less against their will—than the scenario implies. Allowing some patients to die while keeping them comfortable and pain-free is not an uncommon practice, and is one that's being increasingly employed with patient and familial consent.[39]

A different and more realistic scenario doesn't focus narrowly on empowerment of the terminally ill; it encompasses a growing pragmatism about the cost-to-benefit ratio of sustaining problematic life, not just in terminal illness but also in advanced age and severe disability. In this scenario, toleration of assisted suicide isn't an independent development but one ominously related to an aging population's impact on health care in particular and on society in general. In this tougher-minded scenario, acceptance of assisted suicide is a shift from beneficence to expediency regarding dependent life. This second scenario also acknowledges an unspoken but very real element in acceptance of assisted suicide: resentment on the part of younger people. For reasons to do with current age distribution in the population, a disproportionate share of wealth in North America is presently in the hands of those in their fifties and sixties, and is likely to remain so for some years. And because of recent economic developments, the prospects and resources of those in their twenties and thirties are much reduced. A consequence is that many younger people resent the lower standard of living and insecurity of employment that they face and that their parents never knew. It's easy for them to feel that the old have had their fair share of what society provides for its members, especially when young and old must compete for so basic a social service as health care. The result is that the young's perception of the old's choosing suicide over lingering death or technologically sustained life may be strongly colored by the seldom verbalized idea that the old *ought* to forfeit the little time left them, given the cost to others of their clinging to life. The idea also may extend to the severely disabled, who regardless of their age may be seen as clinging to lives that are costly to maintain but are perceived by the able-bodied as not worth living. This is what Caplan has in mind when he says that it isn't that "we're going to have a government dictating, you must die," but rather that "the notion will come that the older and disabled who are expensive should do the responsible thing."[40]

It's probable that acceptance and endorsement of assisted suicide at the present time is in some part a response to contemporary economic and demographic strains. But regardless of the causes, if society is in the process of adopting new values that elevate autonomy and downgrade dependency, those values could jeopardize the rationality of self-destruction by unduly depreciating "real benefit" interests in survival. And again, regardless of the causes, we've little choice other than to deal with higher social tolerance of elective death. The central and decisive point is that dying has become discretionary in a way it never was before. Nor is it just a matter of demography and economics, or of more people being willing to end their lives to avoid suffering. The fact is that "[m]ore and more, we are going to die when someone makes the decision that we are going to die."[41] Whether the "someone" is ourselves, our doctors, or our families, once we gained the capacity to delay death through the use of medical technology, we entered an era in which choices have to be made about when death occurs.

A hundred years ago the capacity to delay death was a dream. Now that we have the capacity, we're learning it can be a nightmare and that we need to exercise discretion about its use.[42] It's that need that's most important: we now have to weigh the pros and cons of living as long as it's *possible* to live. We've achieved enough control over death that choices must be made about protracting the process of dying. And as soon as we have to make decisions about whether or not to delay death, we face questions about whether we should sometimes hurry it along. If we decide not to delay death because of the suffering entailed by doing so, the hastening of death to avoid similar suffering imposes itself forcibly on us as an option needing consideration. The result is that we're becoming subjects who must make decisions about our own deaths.[43] But while Camus may be right that whether life is worth living is the most important philosophical question, it isn't a question most people have needed to ask themselves in a practical way. In the 1990s we're faced with two daunting questions: whether clinging to life is worth the suffering, degradation, frustration, and cost entailed by technological delay of death, and whether clinging to life is worth letting the process of dying run its arduous course.

These are obviously large issues, but what's pivotal for us, in light of how people's subjectivities are shaped, is that it's becoming normal to seriously consider at what point life ceases to be worth living; at what point death either shouldn't be delayed or might be hastened. In itself, this development is empowering. The trouble is that it's occurring at a bad time. The timing is problematic enough to make us seriously consider whether our new realism regarding the value of prolonged life may be not an evolutionary step in human understanding but instead is a result of transient economic and demographic constraints. The danger is that our new discretionary power over death's timing and transient constraints are jointly forging values that jeopardize the "real benefit" interests in survival of the dependent, and that thus steepen the slippery slope to abuse of suicide by making us denigrate the merits of living out our lives.

NEW VALUES

Acceptance of the right to refuse life-sustaining treatment was the first step in reconceiving our lives as lived at *our* discretion. Social acceptance of individuals' right to refuse being kept alive is de facto rejection of the traditional view that life is an unrenounceable gift. Once that acceptance is achieved, there's no definitive reason for allowing refusal of life-sustaining treatment but disallowing warranted assisted suicide. If it's possible for people to refuse death-*delaying* treatment to avoid pointless suffering and degradation, then shouldn't they be able to request death-*hastening* treatment for the same reason? The core of assisted-suicide advocacy is the idea that there's no significant difference between the currently recognized right to refuse life-sustaining treatment and the still-disputed right to request life-curtailing treatment. Society accepts that technologically sustained survival can be renounced if too punishing, and protects the right to renounce it. Why should some of its members needlessly endure equally punishing deaths just because those deaths are "natural"?

The standard argument against the established right to refuse treatment being extended to the right to assisted suicide is essentially a moral one. Its basic claim is that when patients refuse treatment, neither they nor their physicians do anything that directly terminates life, whereas assisted suicide is active termination of life. Noninterference in a natural process is supposedly blameless, so neither patients nor physicians can be culpable for simply letting nature take its course. On the other hand, both may be culpable if they themselves cause death. The argument still has force, but it's no longer as apparently conclusive as it once was. First, we recognize that there are too many instances where doing nothing is morally and/or legally furthering something.[44] We can't blithely maintain that doing nothing to prevent death, in cases where life-sustaining treatment is being used or might be used, is categorically different from causing someone's death. Second, where treatment has been initiated, its cessation *does* require positive action by physicians. Turning off a ventilator is an active intervention, even though doing so is only removing a causal factor that was previously introduced. The more critical life-sustaining treatment is to someone's continued survival, the less significant is the difference between doing something to *cause* death and allowing something that *results* in death.

But still more important is a third element, namely, the permissibility of noninterference. Permitting people to be knowingly allowed to die, especially by professionals entrusted with their care, constitutes abandonment of the principle that there's an unconditional moral obligation to do everything possible to sustain life. The moral argument against helping people to die relies heavily on the principle that there's an obligation to sustain life, and the point here is that though many still cling to it, society has abandoned the principle. It's done so by accepting legislation and professional practices that allow physicians—those most directly responsible for life-and-death treatment decisions—to comply with requests for cessation or noninitiation of treatment. Social acceptance of nontreatment has been in the name of personal autonomy. In effect, then, personal autonomy has trumped a moral and religious general prescriptive principle. But if it's permissible to comply with refusal of treatment or requested cessation of treatment, and doing so reflects a subjugation of a moral principle to personal autonomy, then the question that arises is whether we're already on the slippery slope to neglect or depreciation of the interests in survival of the old, the moribund, and the incapacitated.

The worry is that we could become too indifferent or insensitive to "real benefit" interests in dependent life. Enhancement of autonomy entails a proportionate debasement of dependency. If our society is adopting values that elevate autonomy and depreciate the "real benefit" interests of the dependent,[45] then not only will able, independent individuals depreciate the survival interests of the aged, the terminally ill, and the severely disabled, they'll depreciate their *own* interests in survival. The dependent will internalize values that in turn will make living out lives contingent on others' help appear unacceptable and undesirable. Moreover, this reflexive depreciation of "real benefit" interests will be augmented by people's coming to see self-destruction not only as a normal response to repugnant dependency, but also as the only realistic alternative to enduring the minimal and likely grudging care available to them beyond a certain point in age, illness, or debility.[46] Moreover, there's the grim possibility that rather than witnessing and participating in a genuine change in societal and personal values, we're only being hardened by economic and demographic constraints.

The "slippery slope" argument most likely will prove ineffective in preventing eventual legalization of assisted suicide and whatever legalization entails for social values. It's also very likely that the argument's appropriate variant will prove ineffective in preventing acceptance of preemptive suicide when that becomes a public issue. Nonetheless, the "slippery slope" argument shouldn't be dismissed because it is unsuccessful. Instead, it should be reconsidered. The alternatives aren't that the argument either blocks acceptance of assisted and preemptive suicide or proves an utter failure. Another alternative is that the argument serves as an ongoing caution, and so as a needed check on the practices it opposes.[47] The argument may well work better as a balancing mechanism preventing abuse than as a wholly preclusive tactical device.[48] But a still more productive alternative is to reconceive the argument as an admonition, and take to heart what is in fact its essential point, which is that we just don't know where present trends are taking us. We just don't know what legalization of assisted suicide will eventually do, nor how facilitation of preemptive suicide will affect our values. To paraphrase Foucault, while we know what we do, and may even know why we do what we do, it's an unfortunate fact that what we *don't* know is what what we do, does.[49] We don't know the long-term consequences of our actions. Present debate and judicial care in making legislative decisions contribute to anticipating and shaping the results of sanctioning elective death, but we can't know how routine practice of assisted suicide or preemptive suicide ultimately may change us. Still, assisted suicide is almost certain to be sanctioned, and in any case is currently practiced. Preemptive suicide is also an idea whose time seems to have come. Criterial facilitation of preemptive suicide, then, may turn out to be less facilitation of the practice than a crucial safeguard against its abuse.

NOTES

1. Suicide per se isn't illegal in most North American or European jurisdictions. Germany decriminalized suicide as early as 1751, Canada as late as 1972. Battin 1992b:46. However, suicide is still largely seen as shameful, immoral, and impious.

2. Recent polls show support for physician-assisted suicide to be in the 60 percent range. Dr. Keith Wilson, of the University of Ottawa, is presently conducting a survey of the terminally ill's views on physician-assisted suicide. Wilson realized that polls survey the general public and health-care professionals rather than those who would be most affected by availability of assisted suicide. The likelihood is that assisted suicide is seen differently by those for whom it's an abstract possibility and those for whom it's a pressing reality.

3. Preemptive suicide hasn't yet become a public issue.

4. Battin 1996:182.

5. A major problem with nonobjectivist, consensual views of rationality is that we can't tell if new societal values that *appear* misconceived will shortly be

rejected or might be instrumental in redefining our standards, and thus endure. Once objective standards are abandoned, only enough time can establish the soundness of new values.

6. We see this most often in religiously motivated conflict. Self-sacrifice is exalted and individuals are moved to give up their lives for marginal gains or in ineffective gestures.

7. These developments aren't limited to North America; see Kristof 1997; WuDunn 1997. In 2025 Japan will have "twice as many old people as . . . children." In the United States, by 2020, 37.2 percent of health-care spending will be for people over sixty-five; in Japan it'll be 42.9 percent; in Germany it'll be 32.2 percent and in Britain 42 percent. WuDunn, 1997.

8. Michael A. Gross, Florida Asst. Attorney General. Quoted in Navarro 1997.

9. It's arguable that this is no more than a return to practices that were prevalent no longer ago than the beginning of the century, and that most of the rest of the world's population copes in just this manner. However, North American industrialized society doesn't readily accommodate home care of the old.

10. Battin 1987:169; emphasis in original. See also Bayer et al. 1983.

11. Navarro 1997.

12. Drew Smith, analyst for the Public Policy Institute, quoted in Navarro 1997.

13. See Prado and Taylor 1998.

14. Caplan 1996.

15. Hendin 1996.

16. Rosenberg 1996:33.

17. Ibid.

18. The resolution isn't only a proscribed one; many consider it foreign to the practice of medicine.

19. This is why it's so important that potential preemptive suicidists be counseled.

20. Assisted suicide isn't technically legal in Holland; instead, when certain conditions are satisfied, cases of assisted suicide aren't prosecuted or otherwise pursued.

21. Australia's Northern Territories assisted suicide and voluntary euthanasia legislation went into effect in July 1996, and was struck down on March 25, 1997.

22. Oregon has reaffirmed its original legislative enablement of assisted suicide; see Egan 1997. See also "Florida High Court Upholds State Ban . . ." 1997.

23. Chief Justice William Rehnquist, quoted in Greenhouse 1997b.

24. See Scott 1997.

25. Emanuel and Emanuel 1997.

26. It could be thought at this point that the criteria entail objective or ahistorical standards, but that's a mistake. The relevant contrast is between voguish, unproven values and well-established but less fashionable ones.

27. This includes group values, such as religious or political ones.

28. The commonness in our history of religious and patriotic self-sacrifice shows that strongly held values can regularly override even the interest in survival.

29. It may be that the "real benefit" interests in survival of the old and otherwise dependent appear to be unduly depreciated only from a perspective that's rapidly being abandoned, and that those interests *aren't* depreciated but fairly weighted from a perspective we're in the process of adopting. On the other hand, the depreciation may be real, and the appearance that the interests in question aren't being depreciated may be temporary. We simply can't tell without benefit of significant historical distance. However, given that it's people's lives at stake, our only choice is to defend people's interests in survival against what appears to be undue depreciation.

30. These decades have also seen a key philosophical development, namely, the abandonment of objectivism and "modernism," and espousal of conception of our most basic standards as historical and consensual. As mentioned, consensual conception of rationality leaves us with no other recourse than to history in assessing whether new values are or aren't preferable to those they challenge. See, e.g., Rorty 1982.

31. As Richard Dagger puts it:

Since at least the seventeenth century, the concept of rights has figured prominently in political debate, especially in the English-speaking parts of the world. It is no surprise, then, to find individuals and groups of almost every persuasion stating their cases nowadays in terms of rights. . . . According to a number of commentators . . . people have become too concerned with rights. In the United States in particular, they argue, we are caught in the grip of a crippling preoccupation with rights. . . . [R]ights are by their nature intransigent. . . . If "rights are political trumps," as Ronald Dworkin has said, then it is easy to see how a situation in which everyone is trying to play a trump card is likely to end in deadlock. . . . [T]he concept of rights is too one-sided and individualistic. . . . [And] the ceaseless clamoring for a right to this and a right to that will inevitably weaken all appeals to rights. (Dagger 1997:3–4)

Compare Callahan 1995.

32. Despite some confusion on the part of health-care practitioners and even clinical ethicists, refusing or requesting cessation of life-sustaining treatment isn't committing suicide except in an extended or even metaphorical sense. See Prado and Taylor 1998.

33. Sue Rodriguez was slowly dying of Lou Gehrig's disease and entirely immobilized. She unsuccessfully sought permission for assisted suicide from the British Columbia courts and the Supreme Court of Canada. She eventually did get the help she wanted, but illegally.

34. There would be conditions to be satisfied, of course, before assistance could be provided. Additionally, it bears mention that legitimate reasons for requesting assistance in suicide needn't be only physical incapacity.

35. In fact, the near certainty that preemptive suicide will be argued for is precisely one of the consequences of legalizing assisted suicide that "slippery slope" adherents fear. In their view, application of the assisted suicide arguments to self-destruction in old age is an expected attempt to coerce the aged to do "the responsible thing."

36. I use the term "subject" and its derivative forms in Foucault's deliberately ambiguous manner, to mean both *the subject of experience* and *the governed and disciplined subject*. See Prado 1995.

37. See Foucault 1979, 1980; see also Prado 1995.

38. Foucault's notion of "power" is that of constraints on action itself; power "is a way in which certain actions modify others." "Power" isn't a coercive force bearing on individuals, compelling them to behave or not behave in specific ways. Instead Foucault's notion is of "a mode of action which does not act directly and immediately on others. Instead it acts upon their actions." "Power" is a "set of actions upon other actions"; it's "a total structure of actions brought to bear upon possible actions," a structure or environment that enables some actions and inhibits others. Foucault 1983:219–220.

39. See Fein 1997b; Hoefler 1997; Kolata 1997e, 1996a; Scott 1997; Stolberg 1997a.

40. Caplan 1996. Caplan doesn't oppose assisted suicide in principle; he opposes its likely abuse: "until . . . I'm convinced that assisted suicide is the . . . option of last resort in the way that I think many of its proponents hope and wish it to be, . . . I'm going to stand against it."

41. Marshall Perron, author of Australia's short-lived legislation on assisted suicide. Mydans 1997. As noted above, the legislation was enacted by the Northern Territories in July 1996 and overturned in March 1997.

42. See Brickman 1995.

43. We already prepare "living wills" or advance directives regarding treatment if we become incapacitated.

44. Nonintervention is often culpable, and may be what the courts call "careless disregard," that is, failing to do something within one's power, such as saving a drowning person or stanching an accident victim's hemorrhage.

45. It's already the case that health-maintenance organizations limit elderly patients' appeals of adverse decisions regarding access to certain forms of treatment. Pear 1997.

46. Many people see these developments as monstrous, but the loss of institutional care is, in effect, a return to a time when dying was a family burden rather than a social one.

47. See Prado and Taylor 1998.

48. There's a parallel here with abortion. Though sometimes conducted in deplorable form, continuing opposition to abortion serves to check the practice by keeping arguments against abortion before the public.

49. Dreyfus and Rabinow 1983:187.

8

THEORY AND VALUE

Prudence and courage should engage us
to rid ourselves . . . of existence,
when it becomes a burden.

Hume, "On Suicide"

As indicated in the last chapter, we seem to be in the process of changing our values about elective death. Historical changes of this scope pose a deep question for us to the extent that we don't really understand them. The most we seem able to do is conceive change of this magnitude as characterizing a distinct era, as heralding something of special historical import and significance, or as a transition to something only dimly imagined.[1] We could follow Immanuel Kant and see such change as the end of something, as our leaving something behind through the gaining of a new maturity or sophistication. However, these are attempts to understand the form of change, not its content. Our immediate problem is that the content of the change that concerns us could be either a desirable maturing regarding life and death or an undesirable depreciation of dependent life. It could be that we're coming to adopt William Butler Yeats's advice and learning to cast a cold eye on life and death.[2] We may be learning Seneca's and Hume's lesson that a time comes when life is best willingly surrendered. On the other hand, we may be being driven to think too little of dependent life by factors that are only contingently related to the value of human existence. The most notable example of such factors is the economics of health care. The concern is that what's happening might not have very much to do with how individuals assess the personal costs of continued survival. Instead, it may have more to do with how others respond to their dependency. Nor need it be only social and familial hardships that are prompting the depreciation of dependent life, if that is indeed what's happening. It could be that those hardships are only secondary factors. It may be that our time's high valuation of autonomy, and hence of personal independence, is the main impetus to negative reconception of the value of dependent life. Autonomy is hard to achieve when people are dependent on others for their very survival, and as said in the last chapter, enhancement of autonomy inevitably results in a proportionate debasement of dependency. Exalted valuation of autonomy and independence isn't as extraneous a factor as economic ones, but it may well be transient and ill conceived.

The fact is that we don't know the nature of the change we're witnessing. Today's permissive shift in attitude toward assisted suicide and euthanasia may be only a causal consequence of economic and demographic factors and not a cultural maturing regarding life's final stages. This means that we have to proceed with utmost caution in offering criterial facilitation of preemptive suicide, since doing so contributes to expanding the tolerant attitude toward assisted suicide in medical contexts to other forms of elective death. However, the attitudinal change is real enough, choosing hastened death over punishing life is becoming more prevalent, and doing so is bound to exceed current de facto boundaries. For these reasons, provision of criteria for rational preemptive suicide serves less to encourage elective death than to enable better governance of one form of the practice. Unfortunately, formulation of the criteria isn't enough; they must be shown to be workable. We've seen that this is a matter of establishing that the criteria do apply to cases of self-destruction, of showing that suicide *can* be rational. Above, I argued that articulation of the criteria itself counters the common view that anticipatory self-destruction is irrational; it does so by showing under what conditions it's warranted to judge preemptive suicide rational. However, we need to look at another sort of opposition to the rationality of suicide.

THE ROLE OF THEORY

Despite the profound change that's taking place regarding elective death, increased preparedness to consider suicide acceptable is limited to self-destruction in the context of immediate and genuine—that is, not pathological—hopelessness. The paradigm of acceptability is requested cessation of treatment in a case where life is being technologically prolonged and doing so causes more anguish than can be compensated for by sheer survival. Somewhat more problematic, but increasingly acceptable, is assisted suicide in equally hopeless medical cases.[3] More generally, the view is that it's only surcease or nobly sacrificial suicide that's ever really justified. This view is obstructive and may be preclusive with respect to preemptive suicide. Hopelessness isn't the operant reason for anticipatory self-destruction except in an extended sense that doesn't apply here. It could be argued that a reflective aging individual may experience hopelessness regarding eventual diminishment, but the fact that the diminishment is eventual—that is, still future—is the key point. The consequence is that as long as acceptance of elective death is limited to surcease suicide, reflective aging individuals wanting to avoid personal diminishment won't receive the counseling and support they need to make sound, well-informed decisions about the disposition of their lives.

Previous chapters have attempted to show how preemptive suicide in advanced age can be rational even though it's anticipatory rather than surcease self-destruction. The target in those chapters is the common conviction that willful forfeiture of life generally isn't rational if done for less than immediately pressing and compelling reasons. However, the common conviction isn't the only obstacle to establishment of preemptive suicide as rational. Something needs to be said, even if briefly, about theoretical opposition to the rationality of most forms of suicide.

Recall that the criteria for rational preemptive suicide establish preemptive suicide as rational if suicide is (1) soundly deliberated, (2) cogently motivated, (3) prescribed by well-grounded values without undue depreciation or untimely contravention of survival's value, and (4) in the agent's best interests. The basic claim is that if the criteria are met, self-destruction is rational even though done only in anticipation of unacceptable self-diminishment. The first point to make here is that what the criteria for rational preemptive suicide actually do is authorize use of a certain description. The criteria don't identify matters of fact. While the criteria may justify describing particular cases of self-destruction as rational preemptive suicide, those descriptions remain essentially conditional because they're about states of mind, and states of mind aren't directly accessible to anyone but the suicidists themselves. Third-person judgments about suicidal reasoning, motivation, and even timing must always be conditional. But as important as the obvious privacy of states of mind is that they're by nature complex and ill defined, and may have unconscious aspects at odds with their apparent natures and objectives. Unconscious factors may be strong enough to render intentions and desires self-deceptive. States of mind simply don't have the definiteness, transparency, and stability necessary to make them proper subjects of categorical judgments, whether those judgments are third- or first-person ones.

Another problem with making judgments about states of mind is that even if decisions, intentions, and desires are fairly well defined, resolute, and not undermined by unconscious aspects, they can be undermined in a moment by second thoughts or just a change of mood. In addition, the ambivalence inherent in deciding to take one's own life must always make problematic any judgments about those decisions, whether the judgments are made by others or by suicidists themselves. In the end, the foregoing chapters and provision of criteria for rational preemptive suicide can only show how rational preemptive suicide is possible. Theoretical claims against the rationality of suicide can't be countered with definitive demonstration that any particular case of suicide, preemptive or otherwise, is in fact rational.

Theoretical accounts of suicide purport to show that suicidists' and their peers' judgments about the rationality of any form of suicide are essentially rationalizations of operant determinants that go unrecognized. Theoretical accounts preclude self-destruction's rationality by claiming that all or most suicides are caused, regardless of how it may appear to suicidists or their peers. If self-destruction is indeed an effect, it can't be rational because it isn't an autonomous act. With the possible exception of the clearest cases of surcease suicide,[4] theoretical explanations construe self-destruction as a phenomenon due to causes that covertly govern individuals' actions. These theoretical accounts basically say that while some suicides may appear rational to suicidists and their peers, they're the result of social, psychological, or historical forces. These forces are portrayed as undiscerned by suicidists and as shaping and governing their self-destructive deliberations and actions. The result is that in these theoretical views, suicide isn't *ir*rational but always *a*rational because it is an effect rather than an act.

Depending on the theory, causal explanation of suicide ranges from postulation of influences of varying strength on suicidists' deliberations and actions to predication of intractable determinants that render deliberation and volition illusory. The two most prevalent and important theoretical explanations of suicide originate with Emile Durkheim and Sigmund Freud. Both offer comprehensive causal explanations of suicide, and neither account allows preemptive suicide to constitute a special case of

reasoned, as opposed to caused, self-destruction. In both views, deliberations by suicidists can only be rationalizations because the actions they
concern are caused, and so aren't the results of those deliberations. Again
depending on the theory, the causal determinants of suicide are either
external or internal. In Durkheim's sociological analysis of suicide, the
focus is on the dynamics of suicidists' relations to their society, and hence
on societal influences on them. In Freud's psychological analysis, the focus
is on internal dynamics and resolution of unbearable inner tensions.[5] The
challenge posed to rational preemptive suicide by Durkheim's and Freud's
analyses, as well as those by others, such as Marx's, is the same: causal
construal of suicide preclusive of suicide's being rational. Self-destructive
actions, whether preemptive or not, may be explained in terms of Durkheim's "egoistic" self-destruction, wherein suicide is due to "excessive
individualism"[6] rather than to sound reasoning and motivation. Such
explanation subjugates the rationality of those actions to forces over which
suicidists have little or no control and of which they're largely unaware.[7]
Self-destructive actions, whether preemptive or not, may be explained in
Freudian terms as products of greatly stressful internal conflicts. The
rationality of those actions is subjugated to dissonance-reducing psychological mechanisms over which individuals have no control, and of which
they're unaware except as experience of inner turmoil.[8]

The vulnerability of preemptive suicide to causal explanation affects all
of the criteria for rational preemptive suicide to some extent. However, it's
the first criterion, which deals with sound deliberation, that's most decisively affected. This is clear when we consider how the mere presence of
causes vitiates deliberation. Each of the theories has the causes of suicide
presenting themselves to suicidists in some form of false consciousness,
mainly as compelling values prescribing suicide. It's conceivable that the
values thus presented are in fact well-grounded ones. It's even possible that
in practice the values presented function in ways that would actually
constitute cogent motivation, that they wouldn't depreciate suicidists'
interests unduly, and that they would allow for good timing of suicide. But
even if that were the case, deliberation of suicide based on those values still
would be rationalization of masked causes. At most the presented values
would be coincidentally a basis for sound deliberation if the postulated
causes were absent. Since according to the theories, suicide is an effect of
causes that the presented values mask, deliberation based on those values
could only mimic sound deliberation. If suicide is caused, and its causes are
masked by false consciousness, it's deliberated and committed both in
ignorance of operant determinants and in the false belief that it's an

autonomous act. That means the first criterion is twice contravened and the resulting action isn't rational.

Causal theories of suicide preclude the possibility of genuinely rational, autonomous preemptive self-destruction and are therefore incompatible with the proffered criteria. However, it's hopeless to attempt wholesale refutation of causal theories to support the criteria. What can be done is to clarify just what it means to describe preemptive suicide as rational. In that way, the burden of proof is shifted to theorists to establish that description of preemptive suicide as rational is never warranted.

A PRACTICAL DEFINITION OF RATIONALITY

The project of showing that preemptive[9] suicide can be rational is basically a matter of providing the wherewithal to judge that some cases of suicide committed for anticipatory reasons are instances of rational self-inflicted death. It's a mistake to think that the criteria for rational preemptive suicide test whether it meets the standards of a postulated Rationality. This mistake leads one to expect an independent account of rationality, and thereby confuses matters by raising an intractable philosophical issue about the nature of human rationality. It must be appreciated that the criteria themselves provide a contextual definition of the relevant sense in which preemptive suicide is rational. The criteria don't reflect something separate from themselves to which some cases of suicide conform. The point is that what we mean by saying preemptive suicide is rational just is that it's soundly deliberated, cogently motivated, prescribed by well-grounded values without undue depreciation of survival's value, and in the agent's best interests. What this comes to, in practical terms, is that showing some cases of preemptive suicide to be rational is showing that, contrary to the common view, they aren't *ir*rational,[10] and, contrary to theoretical accounts, they aren't *a*rational or caused events. In other words, the criteria for rational preemptive suicide provide the means to categorize some cases of suicide as not pathological, coerced, or otherwise caused behavior. The ultimate authority for this categorization isn't ahistoric rationality; the authority is reasoned consensus.

What it means to say the criteria for rational preemptive suicide are consensual is that the only appeal is to established communal standards and assessorial methodologies. This is the point Richard Rorty makes against traditional conceptions of ahistoric rationality in saying, "there is . . . no criterion that we have not created in the course of creating a practice." Rorty adds that conformity to standards is no more, though certainly no less, than "obedience to our own conventions."[11] The criteria say what we agree must be the case for something to be rational preemptive suicide. But this isn't to say that the criteria are arbitrary. To think that is to make the mistake of those who see extreme relativism as the only alternative to apodictic certitude. In themselves, the criteria are intended to form part of assessorial methodologies that have been progressively refined over centuries, and that are amply corroborated by their efficacy and reliability. These methodologies are historical in being self-correcting in their repeated application.

More important in the present context is that the methodologies are historical in being sensitive to changes in the standards that determine the ends they serve. That's the real issue here; it isn't about rationality but about our values. The proposal that soundly deliberated, cogently motivated, and interest-serving preemptive suicide can be rational doesn't raise deep questions about the nature of rationality. It raises questions about whether our values can accommodate some instances of anticipatory self-destruction as warranted. The criteria provided claim to show how established assessorial methodologies—which aren't themselves at issue—apply to actions that many think aren't assessable as possibly rational. The problem is that some value life as an unrenounceable gift; hence, anyone who forfeits life in other than utterly hopeless circumstances must be acting irrationally—and, for that matter, immorally. The crux of the matter, then, isn't the nature of rationality. The criteria themselves spell out what it means to say preemptive suicide is rational. The crux of the matter is the values assessorial methodologies serve. These values are what determine both the soundness or rationality of means-to-ends reasoning, and the soundness or rationality of actions and intentions in the sense of what best serves our interests. What makes the criteria problematic isn't competing conceptions of rationality but values that disallow that the criteria can be satisfied.

The pivotal role of values is evident in how the priority given to autonomy doesn't extend to unforced[12] self-destruction[13] in the sense that suicide isn't deemed rational except when justified by unbearable and inescapable pain, a pressing and unavoidable moral threat, or occasion for heroic sacrifice. Against this, I maintain that preemptive suicide in less-than-extreme circumstances—that is, that isn't surcease, morally exigent, or sacrificial self-destruction—may be rational. And given that the criteria spell out what it is for preemptive suicide to be rational, when the criteria are satisfied, there are no further questions about rationality itself, the general irrationality of self-destruction, or theoretical causal factors.[14] What it means to say that an instance of anticipatory self-destruction satisfies the criteria is that it's a case of rational preemptive suicide. If preemptive suicide is judged to be soundly reasoned, cogently motivated, prudently timed, and in the suicidist's interests, then it's rational. It's always open to anyone to theorize that in some ultimate sense all our actions are determined by hidden and inaccessible causes, but deterministic theories, whether philosophical or empirical, are known to be only problematically coherent. In any case, postulation of hidden determinants can't preclude that the criteria may be satisfied. Again, it's always open to anyone to reject the rationality of preemptive suicide because of values that hold life to be sacrosanct. However, unless those values can be demonstrated to be universal, invoking them can't preclude that the criteria may be satisfied. The criteria say what counts as rational anticipatory self-destruction "on the basis of reasoning which is *by all usual standards* adequate,"[15] and that's all that's required to make the methodological point. The trouble is that it isn't enough to deal with the determining role of values; that requires more to be said.

MAKING SENSE

Preemptive suicide in advanced age is the forfeiture of worthwhile life for anticipatory reasons. Since preemptive suicide is precisely suicide committed prior to compelling reasons or contextual coercion, it's inevitable that some worthwhile life will be forfeited in its commission. This is what gives credence to common and theoretical views of life's forfeiture as not rational. Ideally, the minimum of worthwhile life would be forfeited, and the argument is that if the amount of life forfeited is small enough, and balanced by unacceptable diminishment, preemptive suicide can be rational. But no one can know with certainty when life becomes too precarious with respect to personal diminishment, so no one can time preemptive suicide to sacrifice the precise minimum of good time left. The upshot is that despite what's been said, the rationality of preemptive suicide remains doubtful to many. Preemptive suicide is done because of expected but not yet realized developments, and many think that just isn't good enough. They see the enormity of the action as rendering anticipatory reasons inadequate. That's why preemptive suicide invites causal explanation. It appears that if there aren't compelling, immediate pressures to forfeit life, its forfeiture must be caused, because forfeiture of worthwhile life just doesn't make sense. In other words, the value put on life seems to rule out its being relinquished for anything but the most immediately pressing and forceful reasons.

What many do think makes sense with respect to anticipatory self-destruction is to make suicide contingent on the actual onset of the feared condition. The thinking is that the sort of diminishment feared by reflective aging individuals is gradual and allows time for decisions to be made after initial diagnosis. Given that we never know how particular situations will work out, suicide may seem always precipitous if done for anticipatory reasons.[16] The tendency is to think that it makes better sense to see just how bad things get before forfeiting life. There's a complementary tendency to hope that even the worst situations will improve.[17] Therefore, the obvious solution appears to be to forgo preemptive suicide in favor of surcease suicide. However, while that option is acceptable in cases of terminal illness and similar circumstances, it's much more dubiously appropriate with respect to the diminishment of intellectuality that reflective aging individuals seek to avoid. The reason is that the feared diminishment most likely would preclude surcease suicide once discernible because of real or suspected impairment of the ability to reason soundly and to make autonomous choices. The result is that to take the "sensible" course and wait for the actual onset of diminishment is in effect to opt for eventual compassionate euthanasia. Once diminishment is discerned or diagnosable, as opposed to only anticipated, the responsibility for elective death must shift to others.

As is becoming clear, it's values that prevent preemptive suicide from making good sense. Satisfaction of the criteria for rational preemptive suicide exhausts the philosophical questions about the coherency of choosing to die for anticipatory reasons. To demand more would be to misguidedly require unquestionable detection of impossibly determinate reasons, motives, and intentions in the minds of individuals during their deliberations *and* at the moment of their self-inflicted deaths. The legitimate questions that remain, once the criteria are satisfied, aren't about coherency but about values; more specifically, they're about relative evaluations of situations and prospects. There's neither need nor possibility of getting into preemptive suicidists' minds to complete assessment of their suicides as rational or otherwise. Assuming they're competent, the locus of what is or isn't rational about preemptive suicide isn't potential preemptive suicidists' mental states. It's what they're prepared to die to avoid; it's what they are or aren't willing to be and to bear. Again assuming competence, the counterpoint to preparedness to commit preemptive suicide isn't a more rational stance; it's valuing life regardless of what it may bring. Since reflective aging individuals see age-related personal diminishment as the end of themselves as persons, it isn't relevant to argue that it's irrational for them to forfeit lives that still could be rewarding to some extent. We saw earlier that reflective aging individuals aren't willing to continue living even reasonably good lives as diminished others. Though to others it may appear that the lives being forfeited are still worthwhile, if the criteria are met, peers must accept preemptive suicidists' decisions. Assessment of reasoning, motivation, timing, and interests is called for in judging the rationality of preemptive suicide. Appraisal of the soundness of operant values is part of that assessment. What isn't called for is denial or preclusion of the rationality of preemptive suicide based on competing values.

A very important element in value-based resistance to the rationality of preemptive suicide is recognition that human beings are immensely adaptable. We seem able to bear much that we couldn't imagine enduring earlier; we seem able to achieve some contentment or satisfaction in circumstances we would previously have thought unbearable. One's circumstances unquestionably alter personal values, and this enables compensation for situations that would otherwise be intolerable. "A hospice is a place where . . . a pretty hairdo or a good shave . . . take [sic] on vital importance."[18] The point being made is that "[t]he lesson one learns . . . is at once life's most basic and elusive: You live until you die."[19] This is a serious point, because aside from circumstances where only surcease suicide is at issue, it's possible to realize value while one does live. However, reflective aging individuals considering preemptive suicide don't deny this point. They know that they're sacrificing future attainable value by ending their lives in order to die as themselves and not as diminished others. They aren't claiming that their lives as diminished persons will be utterly worthless or unendurable. The point is that they're willing to relinquish whatever value they may still attain to die in a way that both protects them from personal diminishment and affirms their values and identity. They choose to die as the persons they are, rather than to eke out some measure of attainable value as lessened individuals. Moreover, there's something else wrong with appealing to the adaptability of human beings in trying to show that preemptive suicide isn't rational by stressing how life can be worthwhile in circumstances previously thought unacceptable. Diminished or terminal individuals are portrayed as heroically squeezing the last drops of satisfaction from their lives, delighting in simple pleasures like "a pretty hairdo or a good shave." Sentiment aside, the picture painted strongly suggests that people endure the last weeks or months of their final decline by choice. But at present, people have little option but to make the best of their situations precisely because our culture doesn't provide them with suicidal or euthanasic options. Even though assisted (surcease) suicide is being increasingly tolerated, it isn't available to all. The harsh reality is that diminished or terminal individuals have no practical alternative but to endure their situations. To make matters worse, the value it is claimed they achieve usually *is* value only because of their greatly reduced expectations.

With respect to the central issue of clashing relative evaluations of situations and prospects, it must be remembered that the acceptability of age-related changes must be determined in light of what particular individuals are willing to accept,[20] not what others find acceptable. The only legitimate concern regarding relative evaluations is that they and their acceptability be grounded in values that are themselves rational. Reflective aging individuals who contemplate preemptive suicide do so because they reject age-related holistic diminishment. The changes age brings can't be thought of as limited; it isn't as if aging individuals suffer only degeneration of numerous but distinct and delineable capacities. It's persons themselves who change with age. If a stroke partially paralyzes an individual, it's possible that with time and therapy the paralysis can be overcome. Other muscles may be trained to work in ways functionally similar to those affected by the stroke. But the changes that prompt preemptive suicide aren't of this kind. They aren't limited to a set of muscles or even parts of the brain that may respond to therapy. The tragedy of the changes is that they're global. They reduce us rather than being handicapping or even crippling in only some respects. The horror of the diminishment occasioning preemptive suicide is that it makes us into lesser beings who eventually become unaware of the changes in ourselves except in the vaguest and most sporadic ways. As Seneca saw, advanced age is itself a ground for preemptive suicide. It isn't a neutral condition characterized only by contingent maladies. People are themselves lessened by time, not just afflicted with specific ills. Preemptive suicide is value-driven enactment of unwillingness to age beyond a certain point in order not to become lessened.[21]

CONCLUSION

Despite all I've said, it's true that reflective aging individuals can't have certain knowledge of their futures and can never be certain that preemptive suicide doesn't harm them more than continuing to live would. After all, what prompts their readiness to commit preemptive suicide is only fear that lessening changes in themselves will eventuate, and that they *will* be wholly unacceptable. But any one of us may come to judge that survival to an advanced age has seriously jeopardized our continued survival as the persons we are, have molded over a lifetime, and prize being. We may decide that age threatens to diminish us in ways we are unwilling to risk for the sake of dubiously worthwhile survival. So long as our biological nature remains what it is, and we're prey to age-related deterioration, this judgment must be capable of being rational. Preemptive suicide offers a way to appropriate an inevitable event, death, that would otherwise occur as a mere effect. Preemptive suicide not only enables us to avoid being lessened, it adds value to our lives by making our deaths the final assertion of our wills and values. Anticipatory self-destruction, done at the right time and for the right reasons, can be the most fitting last act of self-definition.

NOTES

1. This three-way characterization is taken from Foucault's "What Is Enlightenment?," an essay on Kant's famous one of the same title. Rabinow 1997:304–305.

2. Yeats's self-written epitaph is "Cast a cold eye/On life, on death/Horseman, pass by!"

3. Note the distinction. It's important not to gloss over the difference between requesting that one not be kept alive and actively ending one's own life—even if with assistance.

4. These are, in effect, not exceptions because they are instances of self-destruction caused by contextual coercion.

5. DeSpelder 1987:407–412; Durkheim 1912; Freud 1915.

6. Durkheim 1912:174–232.

7. DeSpelder 1987:409.

8. Freud 1915.

9. Most of what follows applies to suicide per se, but our main concern remains preemptive suicide.

10. Richard Rorty rejects the traditional philosophical conception of rationality. Nonetheless, in a letter to me about the first edition, he grants that "rational" as used therein has "a quite definite sense" that doesn't presuppose a philosophical theory of the nature of rationality. The sense in question is "that used by those who claim that . . . suicide is always *irrational*." The point applies equally to the use of "rational" in this second edition.

11. Rorty 1982:xlii.

12. The reference is, of course, to contextual coercion or the force of circumstance, not the actions of others.

13. Baechler 1975.

14. There may be questions about hidden particular causal factors, such as psychopathological ones.

15. Battin 1982a:301; emphasis added.

16. It's worth emphasizing that the sort of anticipatory reasons at issue have to do with age-related changes and diminishment of ourselves as persons. This point is clear from the context, but it's necessary to acknowledge that there are other anticipatory reasons that would be taken as justifying suicide and not raising the questions we're considering here.

17. Anyone who's been involved in the making of decisions about entering a nursing home will have experienced both tendencies firsthand.

18. Martin 1989.

19. Ibid.

20. Always assuming competence and satisfaction of the criteria.

21. One apparently powerful point that might be made against unwillingness to bear deteriorative changes is that preemptive suicide is restricted by obligations to others. But what this comes to is that potential preemptive suicidists have one more factor to consider in their deliberations. It doesn't mean that preemptive suicide is simply precluded by the existence of responsibilities. We can't allow dependencies to tyrannize individuals who may pay a considerably higher price to remain alive than their responsibilities merit. We must agree with Hume that someone "who retires from life does no harm to society," and that taking one's own life means only that one "ceases to do good; which, if it is an injury, is of the lowest kind." Hume 1963b:109.

BIBLIOGRAPHY

Because of my concern to make this second edition as accessible and timely as possible, I've included many references to newspaper articles and a few to televised programs. My aim is to make productive use of succinct and widely read accounts and commentaries, to reflect the considerable attention the media have recently given to suicide, and to avail myself of the most recent surveys. Newspaper articles having bylines are listed below, with books and learned-journal articles; unsigned newspaper articles and other items are listed separately. Note that since preemptive suicide has not yet become a widely discussed issue, few of the items listed address it directly.

BOOKS AND ARTICLES

Agee, James. [1957] 1985. *A Death in the Family*. New York: Bantam.
Alther, Lisa. 1976. *Kinflicks*. London: Penguin.
Alvarez, A. 1971. *The Savage God: A Study of Suicide*. New York: Penguin.
Anders, George. 1997. *Health Against Wealth: HMOs and the Breakdown of Medical Trust*. New York: Houghton Mifflin.
Angell, Marcia. 1997a. "Editorials: The Supreme Court and Physician-assisted Suicide—the Ultimate Right." *New England Journal of Medicine*, 336(1):50–53.
———. 1997b. "Anguished Debate: Should Doctors Help Their Patients Die?" *New York Times*, June 24. (Excerpted from Angell 1997a.)

————. 1990. "The Right to Die in Dignity." *Newsweek* (July 23):9.

Appleby, Timothy, and Jill Mahoney. 1997. "MDs' Death Role: Murder or Mercy?" (Toronto) *Globe and Mail*, May 9.

Aries, Philippe. 1982. *The Hour of Our Death*. Trans. Helen Weaver. New York: Vintage Books.

Armstrong, David M. 1968. *A Materialist Theory of the Mind*. Oxford: Routledge and Kegan Paul.

Artaud, Antonin. 1995. "On Suicide." *Le Disque Vert*, no. 1 (1925). Quoted in *The Columbia Dictionary of Quotations*. New York: Columbia University Press: Microsoft *Bookshelf*, 1996–1997 CD-ROM edition.

Audi, Robert, ed. 1995. *The Cambridge Dictionary of Philosophy*. Cambridge: Cambridge University Press.

Baechler, Jean. 1975. *Suicides*. Trans. Barry Cooper. New York: Basic Books.

Baltes, Paul, and K. W. Schaie. 1974. "Aging and I.Q.: The Myth of the Twilight Years." *Psychology Today* 7:35–38, 40.

Battin, Margaret Pabst. 1996. *The Death Debate: Ethical Issues in Suicide*. Englewood Cliffs, N.J.: Prentice-Hall. (This is the same work as Battin 1995, with a foreword by Dr. Timothy Quill and repaginated.)

————. 1995. *Ethical Issues in Suicide*. Englewood Cliffs, N.J.: Prentice-Hall. (Revised version of Battin 1982b.)

————. 1994. *The Least Worst Death*. New York: Oxford University Press.

————. 1992a. "Voluntary Euthanasia and the Risks of Abuse: Can We Learn Anything from the Netherlands?" *Law, Medicine and Health Care*, 20(1–2):133–143.

————. 1992b. "Assisted Suicide: Can We Learn Anything from Germany?" *Hastings Center Report*, 22 (March–April): 44–51.

————. 1991. "Euthanasia: The Way We Do It, the Way They Do It." *Journal of Pain and Symptom Management*, 6(5):298–305.

————. 1990. *Ethics in the Sanctuary: Examining the Practices of Organized Religion*. New Haven: Yale University Press.

————. 1987. "Choosing the Time to Die: The Ethics and Economics of Suicide in Old Age." In Spicker et al. 1987:161–189.

————. 1982a. "The Concept of Rational Suicide." In Shneidman 1984:297–320.

————. 1982b. *Ethical Issues in Suicide*. Englewood Cliffs, N.J.: Prentice-Hall.

————, and Arthur G. Lipman. 1996. *Drug Use in Assisted Suicide and Euthanasia*. New York: Pharmaceutical Products Press.

————, and D. J. Mayo, eds. 1980. *Suicide: The Philosophical Issues*. New York: St. Martin's Press.

Bayda, Edward. 1995. "Is Robert Latimer's Life Sentence 'Cruel and Unusual Punishment'?" (Toronto) *Globe and Mail*, July 20.

Bayer, Ronald, Daniel Callahan, John Fletcher, et al. 1983. "The Care of the Terminally Ill: Morality and Economics." *New England Journal of Medicine*, 309:1490–1494.

Baylis, Francoise, Jocelyn Downie, Benjamin Freedman, Barry Hoffmaster, and Susan Sherwin, eds. 1995. *Health Care Ethics in Canada*. Toronto: Harcourt Brace.

Beauchamp, Tom L. 1996. *Intending Death: The Ethics of Assisted Suicide and Euthanasia*. Upper Saddle River, N.J.: Prentice-Hall.

———. 1980. "Suicide." In Regan 1980:67–106.

———. ed. 1975. *Ethics and Public Policy*. Englewood Cliffs, N.J.: Prentice-Hall.

———, and James Childress. 1994. *Principles of Biomedical Ethics*, 4th edition. Oxford: Oxford University Press.

———, and LeRoy Walters. 1989. *Contemporary Issues in Bioethics*, 3rd edition. Belmont, Calif.: Wadsworth.

———, and Seymour Perlin, eds. 1978. *Ethical Issues in Death and Dying*. Englewood Cliffs, N.J.: Prentice-Hall.

Benjamin, Martin, and Joy Curtis. 1986. *Ethics in Nursing*. Oxford: Oxford University Press.

Bennahum, D., G. Kimsma, C. Spreeuwenberg, et al. 1993. "Been There: Physicians Speak for Themselves." *Cambridge Quarterly of Healthcare Ethics*, 2:9–17.

Benrubi, Guy. 1992. "Euthanasia—the Need for Procedural Safeguards." *New England Journal of Medicine*, 326(3):197–199.

Berger, David M. 1987. *Clinical Empathy*. Northvale, N.J.; Aronson. Quoted in Code 1994:83.

Berke, Richard L. 1997. "The Nation: Suddenly, the New Politics of Morality." *New York Times*, June 15.

Betzold, Michael. 1993. *Appointment with Dr. Death*. Troy, Mich.: Momentum Books.

Biggs, H., and K. Diesfeld. 1995. "Assisted Suicide for People with Depression: An Advocate's Perspective." *Medical Law International*, 2:23–37.

Birren, James E. 1968a. "Aging: Psychological Aspects." In David Sill (ed.). 1968. *The International Encyclopedia of the Social Sciences*. Vol. 1. New York: Macmillan.

———. 1968b. "Psychological Aspects of Aging: Intellectual Functioning." *The Gerontologist* 8 (1, Part II): 16–19.

———, and K. Warner Schaie, eds. 1977. *Handbook of the Psychology of Aging*. New York: Van Nostrand.

Bliss, Michael, 1990. "What Price Immortality?" *Report on Business Magazine*, (Toronto) *Globe and Mail* (August):17–19.

Bloch, Sidney, and Paul Chodoff, eds. 1991. *Psychiatric Ethics*, 2nd edition. Oxford: Oxford University Press.

Blythe, Ronald. 1979. *The View in Winter*. New York: Harcourt Brace Jovanovich.

Bond, E. J. 1996. *Ethics and Human Well-Being*. Oxford: Blackwell.

———. 1988. "'Good' and 'Good for': A Reply to Hurka." *Mind*, 97(386):279–280.

Bonsteel, Alan. 1997. "Behind the White Coat." *The Humanist*, 57(2) (March/ April):15–18.

Boswell, James. 1947. "An Account of My Last Interview with David Hume, Esq." (1777). Reprinted as Appendix A in Norman Kemp Smith, ed., *Hume's Dialogues Concerning Natural Religion*, 2nd edition. London: Thomas Nelson and Sons.

Botwinick, Jack. 1967. *Cognitive Processes in Maturity and Old Age*. New York: Springer.

Bradsher, Keith. 1997. "Kevorkian Is Also Painter. His Main Theme Is Death." *New York Times*, March 17. (Article describes the extremely morbid and graphic nature of thirteen paintings shown in a Royal Oak, Michigan, gallery.)

Brandt, R. B., 1975. "The Morality and Rationality of Suicide." In Perlin 1975:61–75.

Bresnahan, James F. 1993. "Medical Futility or the Denial of Death?" *Cambridge Quarterly of Healthcare Ethics*, 2(2):213–217.

Brickman, Harriet. 1995. "Live and Let Die: A Doctor's Best Hopes Can Be a Patient's Worst Nightmare." *New York Times Magazine* (July 2):14.

British Medical Association. 1993. *Medical Ethics Today*. London: BMA.

Brock, Dan. 1989. "Death and Dying." In *Life and Death: Philosophical Essay in Biomedical Ethics*. Cambridge: Cambridge University Press, 144–183.

———. 1986. "Forgoing Life-Sustaining Food and Water: Is It Killing?" In Lynn 1986:117–131.

Brodie, Howard. 1976. *Ethical Decisions in Medicine*. Boston: Little, Brown.

Brody, H. 1992. "Assisted Death—a Compassionate Response to a Medical Failure." *New England Journal of Medicine*, 327(19):1384–1388.

Brody, Jane E. 1997. "Personal Health: When a Dying Patient Seeks Suicide Aid, It May Be a Signal to Fight Depression." *New York Times*, June 18.

Bromley, D. B. 1974. *The Psychology of Human Aging*. London: Penguin.

Brooks, Simon A. 1984. "Dignity and Cost-Effectiveness: A Rejection of the Utilitarian Approach to Death." *Journal of Medical Ethics*, 10(3):148–151.

Brown, Judy. 1995. *The Choice: Seasons of Loss and Renewal After a Father's Decision to Die*. Berkeley, Calif.: Conari Press.

Brown, Newell. 1986. *How Not to Overstay One's Life: To Call It a Day—in Good Season*. Nederland, Colo.: Privately published. Available from Newell Brown, Twin Sisters Road, Magnolia Star Route, Nederland, Colo. 80466.

Bruni, Frank. 1996. "Court Overturns Ban in New York on Aided Suicides: A Historic Shift, Federal Ruling Allows Doctors to Prescribe Drugs to End Life." *New York Times*, April 3.

Bullock, A., O. Stallybrass, and S. Trombley, eds. 1988. *The Fontana Dictionary of Modern Thought*. London: Fontana.

Burgess, J. A. 1993. "The Great Slippery-Slope Argument." *Journal of Medical Ethics*, 19:169–174.

Caine, Eric. 1993. "Self-Determined Death, the Physician, and Medical Priorities: Is There Time to Talk?" *Journal of the American Medical Association*, 270(7):875-876.

Callahan, Daniel. 1995. "When Self-Determination Runs Amok." In Baylis et al. 1995:555–562.

———. 1993. "Pursuing a Peaceful Death." *Hastings Center Report*, 23(4):33–38.

Campbell, Murray. 1991. "Voters Get Say on Right to Die." (Toronto) *Globe and Mail*, October 21.

Campbell, Robert, and Diane Collinson. 1988. *Ending Lives*. Oxford: Basil Blackwell.

Camus, Albert. 1955. *The Myth of Sisyphus and Other Essays*. Trans. J. O'Brien. New York: Knopf.

Caplan, Arthur. 1996. Interview. "The Kevorkian Verdict." Televised program on Kevorkian trial that includes interview with Dr. Timothy Quill, courtroom coverage, and film of Dr. Kevorkian and individuals he later assisted in committing suicide. Produced by WBGH (Boston) Educational Foundation. Aired on *Frontline*, Public Broadcasting System, May 14. Transcripts are available from PBS.

———. 1981. "The 'Unnaturalness' of Aging—a Sickness unto Death?" In Caplan et al. 1981:725–737.

Caplan, Arthur, H. Tristram Engelhardt, Jr., and James J. McCartney, eds. 1981. *Concepts of Health and Disease*. Reading, Mass.: Addison-Wesley.

Capron, Alexander Morgan. 1992. "The Patient Self-Determination Act: A Cooperative Model for Implementation." *Cambridge Quarterly of Healthcare Ethics*, 1(2):97–106.

———. 1986. "Legal and Ethical Problems in Decisions for Death." *Law, Medicine and Health Care*, 14(3–4):141–144, 157.

Carpenter, B. 1993. "A Review and New Look at Ethical Suicide in Advanced Age." *The Gerontologist*, 33(3):359–365.

Carter, Stephen L. 1996. "Rush to Lethal Judgment." *New York Times Magazine*, (July 21):28–29.

Cassell, Eric J. 1991. *The Nature of Suffering and the Goals of Medicine*. New York: Oxford University Press.

———. 1980. *The Healer's Art*. New York: Penguin.

Chappell P., and R. King. 1992. "*Final Exit* and the Risk of Suicide." *Journal of the American Medical Association*, 267(22):3027.

Charlton R., S. Dovey, Y. Mizushima, and E. Ford. 1995. "Attitudes to Death and Dying in the UK, New Zealand, and Japan." *Journal of Palliative Care*, 11(1):42–47.

Checkland, David, and Michel Silberfeld. 1996. "Mental Competence and the Question of Beneficent Intervention." *Theoretical Medicine*, 17:121–134.

————. 1995. "Reflections on Segregating and Assessing Areas of Competence." *Theoretical Medicine*, 16:375–388.

————. 1993. "Competence and the Three A's: Autonomy, Authenticity, and Aging." *Canadian Journal on Aging*, 12(4):453–468.

Childress, James F. 1979. "Paternalism and Health Care." In Robinson and Pritchard, 1979:18.

Choron, Jacques. 1972. *Suicide*. New York: Scribner's.

————. 1963. *Death and Western Thought*. London: Collier-Macmillan.

Ciesielski-Carlucci, C. 1993. "Physician Attitudes and Experiences with Assisted Suicide: Results of a Small Opinion Survey." *Cambridge Quarterly of Healthcare Ethics*, 2:39–44.

Clark, Nina. 1997. *The Politics of Physician Assisted Suicide*. New York: Garland.

Code, Lorraine. 1994. "I Know Just How You Feel." In More and Milligan 1994:77–97.

Cohen, Roger. 1997. "2 'Perfect Little Girls' Stun France in Suicide." *New York Times*, May 30.

Colt, George Howe. 1991. *The Enigma of Suicide*. New York: Summit Books.

Conwell, Yeates, and Eric Caine. 1991. "Rational Suicide and the Right to Die—Reality and Myth." *New England Journal of Medicine*, 325(15):1100–1103.

Coutts, Jane. 1997. "HMOs: Health Service or Horror Show?" (Toronto) *Globe and Mail*, April 19.

————, and Henry Hess. 1996. "Doctor Charged in Man's Suicide." (Toronto) *Globe and Mail*, June 21.

Cowley, Malcolm. 1982. *The View from Eighty*. London: Penguin.

Cox, Donald. 1993. *Hemlock's Cup: The Struggle for Death with Dignity*. Buffalo, N.Y.: Prometheus Books.

Cox, Kevin. 1997a. "Doctor Charged with Murder." (Toronto) *Globe and Mail*, May 8.

————. 1997b. "Families Wondering if Relatives Killed." (Toronto) *Globe and Mail*, May 9.

Crane, Diana. 1975. *The Sanctity of Social Life: Physicians' Treatment of Critically Ill Patients*. New York: Russell Sage Foundation.

Crisp, R. 1987. "A Good Death: Who Best to Bring It?" *Bioethics*, 1(1):74–79.

Crowley, J. 1992. "To Be or Not to Be: Examining the Right to Die," *Journal of Legislation of Notre Dame Law School*, 18(2):347–355.

Dagger, Richard. 1997. *Civic Virtues: Rights, Citizenship, and Republican Virtues*. New York: Oxford University Press.

Dao, James. 1996. "Suicide Ruling Raises Concern: Who Decides?" *New York Times*, April 4.

Daube, David. 1972. "The Linguistics of Suicide." *Philosophy and Public Affairs*, 1:387–437.

Davis, A., L. Phillips, T. Drought, et al, 1995. "Nurses' Attitudes Towards Active Euthanasia." *Nursing Outlook*, 43(4):174–179.

Day, M. 1994. "An Act of Will." *Nursing Times*, 90(10):14.

de Beauvoir, Simone. 1969. *A Very Easy Death*. Harmondsworth, UK: Penguin.

De Spelder, Lynne Ann, and Albert Lee Strickland [1987.] 3rd edition. 1992. *The Last Dance: Encountering Death and Dying*, Mountain View, Calif.: Mayfield.

Degrazia, David. 1995. "Value Theory and the Best Interests Standard." *Bioethics*, 9(1):50–61.

Delden J., L. Pijnenborg, and P. Maas. 1993. "Dances with Data." *Bioethics*, 7:323–329.

Denny, N. W. 1979. "Problem Solving in Later Adulthood." In P. Baltes, and O. G. Brimm (eds.), *Life Span Development and Behavior*, Vol. 2. New York: Academic Press, pp. 37–66.

DeSimone, Cathleen. 1996. *Death on Demand: Physician-assisted Suicide in the United States*. Buffalo, N.Y.: W. S. Hein.

DeSpelder, Lynne, and Albert Strickland. 1987. "Suicide." Chapter 13, *The Last Dance: Encountering Death and Dying*. Palo Alto: Mayfield Publishing Co.

Devettere, Raymond J. 1992. "Slippery Slopes and Moral Reasoning." *Journal of Clinical Ethics*, 3(4):297–301.

Diegner, Leslie F., and Jeffrey Sloan. 1992. "Decision-Making During Serious Illness: What Role Do Patients Really Want to Play?" *Clinical Epidemiology*, 45(9):941–950.

Doerr, Edd. 1997. "Liberty and Death." *The Humanist*, 57(2)(March/April):12–13.

Donnelly, John, ed. 1997. *Suicide: Right or Wrong?* Buffalo, N.Y.: Prometheus Press.

———, ed. 1978. *Language, Metaphysics, and Death*. New York: Fordham University Press.

Downey, Don. 1992. "Waiting for That Final Visitor." (Toronto) *Globe and Mail*, April 8.

———, and K. Calman. 1994. *Healthy Respect: Ethics in Health Care*. Oxford: Oxford University Press.

Downing, A. B., ed. 1969. *Euthanasia and the Right to Death: The Case for Voluntary Euthanasia*. Atlantic Highlands, N.J.: Humanities Press.

Drey, P., and J. Giszczak. 1992. "May I Author My Final Chapter? Assisted Suicide and Guidelines to Prevent Abuse." *Journal of Legislation of the Notre Dame Law School*, 18(2):331–345.

Dreyfus, Hubert, and Paul Rabinow. 1983. *Michel Foucault: Beyond Structuralism and Hermeneutics*. With an afterword by Michel Foucault. Brighton, UK: Harvester Press.

Durkheim, Emile. 1912. *Le Suicide*. Paris: Librairie Félix Alcan. Trans. John Spaulding and George Simpson. 1966. *Suicide: A Study in Sociology*. New York: Free Press.

————. 1897. *Suicide: A Study in Sociology*. Trans. J. A. Spaulding and G. Simpson. New York: Free Press, 1951.

Dworkin, Gerald. 1972. "Paternalism." *The Monist*, 56 (January):76f.

Dworkin, Ronald. 1996. "Sex, Death, and the Courts." *New York Review of Books* (August 8):44–50.

————. 1994. "When Is It Right to Die?" *New York Times*, May 17.

————. 1993. *Life's Dominion—an Argument About Abortion and Euthanasia*. London: HarperCollins.

————. et al. 1997. "Assisted Suicide: The Philosophers' Brief." *New York Review of Books*. (March 27):41–47.

Edwards, Paul, ed. 1967. *The Encyclopedia of Philosophy*, vol. 4. "Intentionality" by Roderick Chisholm. New York: Macmillan/Free Press.

Egan, Timothy. 1997. "Assisted Suicide Comes Full Circle, to Oregon." *New York Times*, October 26.

Eisler, Gary. 1997. "Life Is Precious—Even at the End." *Wall Street Journal*, October 31.

Emanuel, Ezekiel, and Linda Emanuel. 1997. "Assisted Suicide? Not in My State." *New York Times*, July 24.

————. 1993. "Decisions at the End of Life Guided by Communities of Patients." *Hastings Center Report*, 23 (September–October):6–14.

Epstein, Richard. 1997. *Mortal Peril: Our Inalienable Right to Health Care?* Reading, Mass.: Addison-Wesley.

Evans, D., H. Funkenstein, M. Albert, P. Scherr, et al. 1989. "Prevalence of Alzheimer's Disease in a Community Population of Older Persons: Higher Than Previously Reported." *Journal of the American Medical Association*, 262(18):2551–2556.

Farbar, Jennifer. 1995. "Hush of Suicide." *New York Times Magazine* (March 5):27.

Farber, Leslie H. 1969. "The Phenomenology of Suicide." In Shneidman, 1969:109–110.

Feifel, Herman, ed. 1977. *New Meanings of Death*. New York: McGraw-Hill.

Fein, Esther B. 1997a. "A Better Quality of Life, in the Days Before Death." *New York Times*, May 4.

————. 1997b. "Handling of Assisted-Suicide Cases Unlikely to Shift, Officials Say." *New York Times*, June 27.

————. 1997c. "Not Dead Enough to Die: Laws Force Life Support on a Man Who Never Could Consent." *New York Times*, July 25.

————. 1996. "Court Overturns Ban in New York on Aided Suicides: The Decision Offers Relief to Plaintiffs." *New York Times*, April 3.

Feinberg, Joel. 1984. *Harm to Others*. Vol. 1 of *The Moral Limits of the Criminal Law*. New York: Oxford University Press.

————, and Henry West, eds. 1977. *Moral Philosophy: Classic Texts and Contemporary Problems*. Encino, Calif.: Dickenson.

Feldman, Fred. 1992. *Confrontations with the Reaper: A Philosophical Study of the Nature and Value of Death*. New York: Oxford University Press.

"Final Report of the Netherlands State Commission on Euthanasia: An English Summary." 1987. *Bioethics*, 1(2):163–174.

Fletcher, J. 1989. "The Right to Choose When to Die." *Hemlock Quarterly*, (January).

Foley, K. 1991. "The Relationship of Pain and Symptom Management to Patient Requests for Physician-Assisted Suicide." *Journal of Pain and Symptom Management*, 6(5):289–297.

Foucault, Michel. 1988. *Michel Foucault: Politics, Philosophy, Culture: Interviews and Other Writings, 1977–1984*. Ed. Lawrence D. Kritzman. Oxford: Blackwell.

———. 1980. *The History of Sexuality*, vol. 1. Trans. Robert Hurley. New York: Vintage.

———. 1983. "The Subject and Power." Afterword to Dreyfus and Rabinow 1983:208–226.

———. 1979. *Discipline and Punish*. Trans. Alan Sheridan. New York: Pantheon.

Freud, Sigmund. 1915. "Our Attitude Towards Death." Chapter 2, *Thoughts for the Times on War and Death*. In *The Standard Edition of the Complete Works of Sigmund Freud*. Vol. 14, pp. 273–302. London: Hogarth Press. Quoted in Battin 1982a:318, n3.

Fried, T., M. Stein, P. O'Sullivan, et al. 1993. "Limits of Patient Autonomy, Physician Attitudes and Practices Regarding Life-sustaining Treatments and Euthanasia," *Archives of Internal Medicine*, 153:722–728.

Fulton, Robert, et al. 1976. *Death, Grief and Bereavement: A Bibliography, 1845–1975*. New York: Arno Press.

Garret, J., R. Harris, J. Norburn, D. Patrick, and M. Danis. 1993. "Life-sustaining Treatments During Terminal Illness: Who Wants What?" *Journal of General Internal Medicine*, 8:361–368.

Garrett, Thomas M., Harold Baillie, and Rosellen Garrett. 1998. *Health Care Ethics: Principles and Problems*. Upper Saddle River, N.J.: Prentice-Hall.

Garrow, David J. 1997. "Letting the Public Decide About Assisted Suicide: The Court Couldn't Duck Abortion and Contraception Forever. This Moral Issue, Too, Will Be Back." *New York Times*, June 29.

———. 1996. "The Justices' Life-or-Death Choices." *New York Times*, April 7.

Gay, Kathlyn, 1993. *The Right to Die: Public Controversy, Private Matter (Issue and Debate)*. Brookfield, Conn.: Millbrook Press.

Geis, Sally B., and Donald Messer. 1997. *How Shall We Die? Helping Christians Debate Assisted Suicide*. New York: Abingdon Press.

Gentles, Ian, 1995a. *Euthanasia and Assisted Suicide: The Current Debate*. Toronto: Stoddart.

———. 1995b. "Senate Report on Euthanasia: Pro and Con." (Toronto) *Globe and Mail*, June 8.

Genuis, Stephen J., et al, 1994. "Public Attitudes Toward the Right to Die." *Canadian Medical Association Journal*, 150(5):701–708.

Gifford-Jones, W. 1995. "Northern Territory Shows Its Compassion on Euthanasia Issue." (Toronto) *The Financial Post*, December 30.

Gilbert, Susan. 1996. "When Savings Run Out, Some Shun Lifesaving." *New York Times*, August 14.

Gillick, M., K. Hesse, and N. Mazzapica, 1993. "Medical Technology at the End of Life: What Would Physicians and Nurses Want for Themselves?" *Archives of Internal Medicine*, 153:2542–2547.

Gillon, Raanan. 1992. *Philosophical Medical Ethics*. Chichester, N.Y.: John Wiley and Sons.

Glick, Shimon M. 1997. "Unlimited Human Autonomy—a Cultural Bias?" *New England Journal of Medicine*, 336(13):954–956.

Goddard, M. 1992. "Hospice Care in the Future: Economic Evaluation May Be Useful." *Cancer Topics*, 9(1):10–11.

Goldberg, Carey. 1997a. "Oregon Moves Nearer to New Vote on Allowing Assisted Suicide." *New York Times*, June 10.

———. 1997b. "Oregon Braces for New Right-to-Die Fight." *New York Times*, June 17.

Gorovitz, Samuel, et al., eds. 1983. *Moral Problems in Medicine*, 2nd edition. Englewood Cliffs, N.J.: Prentice-Hall.

Graber, Glenn, and Jennifer Chassman. 1993. "Assisted Suicide Is Not Voluntary Active Euthanasia, but It's Awfully Close." *Journal of the American Geriatrics Society*, 41(1):88–89.

Greenhouse, Linda, 1997a. "High Court Hears 2 Cases Involving Assisted Suicide. Justices, in an Unusually Personal Session, Reveal Their Reluctance to Intercede." *New York Times*, January 9.

———. 1997b. "Court, 9–0, Upholds State Laws Prohibiting Assisted Suicide: No Help For Dying." *New York Times*, June 27. (This is the main front-page story and is accompanied by other articles and excerpts from the Supreme Court's unanimous decision.)

———. 1997c. "Benchmarks of Justice: In 9 Extraordinary Months, the High Court Developed a Vast Panorama of Landmarks." *New York Times*, July 1.

———. 1997d. "Assisted Suicide Clears a Hurdle in Highest Court." *New York Times*, October 15.

———. 1996a. "High Court to Say if the Dying Have a Right to Suicide Help." *New York Times*, October 2.

———. 1996b. "An Issue for a Reluctant Court." *New York Times*, October 6.

———. 1996c. "Clinton Administration Asks Supreme Court to Rule Against Assisted Suicide: Contrasting Life Support Withheld and Death Brought About." *New York Times*, November 13.

————. 1995. "Justices Decline to Hear Appeals Involving Assisted Suicide."
    New York Times, April 25.

Grollman, Earl A. 1970. *Talking About Death*. Boston: Beacon Press.

Gross, Jane. 1997a. "Doctor at Center of Supreme Court Case on Assisted Sui-
    cide." *New York Times*, January 1. (On Dr. Timothy Quill.)

————. 1997b. "Wanting a Chance to Choose Their Time: Breast Cancer
    Patients Say Court Overlooked Them on Assisted Suicide." *New York
    Times*, June 30.

Gunnell, D., and S. Frankel. 1994. "Prevention of Suicide: Aspirations and
    Evidence." *British Medical Journal*, 308:1227–1233.

Gutmann, Stephanie. 1996. "Death and the Maiden." *The New Republic* (June
    24):20–21, 24, 28.

Haberman, Clyde. 1997. "The Suicidal Still Call Out in Desperation." *New York
    Times*, January 31.

Hamel, Ronald, and Edwin DuBose, eds. 1996. *Must We Suffer Our Way to Death?
    Cultural and Theological Perspectives on Death by Choice*. Dallas: Southern
    Methodist University Press.

Harman, Gilbert. 1986. *Change in View: Principles of Reasoning*. Cambridge, Mass.:
    MIT Press.

Hendin, Herbert. 1996. *Seduced by Death: Doctors, Patients, and the Dutch Cure*.
    New York: W. W. Norton.

————, Chris Rutenfrans, and Zbigniew Zyliez. 1997. "JAMA: Another Journal
    Warns of Abuses in the Netherlands." *New York Times*, June 24.

Henig, Robin M. 1981. *The Myth of Senility: Misconceptions about the Brain and
    Aging*. New York: Doubleday.

Hentoff, Nat. 1996. "Front-Line Resistors Fight Kevorkian's Easy Death."
    (Toronto) *Globe and Mail*, August 24.

Hess, Henry. 1997. "Doctor Faces New Charges: Hearing Delayed in Case of
    AIDS Patient's Suicide and Physician's Actions." (Toronto) *Globe and
    Mail*, February 4.

Hinton, John. 1967. *Dying*. New York: Penguin.

Hoefler, James. 1997. *Managing Death: The First Guide for Patients, Family Mem-
    bers, and Care Providers on Forgoing Treatment at the End of Life*. Boulder,
    Colo.: Westview Press; New York: HarperCollins.

————. 1994. *Culture, Medicine, Politics, and the Right to Die*. Boulder, Colo.:
    Westview Press.

Hoffmeister, F., and C. Muller (eds.). 1979. *Brain Function in Old Age: Evaluation
    of Change and Disorder*. New York: Springer.

Hofsess, John. 1995. "How Will the Senate Committee See Assisted Suicide?"
    (Toronto) *Globe and Mail*, May 4.

————. 1992. "Killing Off the Right to Die." (Toronto) *Globe and Mail*, February
    27.

Honderich, Ted, ed. 1995. *The Oxford Companion to Philosophy*. Oxford: Oxford University Press.

Hood, Ann. 1997. "Rage Against the Dying of the Light." *New York Times*, August 2.

Hook, Sidney. 1988. "The Uses of Death." *New York Review of Books*, (April 28):22–25.

Howe, Edmund G. 1992. "Caveats Regarding Slippery Slopes and Physicians' Moral Conscience." *Journal of Clinical Ethics*, 3(4):251–256.

Hudson, Liam. 1996. "The Age of Alzheimer's." *Times Literary Supplement*, (January 12):7–8.

Hume, David. 1963. "My Own Life." (1776). In Hume's *Essays: Moral, Political and Literary*. Oxford: Oxford University Press.

———. 1826. "Essay on Suicide." (1776). In *The Philosophic Works of David Hume*. Edinburgh: Black and Tait. Quoted in Battin, 1982a:312.

Humphry, Derek. 1994. "Suicide by Asphyxiation After the Publication of *Final Exit*." *New England Journal of Medicine*, 330(14):1017.

———. 1993a. *Lawful Exit: The Limits of Freedom for Help in Dying*. Junction City, Oreg.: Norris Lane Press.

———. 1993b. "Derek Humphry Discusses Death with Dignity with Thomasine Kushner." *Cambridge Quarterly of Healthcare Ethics*, 2(1):57–61.

———. 1992a. *Final Exit: The Practicalities of Self-Deliverance and Assisted Suicide for the Dying*. New York: Dell.

———. 1992b. *Dying with Dignity*. New York: Birch Lane Press.

———. 1992c. "The Last Choice." *Hemlock Quarterly* (October):4.

———, and A. Wickett. 1986. *The Right to Die—Understanding Euthanasia*. New York: Harper & Row. Reprinted Eugene, Oreg: Hemlock Society, 1990.

Illich, Ivan. 1976. *Limits to Medicine*. New York: Marion Boyars.

Jacobson, Stanley. 1995. "Depression as a Healthy Response." (Toronto) *Globe and Mail*, June 10.

James, William. 1956. *The Will to Believe and Other Essays in Philosophy*. New York: Dover.

———. 1897. "The Will to Believe." In James's *The Will to Believe and Other Essays in Popular Philosophy*: 1–31. New York: Longman's Green.

Jamison, Stephen. 1996. *Final Acts of Love: Families, Friends, and Assisted Dying*. New York: Putnam Publishing Group.

Jarvik, Lissy. 1979. *Psychological Symptoms and Cognitive Loss in the Elderly*. New York: Halsted.

Jecker, N., and L. Schneiderman. 1994. "Is Dying Young Worse Than Dying Old?" *The Gerontologist*, 34(1):66–72.

Johnson, Linda A. 1997. "Kevorkian Aids N. J. Woman: MS Patient Ends Life in Mich." *The Times* (Trenton, N.J.), July 3. (Despite the headline, two women's bodies were found; both were apparent suicides and victims of multiple sclerosis.)

Johnston, Brian. 1994. *Death as a Salesman: What's Wrong with Assisted Suicide*. Sacramento, Calif.: New Regency.

Judis, John B. 1997. "Careless: A Poison Pill for Medicare." *The New Republic* (July 28):14–16.

Kant, Immanuel. 1991. "Suicide." In Mappes and Zembaty, 316–319.

Kass, L. 1993. "Is There a Right to Die?" *Hastings Center Report*, (January–February):34–43.

Kastenbaum, Robert J. 1992. *The Psychology of Death*. New York: Springer.

———. 1991. *Death, Society, and Human Experience*. New York: Merrill.

———. 1967. "Suicide as the Preferred Way of Death." In Shneidman, 1976: 421–441.

———. 1964. *New Thoughts on Old Age*. New York: Springer.

———, and Beatrice Kastenbaum, eds. 1989. *Encyclopedia of Death*. Phoenix, Ariz.: Oryx Press.

Kaufmann, Walter, ed. 1954. *The Portable Nietzsche*. New York: Viking Press.

Kaveny, M. Cathleen, and John P. Langan. 1996. "The Doctor's Call." *New York Times*, July 15.

Kearl, Michael C. 1989. *Endings: A Sociology of Death and Dying*. New York: Oxford University Press.

Keizer, Bert. 1997. *Dancing with Mister D: Notes on Life and Death*. New York: Doubleday.

Kellogg, F., M. Crain, J. Corwin, and P. Brickner. 1992. "Life-Sustaining Interventions in Frail Elderly Persons—Talking About Choices." *Archives of Internal Medicine*, 152: 2317–2320.

Kennedy, I., and A. Grubb. 1994. *Medical Law, Text with Materials*, 2nd edition. London: Butterworth. (Contains the Kings College/Terrence Higgins Trust living will document, pp.1365—1368.)

Kevles, Daniel J. 1995. "We All Must Die; Who Can Tell Us When?" *New York Times Book Review* (May 7):7.

Kluge, Eike-Henner, ed. 1993. *Readings in Biomedical Ethics*. Scarborough, Ontario: Prentice-Hall.

———. 1975. *The Practice of Death*. New Haven: Yale University Press.

Knight, Ben. 1996. "Death with Dignity: Our Last Right." In *The Readers Showcase*. Toronto: Coles/Smithbooks.

Kolata, Gina. 1997a. "Alzheimer Patients Present a Lesson on Human Dignity." *New York Times*, January 1.

———. 1997b. "Living Wills Aside, Dying Cling to Hope." *New York Times*, January 15.

———. 1997c. "Ethicists Struggle Against the Tyranny of the Anecdote." *New York Times*, June 24.

———. 1997d. "Group Proposes a New System on Liver Transplant Priorities." *New York Times*, June 27.

————. 1997e. " 'Passive Euthanasia' in Hospitals Is the Norm, Doctors Say." *New York Times*, June 28.

————. 1997f. "When Morphine Fails to Kill." *New York Times*, July 23.

————. 1996a. "1 in 5 Nurses Tell Survey They Helped Patients Die," *New York Times*, May 23.

————. 1996b. "In Shift, Prospects for Survival Will Decide Liver Transplants." *New York Times*, November 15.

Krausz, Michael, ed. 1989. *Relativism: Interpretation and Confrontation*. Notre Dame, Ind.: University of Notre Dame Press.

Kristof, Nicholas. 1997. "Japanese Parents Wonder Who Will Look After Them: As the Baby-Boom Generation Approaches Retirement, Untraditional Children Are No Longer Sharing Their Homes and Caring for Older Family Members." (Toronto) *Globe and Mail*, August 14.

Kristol, Elizabeth. 1993. "Soothing Moral Shroud." *Washington Post*, December 3.

Kübler-Ross, Elisabeth. 1969. *On Death and Dying*. New York: Macmillan.

Kung, Hans, and Walter Jens. 1995. *Dying with Dignity: A Plea for Personal Responsibility*. New York: Continuum.

Kushner, Howard. 1989. *Self-Destruction in the Promised Land*. New Brunswick, N.J.: Rutgers University Press.

Ladd, John, ed. 1979. *Ethical Issues Relating to Life and Death*. New York: Oxford University Press.

Laurence, Margaret. 1964. *The Stone Angel*. Toronto: McClelland and Stewart.

Leary, Warren E. 1997. "Not Enough Is Done to Ease End of Life, Panel Says." *New York Times*, June 5.

Lee, M., and L. Ganzini. 1994. "The Effect of Recovery from Depression on Preferences for Life-Sustaining Therapy in Older Patients." *Journal of Gerontology*, 49(1):M15-M21.

Lessenberry, Jack. 1996a. "Specialist Testifies Depression Was Issue in Kevorkian Cases." *New York Times*, April 23.

————. 1996b. "Many Turning to Internet for Aid with Suicide." *New York Times*, July 15.

————. 1996c. "Kevorkian Indicted on Charges of Helping in Three Suicides." *New York Times*, November 1.

————. 1996d. "Kevorkian Is Arrested and Charged in a Suicide." *New York Times*, November 7.

————. 1996e. "Prosecutor Goes Against Tide, Going After Kevorkian." *New York Times*, November 25.

Levin, Jack, and William Levin. 1980. *Ageism: Prejudice and Discrimination Against the Elderly*. Belmont, Calif.: Wadsworth.

Levin, Martin. 1996. "Verdicts on Verdicts About Easeful Death." (Toronto) *Globe and Mail*, August 10.

Lockwood, Michael, ed. 1985. *Moral Dilemmas in Modern Medicine*. Oxford: Oxford University Press.

Loewy, E. H. 1995. "Compassion, Reason, and Moral Judgement." *Cambridge Quarterly of Healthcare Ethics*, 4(4):466–475.

Logue, Barbara. 1993. *Last Rights: Death Control and the Elderly in America*. Oxford: Maxwell Macmillan.

Lown, Bernard. 1997. *The Lost Art of Healing*. New York: Houghton Mifflin.

Lynn, Joanne, ed. 1986. *By No Extraordinary Means: The Choice to Forgo Life-Sustaining Food and Water*. Bloomington: Indiana University Press.

MacIntyre, Alisdair. 1977. "Epistemological Crises, Dramatic Narrative and the Philosophy of Science." *The Monist* 60(4): 453–72.

Makin, Kirk. 1997. "Exemptions Rarely Needed, Experts Say: Mandatory Sentences Disappearing as Judges Given Penalty Latitude for Most Crimes." (Toronto) *Globe and Mail*, December 2.

Malcolm, Andrew. 1990. "What Medical Science Can't Seem to Learn: When to Call It Quits." *New York Times*, December 23.

Maltsberger, John, and Mark Goldblatt, eds. 1996. *Essential Papers on Suicide*. New York: New York University Press.

Mappes, Thomas A., and Jane S. Zembaty, eds. 1991. *Biomedical Ethics*, 3rd edition. New York: McGraw-Hill.

Marcus, Eric. 1996. *Why Suicide: Answers to 200 of the Most Frequently Asked Questions About Suicide, Attempted Suicide, and Assisted Suicide*. San Francisco: HarperCollins.

Markoff, John. 1990. "Programmed for Life and Death." *New York Times*, August 26.

Marshall, Andrew. 1994. "A Nasty Piece of Work: Wataru Tsurumi's Suicide Manual Makes a Killing." *Intersect*, (May): 26–28.

Martin, Douglas. 1989. "Creating Beauty out of Suffering as Life Fades." *New York Times*, February 18.

Martin, R. M. 1980. "Suicide and Self-sacrifice." In Battin and Mayo 1980:48–68.

McDougall, Burnley. 1994. "Challenging the Oath of Hippocrates." (Toronto) *Globe and Mail*, March 8.

McGough, P. 1993. "Washington State Initiative 119: The First Public Vote on Legalizing Physician Assisted Death." *Cambridge Quarterly of Healthcare Ethics*, 2:63–67.

McIntosh, John L., and Nancy J. Osgood. 1986. *Suicide and the Elderly*. Westport, Conn.: Greenwood Press.

McKee, Patrick. 1988. "The Aging Mind: View from Philosophy and Psychology." *The Gerontologist*, 28(1):132–133.

McLean, Sheila A. M., 1989. *A Patient's Right to Know—Information Disclosure, the Doctor and the Law*. Brookfield, Vt.: Dartmouth.

———, ed. 1996a. *Contemporary Issues in Law, Ethics and Medicine*. Brookfield, Vt.: Dartmouth.

———. 1996b. *Death, Dying and the Law*. Brookfield, Vt.: Dartmouth.

McNulty, C. 1995. "Mentally Incapacitated Adults and Decision-Making: A Psychological Perspective—Comments on Law Commission Consultation Papers, Numbers 128, 129 and 130." *Medicine, Science and the Law,* 35(2):159–164.

Meier, D., and C. Cassel. 1983. "Euthanasia in Old Age—a Case Study and Ethical Analysis." *Journal of the American Geriatrics Society,* 31(5): 294–298.

Menninger, Karl. 1966. *Man Against Himself.* New York: Harvest/HBJ.

Mezey, M., L. Evans, Z. Golub, E. Murphy, and G. White. 1994. "The Patient Self-Determination Act: Sources of Concern for Nurses." *Nursing Outlook,* 42(1):30–38.

———, and B. Latimer. 1993. "The Patient Self-Determination Act—an Early Look at Implementation." *Hastings Center Report,* 23(1) (January–February):16–20.

Miles, S., and A. August. 1990. "Courts, Gender and the 'Right to Die.'" *Law, Medicine and Health Care,* 18:85–95.

Mitford, Jessica. 1963. *The American Way of Death.* New York: Simon and Schuster.

Miyaji, N. T. 1993. "The Power of Compassion: Truth-Telling Among American Doctors in the Care of Dying Patients." *Social Science Medicine,* 36(3):249–264.

Montaigne, Michel de. 1995. *Essays,* Book 2, Chapter 3, "A Custom of the Isle of Cea." Trans. John Florio. Quoted in *The Columbia Dictionary of Quotations.* New York: Columbia University Press; Microsoft *Bookshelf,* 1996–1997 CD-ROM edition.

More, Ellen Singer, and Maureen A. Milligan, eds. 1994. *The Empathic Practitioner: Empathy, Gender, and Medicine.* New Brunswick, N.J.: Rutgers University Press.

Moreno, Jonathan D. 1995. *Deciding Together: Bioethics and Moral Consensus.* New York: Oxford University Press.

Morgentaler, Henry. 1982. *Abortion and Contraception.* New York: Beaufort Books.

Motto, Jerome. 1972. "The Right to Suicide: A Psychiatrist's View." *Life-Threatening Behavior* 2(3): 183–88. New York: Behavioral Publications.

Mullens, Anne. 1996. *Timely Death: Considering Our Last Rights.* New York: Alfred A. Knopf.

Munson, Ronald. 1988. *Intervention and Reflection: Basic Issues in Medical Ethics,* 3rd edition. Belmont, Calif.: Wadsworth.

Mydans, Seth. 1997. "Assisted Suicide: Australia Faces a Grim Reality." *New York Times,* February 2.

Narveson, Jan. 1993. *Moral Matters.* Peterborough, Ontario: Broadview Press.

———. 1986. "Moral Philosophy and Suicide." *Canadian Journal of Psychiatry,* 31:104–107.

Navarro, Mireya. 1997. "Assisted Suicide Decision Looms in Florida." *New York Times*, July 3.

Niebuhr, Gustav. 1996. "Dying Cardinal Lobbies Against Suicide Aid." *New York Times*, November 13.

Nietzsche, Friedrich, 1967. *Will to Power*. Walter Kaufmann (ed.). New York: Random House.

———. 1954. *Thus Spake Zarathustra*. (Part One, 1883). In Kaufmann 1954: 103–439.

Nuland, Sherwin B. 1997. "How We Die Is Our Business." *New York Times*, January 13.

———. 1994. *How We Die: Reflections on Life's Final Chapter*. New York: Alfred A. Knopf.

Oates, Joyce Carol. 1980. "The Art of Suicide." In Battin and Mayo 1980:161–68.

Outhit, Jeff. 1997. "Homes May Refuse Frailest Seniors: Sickest Seniors in Middle of Funding Dispute." *Kingston Whig-Standard*, February 13. (Outhit's front-page article gives the Ontario Association of Non-Profit Homes and Services for Seniors' definition of a "heavy care resident" as one needing "close to total assistance to manage the activities of daily living, continence care, or behavior." It also specifies "heavy care" as requiring "3.5 hours of care per day or more, including intervention every 15 minutes." It is "heavy care" seniors who may be denied admission to homes for the aged.)

Ozar, David. 1992. "The Characteristics of a Valid 'Empirical' Slippery Slope Argument." *Journal of Clinical Ethics*, 3(4):301–302.

Palmore, Erdman. 1971. "Attitudes Toward Aging as Shown by Humor." *The Gerontologist* 11:181–86

Pear, Robert. 1997. "H.M.O.'s Limiting Medicare Appeals, U.S. Inquiry Finds: Government Is Told by Court to Clarify Its Guidelines on Elderly Patients' Rights." *New York Times*, March 18.

———. 1996. "Managed Care Officials Agree to Mastectomy Hospital Stays: Health Plans Act to Head Off Federal Regulations." *New York Times*, November 15.

Pellegrino, Edmund D. 1993. "Compassion Needs Reason Too." *Journal of the American Medical Association*, 270(7):874–875.

———. 1992. "Doctors Must Not Kill." *Journal of Clinical Ethics*, 3(2):95–103.

Pence, G. E., ed. 1995. *Classic Cases in Medical Ethics*, 2nd edition. New York: McGraw-Hill.

Perlin, Seymour, ed. 1975. *A Handbook for the Study of Suicide*. Oxford: Oxford University Press.

Pohier, Jacques, and Dietmar Mieth. 1985. *Suicide and the Right to Die*. Edinburgh: T. and T. Clark.

Powell, Tia, and Donald B. Kornfeld. 1993. "On Promoting Rational Treatment, Not Rational Suicide." *Journal of Clinical Ethics*, 4(4):334–335.

Prado, C. G. 1995. *Starting with Foucault: An Introduction to Genealogy*. Boulder, Colo.: Westview Press; San Francisco: HarperCollins.

————. 1990. *The Last Choice: Preemptive Suicide in Advanced Age*. Westport, Conn.: Greenwood Press.

————. 1988. "Aging and Narrative." In James Thorton and Earl Winkler (eds.), *Ethics and Aging*, pp. 215–22.

————. 1986. *Rethinking How We Age: A New View of the Aging Mind*. Westport, Conn.: Greenwood Press.

————. 1984. *Making Believe: Philosophical Reflections on Fiction*. Westport, Conn.: Greenwood Press.

————. 1983. "Ageing and Narrative." *International Journal of Applied Philosophy*. 1(3):1–13.

————, and S. J. Taylor. 1998. *Assisted Suicide: Theory and Practice in Elective Death*. Atlantic Highlands, N.J.: Humanities Press.

Quill, Timothy. 1996. *A Midwife Through the Dying Process: Stories of Healing and Hard Choices at the End of Life*. Baltimore: Johns Hopkins University Press.

————. 1995. "You Promised Me I Wouldn't Die Like This!—a Bad Death as a Medical Emergency." *Archives of Internal Medicine*, 155:1250–1254.

————. 1993a. *Death and Dignity: Making Choices and Taking Charge*. New York: W. W. Norton.

————. 1993b. "Doctor, I Want to Die. Will You Help Me?" *Journal of the American Medical Association*, 270(7):870–873.

————. 1991. "Death and Dignity—a Case of Individualized Decision Making." *New England Journal of Medicine*, 324(10):691–694.

————, C. Cassel, and D. Meier. 1992. "Care of the Hopelessly Ill—Proposed Clinical Criteria for Physician Assisted Suicide." *New England Journal of Medicine*, 327(19):1380–1384.

————, and Betty Rolin. 1996. "Dr. Kevorkian Runs Wild," *New York Times*, August 29.

Rabinow, Paul, 1997. *Michel Foucault: Ethics—Subjectivity and Truth*. New York: The New Press.

Rachels, James. 1986. *The End Of Life: Euthanasia and Morality*. Oxford: Oxford University Press.

Regan, Tom, ed. 1980. *Matters of Life and Death*. Philadelphia: Temple University Press.

Richards, Bill. 1997. "Right-to-Die Opponent Heats Up Oregon Vote." *Wall Street Journal*, November 4.

Roberts, David. 1997. "Latimer Receives 1 Year in Jail: Judge Waives Life Sentence." (Toronto) *Globe and Mail*, December 2.

Robinson, Paul. 1984. *Criminal Law Defenses*. St. Paul, Minn.: West.

Robinson, Wade L., and Michael S. Pritchard, eds. 1979. *Medical Responsibility*. Clifton, N.J.: Humana Press.

Rorty, Richard. 1992. "A Pragmatist View of Rationality and Cultural Difference." *Philosophy East and West*, 42(4):581–596.
———. 1989. *Contingency, Irony, and Solidarity*. Cambridge: Cambridge University Press.
———. 1982. *The Consequences of Pragmatism*. Minneapolis: University of Min-
nesota Press.
Rosen, Jeffrey. 1997. "Nine Votes for Judicial Restraint: The Court Rejects a
'Right to Die'—and the Legacy of Roe v. Wade." *New York Times*, June
29.
———. 1996. "What Right to Die?" *The New Republic* (June 24):28–31.
Rosenberg, Charles E. 1996. "Slippery Slope: Seduced by Death." *New York Times
Book Review* (November 24):33.
Rosenthal, Elizabeth. 1997. "When a Healer Is Asked, 'Help Me Die,' " *New York
Times*, March 13.
Ross, Oakland. 1991. "The Right to Die: Going Gently." (Toronto) *Globe and
Mail*, September 14.
Roy, David J., John R. Williams, and Bernard M. Dickens. 1994. *Bioethics in
Canada*. Scarborough, Ontario: Prentice-Hall.
Sabatino, Charles. 1993. "Surely the Wizard Will Help Us, Toto? Implementing
the Patient Self-Determination Act." *Hastings Center Report*, 23 (Janu-
ary–February):12–16.
Sacks, M., and I. Kemperman. 1992. "*Final Exit* as a Manual for Suicide in
Depressed Patients." *American Journal of Psychiatry*, 149(6):842.
Salmon, Phillida. 1985. *Living in Time*. London: J. M. Dent and Sons.
Sandel, Michael. 1997. "The Hard Questions: Last Rights." *The New Republic*
(April 14):27.
Sanders, Stephanie. 1992. "A Time to Live or a Time to Die?" *Nursing Times*,
88(45):34–36.
Savulescu, Julian. 1994. "Rational Desires and the Limitation of Life-Sustaining
Treatment." *Bioethics*, 8(3):191–222.
Scanlon, T. M., 1975. "Preference and Urgency." *The Journal of Philosophy*.
72:655–669.
Schafer, Arthur. 1990. "Treading the Finest of Lines." (Toronto) *Globe and Mail*,
August 16.
Scheper, T., and S. Duursma. 1994. "Euthanasia: The Dutch Experience." *Age and
Aging*, 23:3–8.
Scott, Janny. 1997. "An Issue That Won't Die: Court's Ruling on Doctor-Assisted
Suicide Leaves Some Basic Questions Unresolved." *New York Times*, June 27.
Sedler, Robert. 1993. "The Constitution and Hastening Inevitable Death." *Hast-
ings Center Report*, 23(5):20–25.
Selzer, Richard. 1994. *Raising the Dead*. New York: Whittle/Viking.
Seneca. 1969. *Letters from a Stoic*. Letter 77. Trans. Robin Campbell. Baltimore:
Penguin.

Shapiro, R., A. Derse, M. Gottlieb, D. Schiedermayer, and M. Olson. 1994. "Willingness to Perform Euthanasia: A Survey of Physician Attitudes." *Archives of Internal Medicine*, 154:575–584.

Shavelson, Lonny. 1995. *A Chosen Death: The Dying Confront Assisted Suicide*. New York: Simon and Schuster.

Shenon, Philip. 1995. "Australian Euthanasia Legislation Sparks Mixture of Relief, Rage." (Toronto) *Globe and Mail*, July 29.

Shipp, E. R. 1988. "New York's Highest Court Rejects Family's Plea in Right-to-Die Case" (and transcript excerpts) and "Many Courts Have Upheld Right to Die." *New York Times*, October 15.

Shneidman, Edwin. 1996. *The Suicidal Mind*. New York: Oxford University Press.

———. 1993. *Suicide as Psychache: A Clinical Approach to Self-Destructive Behavior*. Northvale, N.J.: Aronson.

———. 1984. *Death: Current Perspectives*, 3rd edition. Mountain View, Calif.: Mayfield. (Battin 1982a doesn't appear in the 1995 4th edition of this anthology.)

———. ed. 1976. *Suicidology: Contemporary Developments*. New York: Grune and Stratton.

———. 1969. *On the Nature of Suicide*. San Francisco: Jossey-Bass.

Siegler, Ilene, 1976. "Aging I.Q.s." *Human Behavior* 5:55.

Simpson, Michael A. 1987. *Dying, Death, and Grief: A Critical Bibliography*. Pittsburgh: University of Pittsburgh Press.

———. 1979. *The Facts of Death*. Englewood Cliffs, N.J.: Spectrum/Prentice-Hall.

Skegg, P. 1984. *Law, Ethics and Medicine—Studies in Medical Law*. Oxford: Clarendon Press.

Sobel, Dava. 1991. "They Rarely Leave a Note." *New York Times Book Review* (April 14):9.

Southard, Samuel. 1991. *Death and Dying: A Bibliographical Survey*. New York: Greenwood Press.

Spicker, Stuart, Stanley Ingman, and Ian Lawson, eds. 1987. *Ethical Dimensions of Geriatric Care: Value Conflicts for the 21st Century*. Dordrecht, Netherlands: Reidel.

Steinfels, Peter. 1997a. "Perspective: Doctor-Assisted Suicide." *New York Times*, January 11.

———. 1997b. "Beliefs: The Issue of Doctor-Assisted Suicide Is Put on the Scales of Justice, and Philosophers Weigh In." *New York Times*, April 5. (Article on Dworkin et al. 1997.)

———. 1997c. "Beliefs: The Justices of the Supreme Court, Preparing Landmark Opinions, Are Now Writing About Doctor-assisted Suicide. They're Hardly Alone." *New York Times*, June 14.

———, and R. M. Veatch, eds. 1975. *Death Inside Out*. Hastings Center Report. New York: Harper & Row.

Stillion, Judith M. 1989. *Suicide Across the Life Span—Premature Exits.* New York: Hemisphere.

Stolberg, Sheryl Gay. 1997a. "Considering the Unthinkable: Protocol for Assisted Suicide." *New York Times,* June 11.

———. 1997b. "The Good Death: Embracing a Right to Die Well." *New York Times,* June 29.

———. 1997c. "Cries of the Dying Awaken Doctors to a New Approach, Palliative Care." *New York Times,* June 30.

Stout, David. 1997. "From Emotional to Intellectual, Secular to Religious." *New York Times,* June 27. (Article on reactions to Supreme Court's decision to uphold state laws prohibiting physician-assisted suicide.)

Stryker, Jeff. 1996. "Right to Die: Life After Quinlan." *New York Times,* March 31.

Sudnow, David. 1967. *Passing On: The Social Organization of Dying.* Englewood Cliffs, N.J.: Prentice-Hall.

Sutherland, John. 1992. "How to Die." *London Review of Books* (February 13): 8–9.

Tallis, Raymond. 1996. "Is There a Slippery Slope?—Arguments for and Against the Various Definitions of Euthanasia." *Times Literary Supplement* (January 12):3–4.

Teengel, Erwin. 1964. *Suicide and Attempted Suicide.* New York: Penguin.

Thorton, James, and Earl Winkler, eds. 1988. *Ethics and Aging.* Vancouver: University of British Columbia Press.

Tierney, John. 1982. "The Aging Body." *Esquire.* May 1982, pp. 45–57. (Though published in a popular magazine, this article is very concise and illuminating and clearly well-researched.)

Tolchin, Martin. 1989. "When Long Life Is Too Much: Suicide Rises Among [the] Elderly." *New York Times,* July 19.

Toulmin, Stephen. 1989. "How Medicine Saved the Life of Ethics." (1973). Reprinted in Beauchamp and Walters 1989:45–53.

Urofsky, Melvin I., and Philip E. Urofsky, eds. 1996. *The Right to Die: A Two-Volume Anthology of Scholarly Articles.* New York: Garland.

Van Biema, David. 1997. "Fatal Doses: Assisted Suicide Soars in an Afflicted Community." *Time* (February 17):53.

van der Burg, Wibren. 1992. "Slippery-Slope Argument." *Journal of Clinical Ethics,* 3(4):256–269.

Van Hoof, Anton. 1960. *From Autothanasia to Suicide: Self Killing in Classical Antiquity.* London: Routledge.

Veatch, Robert M. 1989a. *Death, Dying and the Biological Revolution: Our Last Quest for Responsibility.* New Haven: Yale University Press.

———. 1989b. *Medical Ethics.* Boston: Jones and Bartlett.

Vesey, Godrey, and Paul Foulkes. 1990. *Collins Dictionary of Philosophy.* London: Collins.

Vries, B., S. Bluck, and J. Birren. 1993. "The Understanding of Death and Dying in a Life-Span Perspective." *The Gerontologist*, 33(3):366–372.

Wal, G., and R. Dillman. 1994. "Euthanasia in the Netherlands." *British Medical Journal*, 308:1346–1349.

Walton, Douglas N. 1979. *On Defining Death: An Analytic Study of the Concept of Death in Philosophy and Medical Ethics*. Montreal: McGill-Queen's University Press.

Wass, Hannalore, Felix Berardo, and Robert Neimeyer, eds. 1987. *Dying: Facing the Facts*, 2nd edition. New York: Hemisphere.

Watts, D., and T. Howell. 1992. "Assisted Suicide Is Not Voluntary Active Euthanasia." *Journal of the American Geriatrics Society*, 40(10):1043–1046.

Weber, Arnold. 1997. "A Kinder, Gentler Way to Suicide." (Toronto) *Globe and Mail*, October 18.

Weir, Robert F. 1997. *Physician-Assisted Suicide*. Bloomington: Indiana University Press.

———. 1992. "The Morality of Physician-Assisted Suicide." *Law, Medicine and Health Care*, 20(1–2):116–126.

Weisman, Avery. 1993. *The Vulnerable Self: Confronting the Ultimate Questions*. New York: Insight Books.

———. 1972. *On Dying and Denying*. New York: Behavioral Publications.

Wennberg, Robert N. 1989. *Terminal Choices: Euthanasia, Suicide, and the Right to Die*. Grand Rapids, Mich.: Eerdman.

Whytehead, Lawrence, and Paul Chidwick, eds. 1980. *Dying: Considerations Concerning the Passage from Life to Death*. Toronto: Anglican Book Centre.

Wilkes, Paul. 1997. "Dying Well Is the Best Revenge." *New York Times Magazine* (July 6):32–38.

———. 1996. "The Next Pro-Lifers." *New York Times Magazine*, (July 21):22–27.

Wilson, Deborah. 1993. "Rodriguez's Final Question: Who Owns My Life?" (Toronto) *Globe and Mail*, May 20.

Wilson, E. O. 1978. *On Human Nature*. Cambridge, Mass.: Harvard University Press.

WuDunn, Sheryl. 1997. "The Face of the Future in Japan: Economic Threat of Aging Populace." *New York Times*, September 2.

Young, E., and S. Jex. 1992. "The Patient Self-Determination Act: Potential Ethical Quandaries and Benefits." *Cambridge Quarterly of Healthcare Ethics*, 2:107–115.

UNSIGNED ITEMS

I've relied most heavily on the *New York Times*, because of its coverage, circulation, and general reputation. The Canadian press is represented mostly by the (Toronto) *Globe and Mail* for the same reasons.

"Latimer's Sentence on Trial (II)." (Toronto) *Globe and Mail*, December 3, 1997.

"Why Latimer Was Sentenced to Only Two Years." (Toronto) *Globe and Mail*, December 2, 1997. (Includes "The Jury's Questions," excerpt from judge's ruling. See Makin 1997; Roberts 1997.)

"Latimer's Sentence on Trial (I)." (Toronto) *Globe and Mail*, December 2, 1997. (See Makin 1997; Roberts 1997.)

"Parliament and Assisted Suicide." (Toronto) *Globe and Mail*, November 8, 1997.

"Kevorkian Lawyer Cited in Note on Body." *New York Times*, October 15, 1997.

"Dying with Dignity—and Privacy." *Toronto Sunday Star*, September 28, 1997.

"H.M.O.'s Seen as Easing Death for the Elderly." *New York Times*, September 24, 1997.

"Kevorkian in New Suicide." *New York Times*, September 22, 1997.

"Kevorkian Is Called Irresponsible for Role In Woman's Suicide." *New York Times*, September 9, 1997.

"Florida High Court Upholds State Ban on Assisted Suicide" *New York Times*, July 18, 1997.

"Two Days That Shaped the Law." *New York Times*, June 28, 1997. (Editorial on four key Supreme Court decisions, including the assisted-suicide decision. Stresses continuing debate on the issue.)

"Woman's Kin Hires Kevorkian Lawyer." *New York Times*, June 28, 1997.

"Doctors Design Rules on Care for the Dying." *New York Times*, June 23, 1997.

"Mistrial Declared in Kevorkian Case After Lawyer's Statement." *New York Times*, June 13, 1997.

"Kevorkian Trial: Jury Selection Begins. . . ." *USA Today*, June 9, 1997.

"It's Young vs. Old in Germany as the Welfare State Fades." *New York Times*, June 4, 1997.

"Health and the Aged." (Toronto) *Globe and Mail*, May 10, 1997.

"Kevorkian Lawyer Tied to Suicide in Michigan." *New York Times*, April 10, 1997.

"Stop Aid, State Tells Kevorkian." *New York Times*, April 5, 1997.

"Australia Strikes Down a State Suicide Law." *New York Times*, March 25, 1997.

"Congress Weighs More Regulation on Managed Care." *New York Times*, March 10, 1997. (Article addresses the question of HMO opposition to regulation and the government's concern to protect patients' options and treatment, asking "If everybody backs patients' rights, why so much discord?")

"Kevorkian Lawyer Gives Rationale for a Suicide." *New York Times*, March 8, 1997.

"Suicide Law Withstands a Challenge." *New York Times*, February 28, 1997. (Oregon law upheld.)

"Kevorkian Is Silent on 2 More Deaths." *New York Times*, February 4, 1997.

"Assisted Suicide and the Law." *New York Times*, January 6, 1997.

"Court Denies Kevorkian Has a Right to Aid Suicide." *New York Times*, January 6, 1997

"Before the Court, the Sanctity of Life and Death." *New York Times*, January 5, 1997. (Includes disturbing comparative photographs of Mary Bowen Hall.)

"Missouri Drops an Assisted-Suicide Case." *New York Times*, December 27, 1996.

"Clinton Administration Asks Supreme Court to Rule Against Assisted Suicide: Contrasting Life Support Withheld and Death Brought About." *New York Times*, November 13, 1996.

"Another Body Left at Hospital by Kevorkian." *New York Times*, October 18, 1996.

"Till Death Do Us Part," *Dateline*, NBC, September 27, 1996. (Program on George Delury's assisting the suicide of his wife, Myrna Lebov, on July 4, 1995.)

"Australian Man First in World to Die with Legal Euthanasia." *New York Times*, September 26, 1996.

"Clash in Detroit. . . ." *New York Times*, August 20, 1996.

"Question of Family Violence Arises in a Kevorkian Suicide Case." *New York Times*, August 18, 1996.

"A.M.A. Keeps Its Policy Against Aiding Suicide." *New York Times*, June 26, 1996.

"Doctor Charged in Man's Suicide: AIDS Specialist Prescribed Pills." (Toronto) *Globe and Mail*, June 21, 1996.

"Doctor Charged in Man's Suicide." (Toronto) *Globe and Mail*, June 21, 1996.

"Man Ordered to Live with Wife Who Had Consulted Kevorkian." *New York Times*, June 12, 1996.

"Kevorkian Assists Woman from New Jersey in Dying." *New York Times*, June 12, 1996.

"Man Who Helped Wife Die to Serve 6 Months." *New York Times*, May 18, 1996.

"Jury Acquits Kevorkian in Common-Law Case; 'This Will Be the Last Kevorkian Trial,' a Lawyer Says." *New York Times*, May 15, 1996.

"Dr. Kevorkian on Trial, with Hints of the Future." *New York Times*, May 14, 1996.

"Kevorkian Back at Trial as Talk of Detroit Is of Another Suicide." *New York Times*, May 10, 1996.

"Tape Recalls a Canadian's Gratitude to Kevorkian." *New York Times*, May 9, 1996.

"Bastable Tried to 'Wake Up Parliament': Assisted Suicide Hastened by Chrétien Snub of Meeting Attempt, Right to Die Society Says." (Toronto) *Globe and Mail*, May 9, 1996.

"Doctor Death Ignores Legalities on Mission of Mercy." (Toronto) *Globe and Mail*, May 9, 1996.

"Kevorkian Repeatedly Disrupts His Trial, Calling It a Lynching." *New York Times*, May 7, 1996.

"Appeals Set Back Kevorkian Trial Repeatedly." *New York Times*, May 5, 1996.

"Press 'Yes' to Die: Why Jan Culhane Hopes to Choose Death by Computer." *Sydney* (Australia) *Morning Herald*, April 17, 1996.

"Lining Up for Battle." *Sydney* (Australia) *Morning Herald*, April 17, 1996.

"Death at Your Fingertips." *Sydney* (Australia) *Morning Herald*, April 17, 1996.

"The Justices' Life-or-Death Choices." *New York Times*, April 17, 1996.

"MDs Can Aid Suicides, U.S. Court Rules." (Toronto) *Globe and Mail*, April 3, 1996.

"The Right to Die." *The Economist* (September 17, 1994):14.

"To Cease upon the Midnight." *The Economist* (September 17, 1994):21–23.

"Dutch Soften Law on Euthanasia." (Toronto) *Globe and Mail*, February 10, 1993.

"Doctor Charged with Murder in Assisted Suicides." (Toronto) *Globe and Mail*, February 6, 1992.

"Suicide Rate for Men Jumps 42% in 20 Years." (Toronto) *Globe and Mail*, March 27, 1991.

"When the Choice Is to Die." (Toronto) *Globe and Mail*, July 24, 1989.

"Survivors." *Currents*, produced by WNET (New York), aired on PBS September 25, 1988.

THE WORLD WIDE WEB

Links to many websites offering relevant material can be found on the Internet. *Yahoo* is a good place to start searching (http://www.yahoo.com). Other useful search engines are *Excite* (http://www.excite.com) and *Altavista* (http://www.al-tavista.digital.com). One of the sites available from *Yahoo* is *The Euthanasia World Directory on the World Wide Web*. Another interesting site is the *New York Times* forum (http://forums.nytimes.com). Also of interest for American articles is http://www.rights.org/~deathnet/USNews_current.html, and for Canadian and international articles is http://www.rights.org/~deathnet/wnews_current.html. Two other sites worthy of note are http://www.efn.org/~ergo/ (Pro-Choice) and http://www.euthanasia.com (Pro-Life). Web addresses change fairly often but can usually be tracked down through *Yahoo*, *Excite*, *Altavista*, and other search engines.

INDEX

About the Author

C. G. PRADO is Professor of Philosophy at Queen's University, Kingston, Canada. He is the author of seven books, two on aging and suicide. He is also the author of some thirty articles and is co-author of a book on assisted suicide.

ISBN 0-313-30584-6

90000>

EAN

9 780313 305849

HARDCOVER BAR CODE